The Life and Times of Raja Mahendra Pratap

Edited by
Dr. Vir Singh

Originals
(an imprint of Low Price Publications)
Delhi-110052

Distributed by
D.K. Publishers Distributors (P) Ltd.
4834/24, Ansari Road, Darya Ganj,
New Delhi-110002
Phones: 51562573-77
e-mail: dkpd@del3.vsnl.net.in
url: www.dkpd.com

First Published 2005

ISBN 81-88629-31-6 (H.B.)
ISBN 81-88629-32-4 (P.B.)

Published by
Originals
(an imprint of Low Price Publications)
A-6, Nimri Commercial Centre,
Near Ashok Vihar Phase-IV,
Delhi-110052
Phones: 27401672, 27452453
e-mail: lpp@nde.vsnl.net.in
url: www.lppindia.com

Printed at
D K Fine Art Press P Ltd.
Delhi-110052

PRINTED IN INDIA

Editorial Note

The saga of struggle for India's Independence is long one. Historians of the freedom movement have extensively dealt with the role of persons and parties. Memorials and monuments have been raised to commemorate the prominent individuals. With the growing regional identities we find newer personalities being brought to centre stage year after year for according a place of honour in the annals of the freedom movement. However, there is one character in the saga, who has not received attention commensurate with his role in the struggle for India's independence. It was Raja Mahendra Pratap who established the first Provisional Government of India in Afghanistan in 1915—much before the declaration in 1929 by the Congress of the goal of complete freedom for India. The yearlong government sponsored celebrations in 1997 of the Golden Jubilee of India's Independence also failed to notice the glaring omission.

It was therefore, in the fitness of things that the Surajmal Memorial Education Society under the guidance of its President, Shri Ram Niwas Mirdha organized a two-day National Seminar on *'The Life and Times of Raja Mahendra Pratap'* on 25th and 26th April 1998 in which more than twenty five scholars from different universities and institutions participated and presented their papers highlighting various aspects of the life and activities of Raja Mahendra Pratap. The present volume is largely the outcome of the above seminar. Some papers on Raja Mahendra Pratap presented in other seminars on Jat history have been incorporated here. A few of the articles already published in the *Raja Mahendra Pratap Abhinandan Grantha* (1976), *Raja Mahendra Pratap Smriti Anka of Premabharati* (1979) and *Raja Mahendra Pratap Janma-Satabdismarika* (1986) have been included for their value as personal reminiscences of contemporaries of Raja Sahib.

Anticipating the proceedings of the Seminar, Shri Ram Niwas Mirdha, in his welcome address stresses on the need for evaluating the role of Indian freedom fighters based abroad. Deliberations on such aspects, he hopes, would throw up suggestions, which could serve as beacon lights for future researchers. Shri Manzoor Ahmed in his inaugural address underlining the secular credentials of Raja Sahib describes him as visionary, philosopher and activist rolled into one. In his opinion Raja Sahib was born ahead of the times in which he lived. In his spirited key-note address Professor Suhas Chakravarti traces the perambulatory course of Raja Mahendra Pratap's activities across several countries and places him in the context of the part played by contemporary revolutionaries working abroad. He reminds us how important it was to conduct research on the life of activities of Raja Sahib, especially in view of the neglect shown by eminent historians of Modern India like Sumit Sarkar. Citing the case of Raja Mahendra Pratap, Professor Chakravarti points out the significance of maintaining individuality and retaining nationalism, retaining your commitment to the nation and at the same time becoming non-communal and secular. He also highlights the contribution of Raja Sahib to technical education and scientific outlook not forgetting to mention his important legacies.

Prof. Ashok Kumar Patnaik puts together the pieces of material available in the National Archives of India, the Nehru Memorial Museum and Library and documents and books from Soviet Russia on the formation of the Provisional Government of India in Afghanistan in 1915. He narrates the background of the formation of the Government and the difficulties negotiated by Raja Mahendra Pratap and his comrades in this mission. Prof. Patnaik has shown how Raja Mahendra Pratap was able to maintain a critical balance while dealing with the Afghans, the Russians and the Germans for their support of the cause of India's freedom.

Dr. Rajpal Singh has described the role played by Indian revolutionaries abroad devoted to the cause of liberating India from foreign rule with special reference to the efforts made by Raja Mahendra Pratap during the period of the first world war and latter. He elaborates the activities of Provisional Government of India at Kabul with the help of Indo-Turco-German mission. We are told how the fond hope of Raja Sahib for receiving full support from the Russians after the revolution proved to be dupe. Dr. Rajpal also recounts how with the radical change in the political scenario in 1918 in favour of the Entente powers no foreign government was prepared to directly espouse the cause of the Provisional Government, which became defunct in course of time.

Prof. A.C. Bose describes the forays of Raja Mahendra Pratap in foreign lands, travelling without an Indian passport for enlisting support from all possible quarters for the cause of liberating India from the British yoke ensuring at the same time that the support if forthcoming did not result in swapping of the masters. A brief account of the Raja's activities or the lack of these has been given by Prof Bose.

Mrs. Yuthika Mishra has traced the activities of Raja Mahendra Pratap from 1919 to 1946 in a chronological way. Covering the period 1919 to 1924 the first phase deals with the efforts of the Raja in seeking support of the left bloc in his struggle against the British. The period 1925 to 1930 was the period of his involvement with the Ghadar Party. The post 1930 period has been shown as the reflective clearly under the influence of Gandhian thought.

Dr. Vir Singh depicts in some details the activities of Raja Mahendra Pratap during the Second World War. The efforts of Raja Sahib to utilize the war situation again to free India have been dealt with elaborately. The formation of the Executive Board of India in Japan by Raja Mahendra Pratap and the attitude of the Japanese towards him have been dealt with in detail. Dr. Singh has also demonstrated how Subhash Chandra Bose was indebted to Raja Mahendra Pratap. The arrest and lodging of the Raja by the American army in the Sugamo prison in Japan in 1945 as war criminal and his subsequent release through the efforts of Mahatma Gandhi and the Congress party have been described.

Shri Shiv Dhyan Singh and Shri Hari Singh narrate personal reminiscences of their contacts with Raja Sahib.

Among the contributors in Hindi Shri Anand Mohan Sahay shares his personal experiences with Raja Mahendra Pratap as a colleague in the Executive Board of India in Japan. Shri Ramesh Verma gives an interpretation of Raja Sahib's philosophy of life. Shri Verma finds enough meeting ground between the Ahimsa of Gandhi Ji and Prema Dharma of Raja Mahendra Pratap. He pleads for a closer examination of the Raja's belief in a World Federation without giving up caste identities, his concept of the originality of Aryan country and religiosity combined with modernity. Shri Akbar Ali Khan, personal assistant to Raja Sahib for over twenty six years recounts his personal experiences with the latter and gives us a peep into some aspects of the life of the Raja. Reproducing the life and activities of Raja Mahendra Pratap Shri Shiv Kumar seeks to establish a similarity of his thoughts with those of Buddha. The Prema Dharma, the World Federation and the New Science of Thought propounded by Raja Sahib, according to Shiv Kumar find a parallel in the threefold *Pitakas* of Buddha. Sadhvi Mahanandamayi delves on the various aspects of Prema Dharma propounded by Raja Sahib. Swami Mahanand Maharaj explains the concept of World Federation as conceived by Raja Mahendra Pratap. Shri Braj Bihari Lal Sharma introduces us to the process of Raja Sahib's evolving the Prema Dharma and the spirituality he experienced. Shri Jyoti Swaroop Singh, Shri Braj Bihari Lal Sharma and Shri Prabhu Dayal Massey record the reminiscences of their personal interaction with Raja Sahib. Dr. Anoop Sharma gives his estimate of the contribution of Raja Mahendra Pratap to society and mankind as a whole. In the end we have a small piece from the thoughts of Raja Mahendra Pratap giving us a peep into his ultimate persona.

I wish to acknowledge with deep appreciation the co-operation of all the scholars for their participation in the seminar and presenting papers.

We express our gratitude to Sh. Om Prakash Chautala, Chief Minister of Haryana, for providing financial help to the Research Centre of the Society. The Society looks forward to his constant encouragement in future also.

I am deeply indebted to Shri Ram Niwas Mirdha for his continuous guidance and encouragement in completing academic projects.

My special thanks are due to Dr. S. S. Rana, the Vice-President of the Society for helping me at every stage in bringing out this publication. But for his help this volume would not have attained the present form.

I also extend my sincere thanks to Shri S. P. Singh, Secretary of the Society for his unstinted help and co-operation.

The Publication of 'The Life and Times of Raja Mahendra Pratap' by Maharaja Suraj Mal Centre for Research and Publication, would be a befitting tribute to him on his Birth Anniversary.

Ist December 2004
Birth Anniversary of
Raja Mahendra Pratap

Dr. Vir Singh
Director
Maharaja Surajmal Centre
for Research and Publication

Contents

अध्यक्षीय स्वागत

रामनिवास मिर्धा

'सूरजमल स्मारक शिक्षा संस्था' जाट समुदाय के इतिहास व उससे सम्बन्धित क्षेत्र को विस्तृत रूप से जानने के लिए शोध कार्य को बढ़ावा देती है। इसीलिए समय-समय पर सेमिनार का आयोजन भी करती है। इसी शृंखला के अन्तर्गत संस्था के शोध केन्द्र ने 'राजा महेन्द्र प्रताप के जीवन और तत्कालीन युग' पर एक सेमिनार आयोजित किया है जिसका उद्देश्य राजा महेन्द्र प्रताप के जीवन के बारे में और तत्कालीन देश-विदेश की स्थिति की जानकारी प्राप्त करना है। यह विषय हमने इसलिए चुना क्योंकि हमारी मान्यता है कि हमारे देश के अन्दर तो स्वतन्त्रता आन्दोलन हुआ ही लेकिन इसके साथ-साथ विदेशों में भी हमारे देशवासियों ने देश-प्रेम, त्याग और तपस्या से आन्दोलन चलाया। अब जबकि हम आजादी की 50वीं वर्षगाँठ मना रहे हैं तो हमने सोचा कि इस पक्ष को अच्छे रूप में हम आप लोगों के सामने रखें। क्योंकि जो स्वतन्त्रता आन्दोलन देश से बाहर हुए हैं उनके बारे में बहुत कम शोधकार्य हुआ है और बहुत कम विद्वानों ने इस ओर कोई विशेष ध्यान दिया है। यह एक कमी है और मैं समझता हूँ कि इस सेमिनार में जो विचार-विमर्श होगा उसकी वजह से राजा महेन्द्र प्रताप के जीवन के बारे में और विदेशों में भारत के स्वतन्त्रता संघर्ष के विषय में कुछ नए पक्ष सामने आएँगे। इससे शोधकर्त्ताओं को मार्गदर्शन भी मिलेगा कि किस दिशा में शोध कार्य को आगे बढ़ाया जाए।

हम बहुत आभारी हैं डॉ. भीमराव अम्बेडकर विश्वविद्यालय आगरा के कुलपति मंजूर अहमद साहब के जो इस सेमिनार में आए। राजा साहब की कर्मभूमि वृन्दावन आगरा के बहुत पास है। आपके विश्वविद्यालय में राजा साहब के बारे में बहुत काम भी हुआ है। राजा साहब इस क्षेत्र के इतने प्रमुख व्यक्ति रहे हैं कि अगर आपका विश्वविद्यालय उन पर ध्यान दे तो यह एक अच्छी बात है।

हम दिल्ली विश्वविद्यालय के इतिहास विभाग में प्रो. सुहास चक्रवर्ती जी के भी बहुत आभारी हैं कि वे हमारे निमंत्रण पर इस सेमिनार में पधारे। वे अपने

मुख्य वक्तव्य में राजा साहब के बारे में प्रकाश डालेंगे। राजा साहब से सम्बन्धित और उनसे परिचित अनेक महानुभाव दूर-दूर से आए हैं। मैं उनका हार्दिक स्वागत करता हूँ, उन्होंने बहुत तकलीफ की। मैं समझता हूँ कि हमारे इस विचार-विमर्श से बहुत से ऐसे निष्कर्ष निकलेंगे जो राजा साहब के जीवन पर तो प्रकाश डालेंगे ही, साथ ही हमें दिशा मिलेगी कि भविष्य में हम और क्या काम करें व कर सकते हैं। उनसे हमें बहुत ज्ञान और प्रेरणा मिलेगी। इसी विश्वास के साथ इस सेमिनार का आयोजन किया है।

राजा साहब वक्त से पहले पैदा हो गए थे

(उद्घाटन वक्तव्य)

मंजूर अहमद

राजा महेन्द्र प्रताप ने बिना किसी विदेशी सरकार के पिछलग्गू बने भारत के बाहर जाकर 1915 में भारत की प्रथम अस्थाई (Provisinal) सरकार की स्थापना की थी। इस प्रकार वे अपने समय से 15 वर्ष आगे थे क्योंकि कांग्रेस ने पूर्ण स्वतन्त्रता का नारा 1929-30 ई. में लगाया था।

उस समय संसार की दो महान शक्तियाँ थी, जर्मनी और तुर्की। इनके राजाध्यक्षों से वे बराबर के स्तर पर मिला करते थे। तुर्की के सुलतान (खलीफा) से राजा महेन्द्र प्रताप ने कई बार भेंट की जिसमें भारत की समस्याओं के बारे में, अंग्रेजों को बाहर निकालने के बारे में इन्होंने बहुत हिम्मत से बात की। एक आदमी जो मुरसान में पैदा हुआ हो और उसका विश्व दृष्टिकोण इतना विस्तृत हो यह सोचकर हैरत होती है।

राजा महेन्द्र प्रताप से मेरा मानसिक सम्बन्ध तो विद्यार्थी जीवन में ही था। 1966 ई. में जब मैं मसूरी में आई. पी. एस. के प्रशिक्षण के लिए गया था तब मुझे मालूम हुआ कि राजा महेन्द्र प्रताप देहरादून में रहते हैं। तो मैं पहला मौका निकालकर उनसे मिलने पहुँचा। उस समय वे संसद के सदस्य नहीं थे और प्रतिदिन राजपुरा रोड़ पर घूमने जाया करते थे। मैं भी कई बार उनके साथ चला, मैं समझता हूँ कि यह चीज जो मुझे उस जमाने में मिली, वह आज मेरे लिए एक अनमोल दौलत है।

राजा साहब के एक मुस्लिम शिक्षक जन्माष्टमी के दिन रोजा रखते थे। इससे वे बहुत प्रभावित हुए और हिन्दु-मुस्लिम एकता का सबक लिया। आगे चलकर सभी समुदायों को मिलाकर काबुल में भारत की आजाद सरकार की स्थापना की। महाराजा सूरजमल ने जो परम्परा शुरू की थी वह धागे की तरह राजा महेन्द्र प्रताप में भी आई। वह है आजादी की ललक के साथ-साथ सभी

हिन्दुस्तानियों को साथ लेकर चलने का जज्बा। इसका उदाहरण है कि जब सूरजमल ने आगरे पर कब्जा किया तो सभी सरकारी इमारतें उनके कब्जे में आ गई। किसी ने कहा कि इन मस्जिदों पर भी कब्जा कर लीजिए तो उन्होंने कहा कि नहीं, ये तो ईश्वर का घर है। इस पर कोई कब्जा नहीं करेगा, जैसी हैं वैसी ही रहेंगी। उसके मुकाबले में 70 साल बाद अपने को बहुत सभ्य कहलाए जाने वाले राष्ट्र ने जब दिल्ली पर कब्जा किया तो जामा मस्जिद पर भी कब्जा किया और उसमें घोड़े बाँधने लगे।

अक्सर दो लोग होते हैं–*एक्टीविस्ट* अलग और *विजीनरी* अलग। इतिहास में बहुत कम ऐसा हुआ है कि एक आदमी एक्टीविस्ट भी हो और विजीनरी भी। लेकिन यहाँ एक अजीब बात देखने को मिलती है कि एक आदमी विजीनरी है, फिलासफर है और साथ-साथ एक्टीविस्ट भी है–सरकार बनाता है, आजादी के लिए लड़ता है। कुछ लोग कहते हैं संसार में हमेशा जल्दी सोचने वाले, ज्यादा सोचने वाले *यूटोपियन* कहलाते हैं।

राजा महेन्द्र प्रताप ने प्रथम विश्व-युद्ध से हुई तबाही को देखकर सोचा कि संसार को शान्ति के लिए एक इकाई होना चाहिए। हमें राजा महेन्द्र प्रताप के सभी विचारों में से 'विश्व परिवार' की बात सबसे प्यारी लगती है। यह अपने देश की रवायत से एन मुताबिक है। यहाँ तो हम 'वसुधैव कुटुम्बकम्' कहते हैं और दुनिया 'अल्लाह कुनबा है', 'ईश्वर का एक खानदान है' कहते रहे हैं। वैसे तो विश्व परिवार का विचार बहुत पुराना है। परन्तु जिस तरह उन्होंने इसे एक अमली शक्ल देने की कोशिश, एक तालीम के जरिए की वो बहुत अहम है।

राजा महेन्द्र प्रताप एक ऐसी शख्सीयत हैं जिसके अनेक पहलू हैं–एक हीरे की तरह। उन पहलुओं पर काम करने की सख्त जरूरत है। हमारे विश्वविद्यालय से तो उनका बहुत गहरा ताल्लुक रहा है। हमारे विश्वविद्यालय के अलीगढ़ में स्थित बहुत से कॉलेजों को राजा महेन्द्र प्रताप साहब ने बहुत दान दिया था। इसके अतिरिक्त मथुरा में एक कॉलेज कायम किया–प्रेम महाविद्यालय। यह हमारे विश्वविद्यालय पर उनका ऋण है। हम अब तक उस ऋण को उतार नहीं पाए हैं। परन्तु हम उनका सम्मान करते रहें यह कोशिश हमारी जारी है। हमारे विश्वविद्यालय में उन पर शोधकार्य चल रहे हैं। छात्रों ने उनकी शख्सीयत के मुख़तलिफ पहलुओं पर शोधकार्य शुरू कर रखे हैं और वे कार्य तेजी से चल रहे हैं। एक चीज जो हमारा विश्वविद्यालय करने जा रहा है–वह है प्रत्येक वर्ष उनके जन्मदिन पर भाषण शृंखला का अपने परिसर में इन्तजाम, जिससे उनकी शख्सीयत पर, उनकी सियासत पर, उन पर, उनके दर्शन पर प्रकाश डाला जा सके। हम इसमें ऐसे लोगों को बुलाएँगे जिन्होंने उनका दर्शन पढ़ा हो और उनसे दर्खवास्त करेंगे कि उन पर यहाँ आकर चर्चा करें। दूसरा हमारे विश्वविद्यालय

ने एक ब्रज केन्द्र खोलने का आयोजन किया है। उसमें एक प्रकोष्ठ राजा साहब के नाम पर रखेंगे। उनका ब्रज संस्कृति से बहुत लगाव था।

विश्वविद्यालय का यह प्रयत्न होगा जिससे आने वाला हिन्दुस्तान जान सके कि उनके बहादुर बेटे ने इतने पहले इतना सुन्दर सपना देखा था। दरअसल ऐसा लगता है कि वो समय से पहले आ गए थे। एक ग्रीक कवि हैशियाट ने कहा था "या तो मैं समय से पहले पैदा हो गया हूँ या बाद में पैदा हुआ हूँ।" शैली ने कहा था कि "अगर मैं पहले पैदा होता तो इन दीवारों की बुनियाद ठीक से बनाता और बाद में पैदा होता तो तोड़ देता और फिर बनाता। पर मैं तो बीच में पैदा हुआ हूँ। सो मेरी तकदीर में इसे छापना (मिट्टी का लेप करके ठीक करना/पलस्तर करना) लिखा है सो मिट्टी छाप रहे हैं इस पर।" राजा साहब की तकदीर में भी बदकिस्मती से उनकी मरम्मत लिखी थी जो वक्त से पहले पैदा हो गए थे।

मैं सूरजमल संस्था को बधाई देता हूँ कि उन्होंने इस देशभक्त के कार्यों को उजागर करने का बीड़ा उठाया है।

Important legacies of Raja Mahendra Pratap (Key-note Address)

Suhas Chakravarty

I remember years ago when late Mr. P.C. Joshi, member of C.P.I., gave me a document of Indian National Movement, which I translated from Russian to Indian English. It was published by the name of Anatomy of the RAJ. Basically it was a collection of material sent by Russian Legation at Calcutta to St. Petersburg before the Russian revolution. It was collected by the revolutionary government in 1917 and was published with an introduction for their own political purposes but they published it as the perception of the imperial government of Russia about the role of imperial government of Great Britain in India, their success, failure, weaknesses from which they could learn about their role in central Aisa.

In the course of my work I found a few very intersting documents dealing with this strange Raja who is around Tashkent and then he goes to Afganistan to form a provisional government. I wondered why this document was sent to India and discovered that English government was literally pertrified in 1915-16 that such a move is afoot and may be a successful move because the war was on. Secondly the entire army in Delhi or India, particularly in Punjab was armless because most of the ammunition sent to the warfront and the rifles that the army and the police was carrying were marked D.P. i.e. 'Drill Purposes only', it was not firing, shooting ammunition. So they thought that potentialities of sharp shooting of the entire army is not there and if the Afghan soldiers along with this Raja arrive backed by Turks and backed by other forces of the axis powers, the country will be absolutely defenceless.

It was the same period when we find large number of documents regarding a total and very organized operation on behalf of nationalism in India all over the world with a concerted action to create a rising all over India and beyond it for the independence of India. In police and army documents we find Barisal and Siam, Bangkok, Columbo, San Fransisco, Batalia together with Berlin, Turkey, Tashkent, Kabul and Iran all closely interconnected with a conserted move to rise and organize a rising in India. It was significant that British government was very keen to find out the contact point the nexus line. The total cooperation with Gadar Party between Batalia, Siam and then alongwith it to find out its connection with Afghanistan, Turkey and Berlin and the possibilities of something like a Balasor a coming up of arms and ammunition. Two such ships were intercepted in the Bay of Bengal. It was Firojpur which was going to be the cantonment and was going to start the mutiny. It was a very organized affair and the man behind this was one of the important leaders who was moving around from Turkey to Berlin, to Rome, to Albania and then again Russia and having contact with the power elite there with the concerted move to overthrow the British rule with the assistance and support of axis powers.

It was absolutely dangerous situation, serious situation to the British Empire which was nervy, jittery and was on tenter hooks. It is reported that this was the period when the Viceroy in Calcutta used to get up early morning to see whether there was any assasin under his bed. It was a time when Calcutta club was not allowed to be visited by even unchecked Europeans. It was a time when there was a bomb thrown on Harding when he was entering Delhi. It was a period of Ras Bihari Bose, and this was the period of upsurge in nationalism all over Asia and one of the central figures was Raja Mahendra Pratap. I am trying to recapture the period, I just want to show you what is the interconnection of the whole area. It was not one man from the north, it was not a small little Zamindar, it was not a small area in Aligarh but it was a period of interconnection of rising tide of nationalism, thinking in terms of overthrowing the British Empire on which the sun never set and it was purely connected with tremendous interconnection all over the world.

To talk about this man therefore, becomes a very important thing. Research about this man is indispensible and to work out that nexus in different areas of this concerted attack by the scholars, intellectuals is very important. Turn the pages of a text book, any text book, any book whatsoever taught in the higher classes in the school, taught in the universities, taught for the honounrs classes. see the book which is translated and infact had a large number of editions in India, which is the must book for all students in India. I am referring to Sarkar's 'Modern India', no mention of Raja Mahendra Pratap. Just see the struggle of the people all over the world in support of a national consciousness in India for the overthrow of the mightiest empire, the most settled empire of the world. No mention of this great man. What is the reason for this subtle indifference, what is the reason for this conscious effort to obliterate the memory, power metaphor, everything in the name of some form of subaltern consciousness.

Raja Mahendra Pratap was concious of this subaltern position. The word that comes in my mind is that hunger is the essence of human civilization. Hunger must be obliterated, everyone must have bread. If everyone must have bread its simple formulation, he quoted Christ to support his position and underlined meaning, is that socially oriented justice which is meant for every man which means equality–social, economic, political, cultural equality of whole mankind. And that idea he gathered not one the basis of his text books but on the basis of the fact that he made a personal experiment with reality. For about four years he was travelling all over India, wanted to know the realities of the peasants, the workers, the level of education, the lack of technical skill, the essesnce of humanity of Indian civilization and the basis of the unity of man. This was his mission to know the details of India. What Tagore could think of this man, went and saw himself experience the man. He went abroad and for years and years travelled all over Europe, America, went to Latin America, Japan, saw Shanghai and tried to understand not merely the man and his realities, man and his specificities, the local specificities, what is the characteristic of England and what is the essence of France, what is the genius of Germany, what is the weakness of Russia, what is the strength of America, what is the danger of Japan, what is the essence of China. That was a perception of his search for civilizations and their essence. This is the man who said therefore, quality does not mean obliteration of individualism. So here is a man who stands for individualism, social nexus, local specificities of a culture and civilization.

Then he goes for socialism. This is a pluralist culture, a pluralist socialism, a pluralist social dimension, which means that everybody has a place. This man, as the Vice-Chancellor said, was a strange phenomenon, born in Hindu family, trained in Muslim institution, married in Sikh family, what a tremendous entry into different religious forms to find out the essence of the unity of being and this is the essence of the man, totally non-communal and anti-communal, totally committed for the development of Indianness of India, totaly committed to the development of pluralist society and totally committed to socialism because everyman must have his bread. He cannot live with his ideals alone without having his bread. Therefore, he promoted technical education in such areas donating all his money and his properties for the development of technical education for the scientific quest of man for the development of the lacunae that an Indian mind had.

He was trying to implement and underline the need for social reform against untouchability. And now someone will come and say that he was more or less a burgeois because he was a burgeois, he was an aristocrat, tried to become a burgeois. Therefore, he did not bring about a social revolution at all, he did not organize a total annihilation of caste system and did not work for abolition of untouchability. No such political zeal for bringing about social reform was there. There was a man who was thinking in terms of chaging the mind of man. You must realize that you don't have a place for social discrimination on the basis of past history of caste systems. You have to create a condition in which untouchability should not be a part of your consciousness. That was possible because he was understanding the reality of the Indian situation. Like Gandhi he realised that you cannot legislate merely and do away with untouchability. You have to change the Hindu mind, that has governed 2000 years of indoctrination–religious and political and economic indoctrination to use a huge element of population as surplus which can be used at a cheap price. This you must know, you must realise the essence of humanness of all humanity. It is based on one fraternity. Therefore, everyman needs bread, everyman needs culture, everyman needs political combination, everyman must arrive to dissent, everyman must be given his respectability of standing together and at the same time must not have regimentation.

The man met Lenin. He was close acquaintance of Trotsky. Here is the man who could realise Trotsky was basically a Jew and Lenin was basically a Russian. Probably there is an element of difference beteen them on that basis, probably over shooting his understanding. But I am interested in that totality the American sociologists are trying to find out. Sociologists in American world are motivated by political connections. This man was trying to findout these meanings then in those days without any type of apparatus of social behavioural pattern in his hand. He was trying to understand the motive power behind the difference of awkward within the society between different groups of people. Now here is the man having met Lenin, having seen centralized communist party, having seen the lack of democratic centralism, having known the hypocracy of politics of imperalism as well as communism. He realized the importance of democratic dissent and pluralism and admired Nehru, but he was also critic of Nehru. An essential member of Congress Party, he never affiliated himself as a rank and file. He remained always an outsider, sitting on the periphery, raising his fingers at things which were not acceptable to his law of notion, of his own vision. This is the significance of maintaining individuality and retaining nationalism, retaining your commitment to the nation and at the same time becoming non-communal and secular.

I would like to bring to your notice the importance that he gave to technical education and scientific outlook, and this is a most remarkable contribution that a man could think in those days when Gandhi did not think and opposed him at a time when Nehru thought it was superficial to be bothered about this. He thought that it was essential for the Indians to have technical skill for the development of a scientific mind and attitude and that was the product of a stream of conciousness of India which was very much there in Swadeshi movement which impressed him the most. In 1906 when he went to Calcutta Congress he learnt about Swadeshi movement, self reliance which means self reliance of technical know how as well, and this self reliance became the part of his life. He thought that we must build up a society. We must develop our industrial society on the basis of our own skill, our requirement, our need. He was totally opposed to acquisitive principle of pomp and show, opposed such ideas as trying to create a society on the basis of superficial industrialization so that we can borrow and use cosmetics from abroad. He was opposed to all this self reliance. Probably his assessment of America was somewhat rosy and exciting because he saw the Roosevelt government. He saw the intervention of the state at a given point of time in the affairs of the economy to regulate it and thereby bring about some amount of social change. Therefore on that basis he did not understand the potentiality of the remarkable agressiveness of American Capitalism.

But at the same time he realised the super power system. He realised the importance of managing your identity working within the orbit of super power system. His opposition to commonwealth was essesntially rational because he thought there was a basic problem. The problem is India would be British oriented which means western oriented. That means your non-alignment will be diluted by your presence and membership in the commonwealth. These are certainly important lines of thought that he left behind. And infact self-reliance, nationalism, secular-conciousness tried in Indian past development, and integrating the different aspects of Indian genius into one coherent theme, and then placing India on the map of the world are his legacies.

These are the important legacies which are infact thrown and given a tremendous support to the rise of a generation to which I belong who have seen India, Nehru, Gandhi, who have seen the development of *Bandung* and *Panchsheel*. We believe and I believe, I am totally outdated today, people laugh at my stupidity of living in 1950's and I think that world of 1950's and early 60's is a reality of Indian, Modern Indian life which remains the legacy for the future, despite my university's clarion call for subaltern studies and local identities.

Raja Mahendra Pratap and The Provisional Government of India at Kabul (A Unique experiment in Indian National Movement)

—Ashok Kumar Patnaik

The glorious struggle for national liberation had incorporated various streams with different ideas, philosophies and activities throughout its existence and such rich varieties of converging trends had strengthened the unique struggle throughout its history. The Indian revolutionary movement was an important and integral component of that great struggle for freedom. It originated from the anti-British popular movements of the nineteenth century, under the same historical, social economic and psychological conditions that gave birth to the national movement as a whole. In fact, it was the militant arm of the Indian national movement. The pressure of the colonial authorities at home led those patriots to seek safer hide-outs and freedom of activities in a number of foreign countries. The earlier revolutionaries like Shyamaji Krishna Varma and Madame Cama had established their centres at London and Paris respectively in the beginning of the twentieth century and carried on their anti-British propaganda and organization, which attracted other Indian revolutionaries to follow their foot-steps to alien land. A major sub-trend later came up within the ranks of the revolutionaries during the World War I, who wanted to utilize the war situation to their advantage by establishing friendly relationship with various anti-British foreign governments and acquire their active support and assistance both financially and militarily to organise a liberation march from abroad, to free India by armed means. Efforts were made to contact the foreign governments not only on individual basis, but through an established diplomatic framework of state to state relationship in which Indian state would be represented by a government in exile. The legendary hero of such an idea was Raja Mahendra Pratap. President of the Kabul based 'Provisional Government of India,' which was the first Indian national government-in-exile, the first parallel government of the Indian national revolutionaries vis-a-vis the colonial authorities. Such novel experiment was later followed by Netaji Subash Chandra Bose during World War II years through 'Azad Hind Government'. Though scanty materials are available on the first national government-in exile, yet from the works of Raja Mahendra Pratap and the colleagues in his government, documents in the National Archives of India (NAI) including the private papers section, Oral History Transcripts in Nehru Memorial Museum and Library, New Delhi, some German documents whose microfilms are available in NAI, a few documents and books from Soviet Russia and their archives throw light on that 'government' of Raja Mahendra Pratap. Major documents can only be available in Afghanistan, which are still hidden from the eyes of the researchers. This constitutes a major limitation of this paper. Yet, from the materials available, enough light can be thrown on the 'Provisional Government' at Kabul.

Composition of the 'Government'

The composition of the 'Government' and characteristic features of leaders made it further interesting. Its President Raja Mahendra Pratap started his political career as a nationalist, attended a session of Indian National Congress and donated a part of his property for the extension of techincal education in India, which clearly speaks about his humanitarian attitude, love for expansion of education, especially technical education and determination to play a politically active role in life than the material luxury and comforts to which he was hereditarily entitled to as the feudal chief of a small princely state of Hathras in U.P. His Patriotic zeal could not be satisfied with these activities and it ultimately led him to leave India for Europe during the World War I. According to an India office report, Mahendra Pratap had gone to Europe on behalf of several Indian princes to ascertain whether military position would make it a favourable moment for revolution in India.[1] At his retreat in Switzerland, he received a letter from Umrao Sing Majithia, an emigre nationalist leader from Punjab, inviting him to Germany.[2] Like most other contemporary Indian revolutionaries functioning from abroad, Mahendra Pratap pinned his hopes on Germany, the enemy of England. There, he submitted a scheme for work in Afghanistan to the German Foreign Office. His scheme referred to a march of German-aided Afghan army to invade India which would be assisted by Indian princes and nationalist leaders, to whom German Foreign Office would write emphasising "community of interest between Germany and India."[3] Raja Mahendra Pratap, while coming as a member of Indo-German Henting Mission under Warner Otto Von Hentig from Berlin to Kabul had Maulavi Barkatullah and carried 27 letters from Reich Chancellor of Germany to Indian Rajas, Maharajas and Nawabs and two important letters from German side to the King of Nepal and Amir of Afghanistan.[4] The Sultan of Turkey, on the way, gave the mission a letter to the Amir of Afghanistan and seven more addressed to various Indian princes through Mahendra Pratap.[5] The faith of Mahendra Pratap on the Indian princes was belied when they handed over these letters to their British colonial masters.

Maulavi Barkutullah started his political career as a Pan-Islamist and left India for Japan in 1910 to join as a Professor of Hidustani language at Tokyo University[6] and published a journal, **The Islamic Fraternity** which was anti-British and Pan-Islamic.[7] Under pressure from British Government when his contract was not renwed beyond March 1914, he left immediately for America to work with the Gadar Party,[8] from where he came to Berlin in search of anti-British assistance.

While Mahendra Pratap and Barkatullah represented the

Indian Independence Committee at Berlin (popularly known as Berlin Committee), another important leader of the Indian nationalists of Kabul was Obeidullah Sindhi, who came to Kabul during mid-1915 with three companions to take part in **jehad** and rouse the whole of Afghanistan to wage war against the British Government.[9] He believed, as a Pan-Islamist and analysing the Muslim reaction against British, especially after the joining of Turkey in World War I against England, that the unity of Persia and Afghanistan would eventually lead to the expulsion of British from India. Now he joined with other Indian revolutionaries and the arrival of Mahendra Pratap and Barkatullah gave an opportunity for all Indian revolutionaries at Kabul to form an organization of the Indians which was supported by Nasrullah, borther of the Amir and many more nobles in the Afghan court, known as war party. Though most of the Muslim revolutionaries who came to Kabul or fled out of India were primarily Pan-Islamists, the secular and liberal leadership of Mahendra Pratap could combine them on a common platform whose prime concern was the liberation of their motherland with the help of friendly anti-British foreign powers. Earlier, Umrao Singh Majithia, who associated with the Kabul mission wrote to Mahendra Pratap in Kabul that they should fight on secular lines.[10] Secularism was the main planks of the future Kabul based 'government' of the Indian revolutionaries.

At Kabul, on 1st December, 1915, the Provisional Government of India was inaugurated with Raja Mahendra Pratap as its life President, Barkatullah as Prime Minister and Obeidullah Sindhi as Home Minister.[11] There were many more holding various positions in the 'Provisional Government'. The 'Provisional Government' issued a proclamation which was sent to India and seized by the British authorities.[12] The proclamation was addressed to Indian rulers and ryots to exploit the war situation which had exhausted the British during two years of fighting. It urged upon the Indian soldiers, police constables and the Indian rulers to get ready for a great upheaval to oust the foreigners from India. It spoke of German and Turkish assurance of assistance in the Indian war of liberation with men and material without any desire to establish their own rule over India. The most important diplomatic manoeuvre did by the 'Provisional Government' was their obtaining a written agreement from Germany and Turkey that along with their other allies, Austro-Hungary and Bulgaria after the expulsion of the British by the Indian people, they themselves would not only recognize the Indian government by the Indians as the legitimate government of the country but also get it approved by the other powers in the post-war peace time. The proclamation urged people of all religions to get united in the mission of expelling the British in India and live happily together like brethren to encourage "arts and science, turn the whole human race into a family by promoting civilization to the highest degree and turn the face of the earth into heaven and make it a fit abode for the pious." The 'Provisional Government was working desperately to bring about a collision between Afghanistan and Great Britain and to prepare India for the acceptance of Afghan invasion.[13] Raja Mahendra Pratap thought that an external invading army would march into India at right time to liberate it and its efforts would be matched by a general uprising of Indian people, soldiers and others. He, in a letter to the Reich Chancellor of Germany, requested for twenty thousand troops only for Indian mission and it would fully cooperate with him.[14] He belived that after arrival of sufficient military help from Germany and Turkey, the Afghan government would join hands with him and the 'Provisional Government' to oust the British from India by military might. The British Indian Government was very much alarmed with the activities of Raja Mahendra Pratap and other Indian revolutionaries at Kabul though the Amir alaways proclaimed his neutrality during the war years. The British intelligence reports maligned the 'Provisional Government' by recording that it declared to accept the Amir of Afghanistan as the permanent ruler of India, if he would declare that he was against the British Government.[15] Knowing the patriotism of Mahendra Pratap and other revolutionaries in the Provisional Government, such accusition seems baseless and malicious. Mahendra Pratap would not have welcomed and tolerated any other colonialism over India by replacing that of the British.

The Provisional Government realised the difficulties it faced to contact the people from abroad. Though the 'government' was secular it issued and utilised religious appeals as a means of mass arousal. It tried to arouse the religious sentiments especially of the Muslims with the help of anti-British Muslim powers like Turkey. Obeidullah tried to involve various Arab states in the anti-British struggle. He sent his friend Maulana Mahamud-ul-Hasan to Arabia to secure a holy writ from religious head calling upon Indian Muslims to rise in revolt against the British. The 'Provisional Government of India' itself issued three proclamations to Indians—one specially to the Muslims, one specially to the Hindus and one to all the Indians. Mahendra Pratap, thus, said :

> *We are doing our best to push forward our cause in the tribal area on the frontier. Maulvi Barkatullah's proclamation to the Mussalmans proved very useful and inspiring. While I hope my proclamation to the Hindus and the proclamation of the Provisional Government to the Indians must have proved of great benefit to our holy cause...*[16]

Mahud-ul-Hasan was able to secure a declaration of Jehad from Ghalib Pasha, the then Turkish military Governor of Hedja, known as Ghalibnama, which was distributed in thousands among the frontier tribes of Indo-Afghan border and among Muslims inside India. A scheme for a pan-Islamic army to be formed under the active guidance of the Turkish Government and the Sheriff of Mecca was chalked out by Obeidullah Sindhi who wrote a series of letters to different influential Muslims in India on 9th July 1916. These letters were intercepted by the British and their discovery led to the famous 'Silk Letter Conspiracy Case'.[17] Thus, no concrete result could be achieved out of these efforts of the 'Provisional Government' to exploit the religious sentiments against the British. Yet, perhaps, except Vir Savarkar, none of the Indian revolutionaries ever thought of establishing a Hindu Raj. Mahendra Pratap as head of the 'Provisional Government' sought to exploit religious sentiments as a means to further the revolutionary activities. Harnessing religion to promote the cause of national liberation with the positive aspect of uniting both the Hindus and Muslims on a common revolutionary platform, was a revolutionary aspect of Mahendra Pratap. It was later revealed that Obeidullah Sindhi, a hard-core Pan-Islamist, joined the 'Provisional Government' to safeguard the interest of the Muslims as he was afraid that a Hindu government if established in India would "eventually drive Islam out of India."[18] By no spark of imagination one can think of Mahendra Pratap to establish a Hindu Raj and never in history his secular credentials were under cloud.

The Provisional Government of India had entered into a treaty with the Amir of Afghanistan,[19] the contents of which are not known. Though the government of Amir did not declare war against England, it did give enough freedom to the 'Provisional Government' to carry on their patriotic duties. The printing of booklets and leaflets, meeting of the Indian revolutionaries, the functioning of the 'Provisional Government', sending some of them secretly into India through Indo-Afghan border were done without any hindrance by the Afghan government, without any positive response from the Amir and despite his German adviser Hentig's advice, the Raja proceeded to seek aid from tsarist Russia as well. He wanted to utilise old Anglo-Russia rivalry in central Asia and befriend Russia in a proposed grand alliance of Germany, Russia and Afghanistan. The 'Provisional Government' sent two unsuccessful missions to Tsar. In March 1916, the 'Provisional Government' sent two of its emissaries, Shamsher Singh and Muhammad Ali with a letter of Mahendra Pratap to the Governor of Russian Turkestan and the Tsar of Russia.[20] Mahendra Pratap himself had written a letter to the Tsar on a gold plate. In the letter to the Governor of Turkestan Mahendra Pratap wrote: "We nourish deep respect for our great neighbour and brother in Asia.

That is why we, naturally count on the friendly help of Russia. Cunning England, your natural rival in Asia, will not remain your friend for long, and we...may sometimes extend to you great help, political as well as economic''.[21] In the letter to the Tsar, he "expressed regret that India's two powerful neighbours should be fighting each other, and hoped that they would soon unite to crush England, the tyrant of the world, and set free the people whom she had enslaved.''[22] Even Mahendra Pratap mentioned about the unique opportunity the war had offered to Russia for joining hands with Afghanistan and "by so doing establish her influence in Asia on a permanent basis.''[23] On getting the hints on this mission, the British government sent a protest letter to the Russian government, requesting it to arrest these two emissaries and hand them over to it. The Tsarist government simply asked the mission to leave Russian territories. Another attempt was made in August 1916, which too, was unsuccessful.[24] The sending of these missions, on the one hand, shows the patriotic zeal of Mahendra Pratap and the 'Provisional Government', who in a frantic bid to oust the British from India thought of a Kaiser-Tsar-Amir confederacy to do the job and, on the other, speaks of their failure to understand the real character of imperialism as a global phenomenon.There might be contradictions among the imperialist powers but on the question of enslaving other nationalities, economic and political exploitation of those peoples for their own benefit they had common approach and thus, the Tsarist government with all its clash of interest with the British was not prepared to come out against the British government and that too, during the war years. Naturally, the efforts of the 'Provisional Government' to achieve the liberation of India from abroad without sufficient home-work, was doomed to be a failure.

Meanwhile, the February Revolution took place in Russia and a new government under prince Kerensky came to power. Mahendra Pratap tried to explore the possibility of getting assistance from the Kerensky government, there. But in reply to his query he was informed that there would be no change in the

Russian foreign policy under the new regime and the Indian revolutionaries should not expect any help from Russia.[25] The turning of the tide in war in favour of British and the impending defeat of Germany and Afghan reluctance to help the Indian revolutionaries led them to seek for aid and assistance elsewhere. The Indian native rulers in a conference had already pledged to help the British government in its war efforts and not to create any problem for it. They assured to arrest the emissaries who would bring the letters of Reich Chancellor of Germany or Sultan of Turkey. Kala Singh the emissary of the 'Provisional Government' was arrested while returing from Nepal, perhaps, sent by Mahendra Pratap to deliver the letter of Reich Chancellor to the king of Nepal. Not only was he unhappy on this score, but also he aid not reccive any financial assistance either from Germany or Turkey[26] to accomplish his mission which was creating great difficulties for him. But the patriotic zeal of Mahendra Pratap and other emigre revolutionaries in Kabul could not be extinguished by such hindrances rather it stiffened their determination to search for new source of support.

The news of victorious October Socialist Revolution in Rusia cheered the Indian revolutionaries who at that time were somewhat depressed on account of mounting British repression at home and the failure of their plan to liberate India with external aid of the German-Afghan-Turkish axis. They welcomed the new revolution and Bolshevik state as a new possible source of assistance to their cause. After three abortive attempts by the 'Provisional Government' to contact the former Russian Government, the October Revolution created a new hope for a favourable response from the Bolshevik government of Soviet Russia.

On 29 November, 1917, the president of the 'Provisional Government' of India, Raja Mahendra Pratap, arrived on the Afghan-Soviet border and asked the Turkestan authorities to allow him to negotiate with the Government of the RSPSR. Stating the Russians as 'true friends of humanity' and looking forward to 'close friendly relations between Russia and India', he expressed the opinion that "nothing but a partnership of Russia and India will make possible, India's true liberation and equilibrium in the Universe."[27] The Soviet Government invited Mahendra Pratap to Petrograd and Raja met there Trotsky[28] and also Joffe. Till then, the 'Provisional Government' was inclined in favour of a major German role in the liberation of India and advocated the idea that "the liberated Russia should cooperate with Germany in order to liberate India."[29] Staying in Petrograd for nearly a month, Mahendra Pratap left for Berlin and reached there on 28 March 1918 to negotiate with the German authorities and discuss further on the strategy for Indian independence with fellow Indian revolutionaries there.

Thus, the interest of Mahendra Pratap and the 'Provisional Government' for the Soviet power was the genuine urge of a nationalist as a possible source of financial, political and moral support. Moreover, he might have been impressed with the decrees and declarations issued by the young Soviet State. The Decree on peace (8 November, 1917) was followed by the Declaration of the Rights of the People of Russia (16 November, 1917) the Appeal of the Council of People's Commissioners to All Muslim Toilers of Russia and the East (20 November, 1917), and the Declaration of the Rights of the Toiling and Exploited People (12 January, 1918). The new Russian Government emphasised the principle of national self-determination and ethnic distinction of minorities. Moreover, The Raja and other Indian revolutionaries appreciated the Soviet recognition of the independence of Finland, Poland and other Baltic states and annuling unequal treaties that the Tsarist Government had entered into with Persia, Turkey and China. The Soviet state's recognition of the independence of Afghnistan enthused the 'Provisional Government'. Yet, till the fall of Kaiser, almost all Indian revolutionaries from Indian Independence Committee at Berlin to the 'Provisional Government' at Kabul had pitched their first preference of hope on Germany. In Berlin, Raja Mahendra Pratap came out with a curious and quixotic plan for organising an international socialist army comprising the German, Austrian, Bulgarian, Turkish and

Russian socialists to march through Soviet Russia to liberate India.[30] It shows that the position of Mahendra Pratap was the logical perception of an Indian nationalist, who, though was impressed with the Soviet state, not sure of Soviet strength in those years to give him sufficient material assistance in his plan of leading an external liberation mission to India. The notion of a decisive role of the military factor in a liberation struggle arose because of both, the real weakness of the movement of the Indian proletariat and the nascent workers' and peasants' movement, and the distinct military character of the major events of the day. In some countries like Persia, China and Korea armed gurillas launched operations against the imperialist troops. The victory of the Red Army in the Civil War and their struggle against the foreign interventionists in Soviet Russia had further strengthened their belief in the armed solution of the Indian question.

After the fall of Kaiser at the end of World War I, Mahendra Pratap as well as the 'Provisional Government' lost all interest in Germany. Now their hope rested on Soviet Russia and Afghanistan and they tried to help in the establishment of diplomatic relationship between both the countries. Prime Minister of the 'Provisional Government', Barkatullah came to Russia as 'Ambassador-Extraordinary' of the Afghan government to establish a permanent relationship between both the countries and met Lenin in Moscow in that connection. Though he came with a different mission, during his stay, he was attracted towards the Soviet State.

The starting of the third Afghan War between British India and Afghanistan on 3 May 1919 thrilled the 'Provisional Government'. It immediately issued a proclamation declaring that the 'Provisional Government' had entered into a compact with the invading forces of Afghanistan and asked the Indian people not to destroy their real interest by fighting against them.[31] The idea of securing independence of India through armed invasion of another country did not get enough support inside the country. The war lasted for a few days only, followed by a peace treaty between British and Afghan Government. Under the circumstance, the hopes of Indian revolutionaries to liberate India with the help of Germany and later by Afghanistan were shattered. Even though the India revolutionaries carried on their activities from Afghan authorities for few more years, they knew the futility of such efforts. The 'Provisional Government' turned to Soviet Russia for getting assistance. Now its next programme was to meet Lenin and other Soviet leaders to seek the Soviet support for the cause of India's independence.

Raja Mahendra Pratap led the first representative body of the Indian revolutionaries to Moscow and met Lenin in July 1919. The delegation included Barkatullah, Abdur Rab, M.P.T. Acharya, Dilip Singh Gill and Ibrahim. Mahendra Pratap had two intentions behind his mission to Moscow. Firstly, he wanted to get effective help form Soviet Russia in a liberation march into India. He said : "What Germans could not do, I thought, will now be done by Soviet Russia and the new Afghanistan (which had proclaimed its independece). Freedom of the one-fifth of mankind appeared very near."[32] Secondly Mahendra Pratap wanted the Soviets to recognize the 'Provisional Government' at Kabul. Both these requests were not accepted by the Soviets. The Soviet Government was not prepared to lend its supoort to the idea of raising liberation army from outside India without preparing the masses inside the country politically and ideologically. On the question of recognition, Soviets hesitated as it was not formed on the Indian territory and worked from there and it had not mustered support of a fairly large cross-section of Indian revolutionary opinion. Mahendra Pratap presented Lenin his book, **Religion of Love**. According to veteran revolutionary Bhupendranath Dutta, Lenin commenting on the book, asked Mahendra Pratap : "In our country too Tolstoy and others tried for the emancipation of the people by propagating religion, but nothing came out of it. So after returning to India you propagate class struggle, that will clear the path of liberation."[33] Later, a similar request was made to the Turkestan Commission of the All Russia Central Executive Committee by Mohammad Ali, Assistant Minister for the Interior and

Mohammad Shafiq Secretary of the same ministry in the 'Provisional Government', in the first half of April 1920. They also sought Soviet assistance for the liberation of India.[34] Though Lenin and the Soviet leadership supported the cause of Indian independence and appreciated their efforts for that, but their own involvement in solving the complicated pan-Islamic problem perhaps could not commit the former for any deep involvement in Indian affairs.

The advice of Lenin to Mahendra Pratap on class struggle was not accepted as such by him, but certainly, a subsequent change in the latter's thinking could be noticed. Earlier during the spring of 1919, the German indologist, H.V. Glasenapp, who worked for the German foreign office reported that Mahendra Pratap was about to publish a booklet exhorting the Germans to join the Spartacists and cooperate with the Russian Bolsheviks, was denounced by the then Social Democratic German Government as an 'eulogist of Trotsky'. His views were described as interference in the 'internal affairs of Germany' and their publication was stopped.[35] On his return from Moscow, Soviet ideological impact became noticeable in number of pronouncements which carried a touch of socialism or rather egalitarian ideas to be more precise. In his appeal to the Indian people from Kabul after his Moscow visit, Mahendra Pratap declared : "Tenants or the land labourers shall become proprietors of all such land that they till. Every family shall possess a permanent residence.[36] Of course. his appeal also contained several provisions for the benefit of the feudal chiefs and propertied classes, but his concern for the common peasants' desire for land and home-reflected the influence of early land reforms in Soviet Russia which he had an opportunity to watch during his stay in that country. While propagating his views about a world federation he expressed his belief in a mystic idea of 'Voluntary Communism'.[37] Lenin and Mahendra Pratap lived in two different worlds with their ideological convictions poles apart. Yet, Mahendra Pratap remained a radical nationalist with a non-class, humanitarian approach, always ready to cooperate with the Soviet

Union to undermine British imperialism.

While Mahendra Pratap led the delegation to Lenin in July 1919, the Prime Minister of the 'Provisional Government' Prof. Barkatullah was already there at Moscow by March 1919. He subsequently worked among the Muslim masses in Soviet Central Asia to win them over to the side of the Bolsheviks in order to fight against counter revolutionaries and foreign interventionists. In that process he travelled extenstively in Soviet Central Asia, talked to the people, gave press interviews, and wrote articles and booklets. In a clarion call to the Muslim population of Soviet Russia, he urged them in the name of Islam, which was threatened by the American, French and England capitalists' action in the holy cities of Constantinople, Mecca and Madina, to oppose the Russian counter-revolutionaries and defend the revolutionary gains.[38] In his own way, he tried to prove that the main propositions of Islam and Communism never contradicted each other, which, at that time, did a great service to the Young Soviet Republic. His articles, "Bolshevik ideas and the Islamic Republic", "Appeal to All the Muslims of Asia", 'Oriental Policy' and finally the pamphlet, 'Bloshevism and Islam' deeply influenced the Muslims in Soviet Russia. In his best written pamphlet, "Bolshevism and the Islamic Nations", though he attributed the origin of socialist theory of Marx and Lenin to the teachings of Plato and put many utopian socialist ideas into it, he called upon the Muslims in a religious way to come forward to support the Soviet power. Evaluating the character of the Soviet power, Barkutullah wrote:

> *The New administration of the extensive territories of Russia and Turkistan has been placed in the hands of the labourers, cultivators and soldiers. Distinction of race, religion and nationality has disappeared. Equal right to life and freedom are ensured to all classes of the nation.*[39]

His pamphlets were distributed in thousands throughout Soviet Central Asia. He did not accept scientific socialism as his ideological base and viewed it as a purely egalitarion doctrine.

Yet he openly called for the abolition of private property as it was "the cause of all evil on earth." He believed that given the national public ownership of land houses and factories, "all products made by every man must be a public asset" and everyone would be able "to take whatever he may need from a public storehouse."[40] Sharply criticising the British Parliament as "a children's toy made to dupe the people", he asserted that the right to be elected actually belonged to the propertied classes only while "labour and workers have been fighting for their rights for six hundred years, but cannot get rid of oppression."[41] Later when Barkatullah published a monthly Persian journal **El Islah** from Berlin, some of his political and ideological views were more explicit. A proscribed copy of the journal of July 1926, kept in the National Archives of India, carried an article which suggested a solution to India's problems of poverty and dependence by strike and appealed "to the students of India to unite with the cultivators, labourers and other poor people, and form a league for the freedom of India and fix complete freedom as their political and socialism as their economic objects." It further advocated "nonpayment of revenue by the peasants", which had not yet been advocated by the Indian nationalists at home, and "strikes by the labourers" as a means to revolution. Significantly, it also categorically demanded the "nationalisation of land", among other things.[42]

The Home Minister of the 'Provisional Government', Maulana Obeidullah Sindhi went to Moscow in 1922, met Chicherin, Soviet People's Commissioner for Foreign Affairs talked to other Soviet leaders and studied the Soviet constitution of 1918. In 1924, on the basis of his study he wrote "The Constitution of the Federated Ruplublic of India" which itself speaks of the ideological influence of the Soviet system on the programme of the Indian revolutionaries. A copy of this 'Constitution' is preserved in Russian archives and has been commented upon by Soviet scholars in their works on Indian revolutionaries.[43] Jawaharlal Nahru also referred to Obeidullah Sindhi's 'Constitution' in his **Autobiography** as an "able attempt to resolve the communal problem."[44] This proposed 'Constitution' of India borrowed many articles from the 1918 Constitution of the RSPSR.

On 10 April, 1920, two representatives of the 'Provisional Government' of India, Mohammed Ali and Mohammed Shafiq were asked in Soviet Russia about the objective of their 'Government'. They replied that it was 'to create an indigenous government in India, instead of the present alien government' and when it would become a reality, it would "handover its portfolio to the body-politic of India formulated by the Indian National Congress and the All India Muslim League, the two well-known representative bodies of India."[45] While detailing out their plan to achieve their objective, they stressed on invoking "the sympathy and moral support of foreign governments", disseminating revolutionary propaganda among "the princes and ruling chiefs of India.", "leaders of public opinion and captains of industries", and the Indian soldiers, and obtain arms and ammunitions to be used for "emergencies that is the general war of independence."[46] On the question of the relationship of their 'Provisional Government' with the Soviet Government, they wrote : "The Provisional Government expects to have the same relations with Soviet Russia as Denkin's and Kolchak's Government have with the Entente, that is to say, Provisional Government that hopes that Soviet Russia will help it carry on war against the English in India."[47] These two members of the 'Provisional Government' with few Indian revolutionaries formed the Indian section of the Council for International Propaganda or commonly known as Sovinterprop based at Taskent and authored many pamphlets, booklets and issued the only issue of its organ, **Zamindar.** Thus, we find the members of the 'Provisional Government' had carried their mission to Soviet Union and other countries with single minded determination to achieve India's independence.

Conclusion

The 'Provisional Government of India' under the leadership of

Raja Mahendra Pratap was a heterogenous conglomeration of various elements, from pan-Islamists to utopian socialists, with varying methods of struggle, from raising an external liberation army with the help of friendly, anti-British foreign governments to arousing the British Indian soldiers, peasants, common people and the ruling native chiefs. But the towering personality of the Raja was able to unite all of them on a common anti-British platfrom, with a common goal of national liberation. When their efforts with Germany and Afghanistan failed to get any concrete result, they came to Soviet Russia in search of material assistance. Though, the Soviets and Lenin were not prepared to give them arms, ammunition and other help in military mission, which to Soviets were futile without a mass awakening and grassroot work among the common people of India, the members of the 'Provisional Government' learnt new lessons during their stay in Soviet Russia and made study of the October Revolution and the developments in Russia after revolution. That realization was well-reflected in their post-Soviet visits, proclamations and documents. Though most of them did not become converts to socialism but remained nationalists, yet they remained friends of Soviet Russia and appreciated most of the changes that occurred there.

Mahendra Pratap was a liberal and never believed in class struggle. He did not impose his ideas and philosophy on his fellow revolutionaries. His 'Provisional Government' had a secular and non-sectarian base with a common binding force of selfless dedicated spirit of sacrifice on the altar of national liberation. It is not to suggest that Mahendra Pratap was above any criticism. References can be made to Mahendra Pratap's acceptance of a leading role of army in Indian liberation struggle (both external army and British Indian army) and his undue faith on the Indian princes to play a patriotic role in the anti imperialist struggle in India. Of course, Mahendra Pratap later corrected those wrong notions from his own life's experience. When we compare Mahendra Pratap and his fellow revolutionaries in the 'Provisional Government' with the mainstream nationalists back at home, we find a contrast. Most of our national leaders of that time thought of helping the British during the war years, which, to them, would expedite India's cause by the British after the war. They had not accepted the proposition of direct assault advocated by Raja Mahendra Pratap by that time. Gandhi, Patel and many other Indian nationalists believed in such a proposition, which was belied when British did nothing to give more power in the hands of the Indians after the war and the Montford Reform of 1919 was far from the nationalists' expectations. But the revolutionaries like Mahendra Pratap and the 'Provisional Government' had realised from the very beginning that India could not achieve her independence by the grace of alien government. She has to fight for it through various means by herself, on several fronts and Mahendra Pratap adopted one path of forming a government-in-exile and explored the possibility of an armed struggle against the British with the assistance of anti-British foreign powers, which remained a major thrust of their activities during and after the World War I.

Mahendra Pratap and the 'Provisional Government' should not be judged by what they achieved in real terms, but it should be judged by the wide-spread interest it created among various foreign governments and their people on the question of India's pitiable colonial subjugation under the British and her struggle for freedom. It thrilled the Indian people, who looked to their dedication and sacrifice with appreciation and reverance which alarmed the British authorities. When the efforts of Raja Mahendra Pratap in forming the 'Provisional Government' during the World War I was repeated by Subash Chandra Bose during the World War II in the form of the 'Azad Hind Government', Indians, staying abroad, joined it in thousands and assisted it, which ultimately, though not totally successful, was able to hoist the Indian tri-colour flag on Indian soil for a few days at Imphal in North-east in 1944. What Raja has dreamt was attained temporarily and finally in 1947, it was fulfilled. 'The Provisional Government of India' ramained as a glorious chapter of our national history and Mahendra pratap remained as a popular hero in mass psyche, not only among the revolutionaries alone but the general people of the country as a whole. The revolutionary movement in particular and national movement in general remained indebted to those valient revolutionaries in the 'Provisional Government' led by Mahendra Pratap, who at a crucial juncture of history during the war years strived for an anti-British front and kept up the morals of revolutionaries and patriots in high spirit with high expectations for the unknown future of India.

References—

1. Political and Secret Department, Vol. No. 4353/1920 India Office Library cited in T.R. Sareen, *Indian Revolutionary Movement Abroad* (Delhi, 1979), p. 172
2. Weekly Report of Director, Criminal Intelligence, 24 Feburary, 1919 Home-Political B, February, 1919 Nov. 181&184, National Archive of India (NAI).
3. Memorandum by Mahendra Pratap, 17 February 1915, German Foreign Office Records (microfilm), Roll No. 397. NAI.
4. Mahendra Pratap *Reflection of an Exile* (Lahore, 1946) P.B.
5. Sareen, n.1, p. 174
6. Foreign Department, Secret Internal, February, 1914, Nos. 11-18
7. Foreign Department, Secret Internal, January, 1913, No. 1, NAI
8. Home-Political A, August 1914, Nos. 7-16, NAI.
9. Foreign Department, Frontier, Confidential A, 1918, Nos. 241-430 NAI.
10. Weekly Report of Director, Criminal Intelligence, 24 February, 1919, Home-Political B, February, 1919, Nos. 181-84, NAI.
11. Mahendra Pratap, *My Life story of Fifty five years* (Dehradun, 1951) p. 51
12. Full text of this proclamation is available in Foreign Department, Frontier, Confidential A, 1918, Nos. 241-430, NAI
13. Ibid.
14. See Mahendra Pratap Papers, NAI.
15. Viceroy to Secretary of State, 15 September, 1916, Foreign Department, Frontier confidential A, 1918, Nos. 241-430, NAI.
16. "Mahendra Pratap : An Account of the Trip from Berlin through Turkey, Persia Afghanistan and Russia". German Foreign

Ministry Archives (microfilm), Real No. 400, NAI.

17. "Reports on the Silk Letter Conspiracy", Political and Secret Document, File No. 4260/1916, IOL,
18. Obeidullah to Mahmud Hassan, 9 July, 1916 Foreign Department, Frontier confidential A, 1921, Nos. 12-13, NAI.
19. Mahendra Pratap n. 11, p. 52
20. Mahendra Pratap to the Governor of Russian Turkestan, 21, February, 1916, Foreign Department, Frontier Confidential A, 1918, Nos. 241-43, NAI.
21. Cited in A.V. Raikov, *Probuzhdenie* (Mascow, 1968) p. 103 (in Russian)
22. Mahendra Pratap to the Governor of Russian Turkestan, no. 20
23. Ibid.
24. Mahendra Pratap n. 11, p. 56
25. Ibid. p. 57
26. "Note by Mahendra Pratap regarding failure of the Kabul Mission", German Foreign office Records, Roll No. 400, NAI
27. See M.A. Persits, *Revolutionaries of India in Soviet Russia* (Moscow, 1983),p. 38
28. Mahendra Pratap, n. 11, p. 57
29. Political and Secret Department, F.N. 4363, 1920, NAI.
30. Mahendra Pratap, n, 4, p. 20
31. Home-Political, B. June, 1919, Proceeding No. 497, Proclamation of the Provisional Government of India, working Report of the Director, Criminal intelligence for the month of May 1919, NAI.
32. Mahendra Pratap speech preserved central Party Archives, Institute of Marxism-Leninism (CPAIML), Persists n. 27, pp. 40-41.
33. Bhupendranath Dutta, *Aprakashita Rajnaitik Itihas* (Calcutta, 1953,) p, 118 (in Bengali)
34. 'A short Account of the History, of the Indian Revolutionary Committee', October, Revolution Central State Archives (ORCSA). 1, f. 486, p. 1-2, cited in Persits, n. 27, p. 42.
35. Glasenapp's Report of 15.4.1919 and the letter of German envoy in Switzerland, Adolf Mueller of 6.5.1919, cited in Manmath Nath Gupta, *History of the Indian Revolutionary Movement* (Bombay, 1972), p. 76
36. Home-Political, 1922, F.N. 73.
37. Mahendra Pratap, *Afghanistan, the Heart of Aryan* (China, n.d.) p. 28 Preserved in the private papers of Mahendra Pratap, Item

No. 4, NAI.

38. *Izvestia turk Ts Ika* (Tashkent), 12 February, 1920, p. 2.
39. Cited in G. Adhikari, ed., *Documents of the History of the Communist Party of India,* Vol, I (Delhi, 1971), pp. 123.
40. Barkatullah's Speech published in *Istiraquin* (Tashkent), 16 April, 1919.
41. Ibid.
42. Home-Political, 1926, File No. 135/V
43. L. V. Mitrokhin and A.V. Raokov, "Obeidullah Sindhi, First constitution of Federated Republic of India", *Mainstream,* Vol. XIII, No. 10, 9 November, 1974, pp 7-9.
44. Jawaharlal Nehru, An Autobiography, (Delhi, 1962) p. 151.
45. "*A short History of the Indian Revolutionary Committee*", n. 34, p. 42
46. Ibid, p. 43
47. Ibid, p. 49.

Indian Revolutionaries Abroad —A study of the Role of Mahendra Pratap and the First Provisional Government of Independent India.

—Raj Pal Singh

The Nationalist Revolutionary strivings for complete independence during the first World War and the Wanderings of Indian revolutionaries abroad helped to minimise the rising tide of communalism and relative parochialism as well as provided a vision of the emergence of international anti-imperialist struggle as well as developed links with the international socialist movement. The First World War brought about really crucial changes in the political life and socio-economic conditions of India. Leaving the detailed scrutiny of multi-dimensional consequences of the War, here an effort has been made to concentrate on the active participation of Indian Revolutionaries Abroad in their efforts to liberate India with sepcial reference to the role played by Mahendra Pratap during these years.

Raja Mahendra Pratap of Hathras in Aligarh district of modern Uttar Pradesh was born on I December 1886. He received his education at the famous Aligrh Oriental Muslim school and grew up as a nationalist revolutionary. The beginning of the First World War in 1914 brought about really crucial changes in his political thinking. After applying for passport stating that he wanted to go to Europe to study the War situation and then would go to U.S.A. to see the World exhibition, he left for Switzerland. When he was in Geneva he came into contact with

Lala Har Dayal and Shyamji Krishan Varma, the famous revolutionaries. In fact, nationalist revolutionaries, who were active in different countries striving for independence, "the War seemed a heaven-sent opportunity draining India of White soldiers and bringing the possibility of financial and military help from German and Turkish enemies of Britain. At this point of time, Indian revolutionaries in non-Entente Europe, who had responded to the call to serve their mother land like M. Prabhakar, Abdur Rahman, A. Siddiqui, Virendranath Chattopadhyaya, Mahammad Mansur and others grouped together at Berlin and founded Indian Independence Committee popularly known as the 'Berlin Indian Committee'. Its explicit object was to "take care of Indians living under the central powers, establish contacts with Indian revolutionaries elsewhere, and to advise the German Government on Indian affairs."[1] The Berlin Indian Committee planned to establish a provisional government.[2] However, it was felt that before doing so they must make the committee more representative of the Indians. "The presence of some well-known figure among them, they thought, would strengthen their moral position, raise their bonafides above doubt, and convince their countrymen that the German could be trusted as their sincere friends"[3] That is why, on learning about the presence of Mahendra Pratap and Har Dayal at Genewa, Virendra Nath Chattopadhyaya hurried down to meet them in Switzerland and invited them to Germany. Mahendra Pratap insisted upon meeting the German Emperor, William II after reaching Berlin. When this condition was agreed upon, he alongwith Chattopadhyaya reached Berlin on 10 February, 1915 and was received in audience by the Kaiser himself, who conferred on him the order of Eagle (2nd class). In fact, he was always shown special courtesy and consideration due to a prince with a commanding presence.[4]

Now many prominent leaders of the Ghadar Party and of other organisations of Indian emigeres had converged in Berlin. Efforts, were made to get as many well known nationalist leaders to join them in Germany as possible. More than once, Lala Lajpat Rai was requested to come and accept the leadership of the

Indian revolutionaries in Germany but he refused to do so. in due course of time the Berlin Indian Committee was not wanting in men of stature as it had the services of persons like Mahendra Pratap, Har Dayal, Virendra Nath Chattopadyaya, Barkatullah Khan, Dr. Jnan Chandra Dasgupta, Jitendranath Lahiri, Bhupendranath Datta and others. Since the German scheme to spread disaffection among the muslims of constantinople and Baghdad against the British and Envar Pasha's plan to organise revolutionary movements by sending German officers to Afghanistan had miserably failed,[5] it was now for the Berlin Indian Committee to show its worth. To Mahendra Pratap, it was the one point of time when a successful *coup detat* appeared not impossible. He "submitted a scheme to the German Foreign office. Accordingly the preparation was made with a view to concluding an alliance with afghanistan, while Mahendra Pratap would carry the letters addressed to twenty-six Indian Princes and one for the King of Nepal given by the German Emperor exhorting them to rise in revolt against the British. Bethmann Hollweg wrote assuringly to Mahendra Pratap that he "may rely on the powerful support of the Imperial Germany."[6] The idea was even supported by well known industrialists of Germany like Albert Ballin and Mannesmann. "They all felt that the fact that Mahendra Pratap was a well known landlord of Kshatriya caste and Baraktullah, a renowned revolutionary and a maulvi, would inspire enthusiasm in Indan princes and Muslims alike. It was further decided, obviously with an eye on Indian sentiment, that Mahendra Pratap would be the formal head of the mission. while Dr. W.O. Von Hentig of the German foreign Office would be in actual charge of its affairs."[7] Enroute to Kabul, Mahendra Pratap had an audience with the Sultan of Turkey and also had meeting with Hilmi Pasha, the Prime Minister of Turkey, Envar Pasha, Talat Pasha and the Sheikhul Islam. The Sultan and his officers issued special orders to their military officers about ensuring safety and security to the mission through Asia Minor to Persia and also to provide all necessary facilities. The Turkish Sultan also gave a letter of introduction of Mahendra Pratap for the Amir (King) of Afghanistan. The Prime Minister of Turkey gave him seven letters for the Indian Princes professing Turkish friendship and a call to rise in revolt against the British. The Sheikh al-Islam gave them a written fatwa urging Hindus and Muslims to work together against the British. The Turkish authorities also agreed to Mahendra Pratap's request to sent one Turkish official with the Mission.

After having braved the hazards of the journey and dangers of the enemy activities, the mission was able to safely enter Kabul on 2 October 1915. The members of the mission were accommodated at the Bagh-i-Babur in Kabul but the Amir Habibullah did not show any interest in its arrival. Attempts of Mahendra Pratap, Barkatullah and Hentig to seek an audience with him at first seemed bleak. However, in view of the public support to the anti-British mission and also sympathetic attitude of the crown princes Inayatullah and Nasrullah Khan, the Amir had to grant the mission an interview on 24 October, 1915. There, in the presence of the Amir's ministers, it was agreed that the German-would train the Afghan army, and that the blue-print of a German-Afghan treaty would be prepared in due course of time.[8] Therefore, a separate meeting was arranged for the Indian delegates on the mission with the Amir, Habibullah. In the meeting Mahendra Pratap raised the issue of Indians interned and Indians in prison of Afghanistan. The Amir promptly acceded to the request to grant guest status to the Indians interned and set free the revolutionary prisoners. Among the persons so set free were Maulana Obeidullah Sindhi of Dar al-Ulum at Deoband, Mathura Singh and a number of the Mujahids. Haji Abdul Razak was appointed by the Prime Minister to deal with the Indian problems.[9]

Although the Indo-Turco-German Mission had been allowed to stay in Kabul, the pro-British Amir, Habibullah did not reveal his real intentions. In view of the presence of a pro-Turkish and anti-British opinion among certain sections of the Afghan people as reflected by the Siraj al Akhbar, a leading newspaper of Kabul, the Amir could not order them to go away. Rather he chose to while away the time of the mission. At this juncture arrival of a considerable number of the muslim revolutionaries in Kabul under the leadership of the Deoband Maulavis to liberate India with Turkish help and the presence of many Indian nationalist revolutionaries, inspired Mahendra Pratap and Barkatullah Khan to take a rather bold decision of considerable symbolic value. This was the anouncement of a Provisional Government of India at Kabul on 1 December 1915 under the leadership of the veteran nationalist revolutionary, Mahendra Pratap. He was designated as its President, Maulana Barkatullah as Prime Minister and Maullana Obeidullah Sindhi as Home Minister.[10] Those Indians who were under detention in Afghanistan were now released and "some of them took up various secretarial jobs under provisional government."[11] The composition of the newly established organisation "attested to a radicalisation of the Indian National liberation movement and a unification of its revolutionary force of diverse orientations. The provisional Government in exile was made not only of representatives of the Ghadar Party and the Berlin Committee, but also of some leading members of the Muslim movement and extreme left-wingers of the Indian National Congress."[12]

In Feburary 1916, Mehendra Pratap and Maulana Obeidullah sent a secret invitation to Abul Kalam Azad to join them at Kabul to wage their fight against the British.[13]

In the meantime, the provisional Government of India issued its manifesto listing there in the promises of the Turko-German help. It also spoke very high of the efforts of the Ghaderites by employing armed resistence against the British. The Provisional Government of independent India exhorted the Hindus and Muslims of India to maintain unity and also called upon the Rajas and Nawabs (rulers of the Indian princely states) to rise against the alien rule. They also appealed the army men to rise in revolt against the British Imperialism.[14]

With a view to achieve its avowed objectives the Provisional Government of India swang into action. Accordingly, an agreement was reached between the Amir of Afghanistan and the Provisional Government of Independent India. The Amir allowed the establishment and functioning of this government from its headquarters at Bagh-i-Babur and also permitted it to estabilish diplomatic relations with other countries.[15]

Mahendra Pratap and his comrades were restless souls of indomitable energy and adventurous temperament. All of them possessed anti-British nationalism in abundance and wanted to use any sort of support from the foreign countries which could be used to promote the cause of Indian freedom. In March 1916, with a view to explore the possibility of securing Russian assistence, Mahendra Pratap in his capacity as the President of the Provisional Government of Independent India despatched a letter to the czar through Mathura Singh and Mirza Muhammad Ali. But they were arrested and handed over to the British.[15] Undetered by this turn of events, Mahendra Pratap sent Kala Singh alias Gujar Singh to Russo-Turkistan to solicit the help of the Czar in August 1916.[16] However, he was denied entry in Russia.[17] It would be pertinent to ask as to why the Provisional Government of Independent India was so eager to get Russian military and financial support. "The reason why they looked to Russia was two-fold : Russia's central Asian possessions lay close to the borders of India and the Anglo-Russian contradictions in the East had come to a head. Under such circumstances Mahendra Pratap's Government strove hard to organise with Russian and Afghan support an all out uprising in India. But the response of both the Czar and the Amir was not upto the expectations of the Provisional Government of Independent India. The members of the Turco-German-Indian Mission after having stayed in Afghanistan for over eight months failed to wean away the Amir from the pro-British policies, the German delegates left for their country in may 1916 but were captured by the British in Iran. In september, 1916 the Provisional Government of Independent India sent a mission to the captial of Turkey. However the Czar's officers in Persia arrested this third mission and handed it over to Britain."[18]

Earlier to it Mahendra Pratap and his cabinet colleague Obeidullah tried to solicit help of the pan-islamite revolutionaries.

They on 9 July 1916 sent letters written on silk clothes and sewn with the bearer's coat for the princes of India exhorting them to rise in revolt against the British. But the emissary was arrested by the Britishers and several revolutionaries were nabbed and severely punished in the Silk-letter conspiracy.[19] In spite of the repeated failures, Mahendra Pratap desperately tried to make some useful contacts with anti-British powers. He managed to send Bethman-Hollweg's letters and the Turkish Sultan's letters alongwith his own notes to India urging the Indian princes to declare their independence from the British yoke and constitute a commonwealth of India. But the British authorities had prior information about this. Hence the move proved futile.[20] However, Mahendra Pratap's emmissery Kala Singh (Gujjar Singh) delivered the above type of letters to the King of Nepal but he remained unmoved.

But Mahendra Pratap and his fellow revolutionaries were not made of the stuff that easily melts due to slightest heating. Following February Revolution of 1917 in Russia, the Provisional Government of Independent India under Mahendra Pratap, once more tried to count on Rassian aid. But in reply to his query Kerensky's Russian Provisional Government informed that there would be no change in Russian foreign policy and that Indian revolutionaries should not expect any help from Russia.[21] This obviously caused a bit of pessimism to the nationalist revolutionary activities. However, following the victory of the October Revolution, Mahendra Pratap wrote that now "the final obstacle has been removed, and I have been glad to find out from the latest newspapers appearing in India that the Russian Government is now led by the noble sons of Russia. English present them as traitors, but in actual fact they are true friends of humanity...." He went on to say that he was anxious to see "close friendly relations between Russia and India" because "we trust that nothing but a partnership of Russia and India will make possible India's true liberation and an equalibrium in the Universe."[22]

Accordingly, Lanin's Government, soon after assuming

power, invited Mahendra Pratap to visit the U.S.S.R. In March 1918, he reached Petrograd (Leningrad) and met Trotsky in the War Office. And finding the Russians pre-occupied in their fight for survival, Mahendra Pratap left for Germany. He arrived at Berlin on 28 March, 1918 and handed over to the Kaiser William II the letter of the Amir of Afghanistan. During the course of his talks with the Emperor of Germany he suggested to organise an international socialist army, comprising the German, Austrian, Bulgarian, Turkish and Russian. He thought that such an army could easily cross Soviet Russia and help India to gain her freedom. The idea was not liked by the German Emperor. Undetered by it, Mahendra Pratap repeated the suggestion before Envar Pasha at Constantinople about a month later, but in vain.[23]

From the above, it is apparent that Mahendra Pratap was knocking at every door from where he could garner support to liberate his motherland from the yoke of the alien rule. He tried his level best to present the case of the independence of India before the American Ambassador. However, he did not listen to him.[24]

On hearing about the murder of King Habibullah of Afghanistan, Mahendra Pratap hurried back from Germany to Afghanistan. He thought that under the changed circumstances there seemed better prospect of the Soviet and Afghan aid for India's struggle for freedom as the government in both the countries seemed to be friendly towards the Provisional Government of Independent India. Enroute he paid a visit to Petrograd where Lanin gave a generous welcome to him. Mahendra Pratap, Barkatullah Khan and other members of the Provisional Government of Independent India in Kabul strived hard to get Russian recognition to their government and Russian military and financial support for their revolutionary activities from then onwards and all through 1919, 1920 and 1921 but no concrete support could be enlisted from outside.

By 1918, the political scenario radically changed in favour of the Entente powers and no foreign country seemed interested in directly supporting the Provisional Government of Independent

India. At first, the new Russian Government of Lenin showed some interest in the affairs of Mahendra Pratap but gradually it also tried to utilize the services of the members of his Government to further consolidate the position of Bolsheviks in the central Asia. In view of it, the First Provisional Government of Independent India in exile established on December1, 1915 at Kabul became inactive and defunct by 1922. Several members of the nationalist revolutionary fervour owing allegiance to it had either been captured by the British or shifted their loyalty to other groups engaged in carrying out their liberation struggle from other places than Kabul. Mahendra Pratap himself had suffered a lot due to his involvement in the freedom struggle from abroad. His estates in India were escheated as revealed by the reply of a question in the central Assembly.[26] He was denied entry into India till the second World War was over. Admittedly Mahendra Pratap and his provisional government failed to garner enough support in India and also from abroad due to inherent shortcomings of the nationalist struggle and countradictions in the objectives of the foreign government promising support to them. However the Saga of sufferings faced and sacrifices made by Mahendra Pratap and other nationalist revolutionaries from abroad kept on arousing the imperative determination of the next generation of freedom fighters. Perhaps, taking a cue from the experiences of the First Provisional Government of Independent India headed by Mahendra Pratap, the Indian revolutionaries led by Subhash Chandra Bose established the Indian National Army and the Second Provisional Government of India and successfully focussed the attention of Indians, both inside India and abroad, towards the need of liberating their motherland. This is not, in anyway, an insignificant achievement of Mahendra Pratap and his government in Exile.

Reference—

1. A.C. Bose, *Indian Revolutionaries Abroad*, Patna (1971). pp. 91
2. Raj Kumar Trivedi '*Turco-German Intrigue in India during the World War-I*' I.H.C. Proceedings, Kurukshetra, 1982. pp. 655
3. A C. Bose, op. Cit. pp. 93

4. *Ibid.*, Mahendra Pratap, *My life Story of fifty five years*, (Delhi) pp. 48-50
5. Raj Kumar Trivedi, op. cit. pp. 656-657
6. *Ibid.* For details, see T.R. Sareen, *Indian Revolutionary Movement Abroad* (1905-1920) (Delhi, 1979), pp. 172 ff.
7. Statement of Guenther Voigt quoted by A.C. Bose, Op. cit., pp. 107.
8. Mahendra Pratap, op. cit. pp. 49-50, A.C. Bose. op. cit. pp. 109-110.
9. Ibid.
10. Mahendra Pratap. Op. Cit, pp. 50-52.
11. A.C. Bose, Op. Cit., pp. 111
12. M.A. Persits, *Revolutionaries of India in Soviet Russia,* Moscow, 1973, pp. 22.
13. Report by C.E.W. Sands cited in A.C. Bose, Op. Cit. pp. 111.
14. Tilak Raj Sareen, op. cit., pp. 274-275.
15. *Ibid.* pp. 180
16. M.A. Parsits, Op. cit. pp. 23; A.C. Bose, op. cit. pp. 113.
17. Mahendra Pratap. op. cit., pp. 56.
18. Records of Central State Military History Archives of USSR quoted by M.A. Persits in op. cit., pp. 23.
19. A.C. Bose, op. cit., pp. 114.
20. Tilak Raj Sareen. op. cit., pp. 183-184.
21. M.A. Persits, op. cit., pp. 23; Mahendra Pratap op., cit., pp. 57; A.C. Basu, op., cit., pp. 114.
22. Letter of Mahendra Pratap in Central State Military History Archives, S. 1936. R.C.F. 234. pp. 131-132 quoted by M.A. Persits, op. cit., pp. 38.
23. Mahendra Pratap, op. cit., pp. 58-59.
24. *Ibid.*
25. Nand Kumar Dev Sharma, *Prem Pujari Raja Mahendra Pratap Singh*, Caltutta (1980 Vikrami samvat), pp. 93.
26. Also see, *Mahendra Pratap Abhinandan granth*, for fuller details of the activities of M.P. abroad and in India.

The Restless Raja – Rebel in Arms and an Apostle of Love

A.C.Bose

The fascinating life of Raja Mahendra Pratap, born at Mursan in Aligarh district on 1.12.1886,[1] is a romantic saga of revolt and renunciation, of ceaseless struggle and sacrifice. Although comparisons are seldom perfect and one is tempted, when studying his colourful career, to think of two world famous princes who five hundred years before Christ renounced all earthly pleasures and powers to announce the eternal truths of love and liberation. Born and brought up as a landlord, who as a class are noted for their avarice and arrogance, he virtually started his adult life by donating five villages with a net income of Rs.27,500.00 (a big amount in those days) for his technical school, Prem Maha Vidyalaya,[2] which was formally inaugurated on 24 May 1909.[3] Both his action and the choice of name for this institution speak volumes about the idealism that was to direct his destiny thereafter. It may not be a pure accident that one of the teachers in his institution was none but Abani Mukherjee who made a name during the first World War as a leading revolutionary and later as a Comintern emissary in Central Asia struggling for India cause. Three years later, when Turkey was involved in the Balkan War with the Christian powers of the region, we find him at Istanbul offering his services to the Turks in distress. The Turks, however, were in no position to appreciate the universality of his human concern and cold-shouldered his offer as something suspicious coming from a non-Muslim.[5] So, he returned home, but his irresistible urge to do all that was possible for the suffering humanity, starting with his own countrymen, would not let him enjoy the pleasures of life with his wife and children. So, he left for Europe, in December 1914, without a passport which reached him later through his travel agents, Thomas Cook – got down at Marseilles and went to Switzerland. He had no chosen destination, no contact with any of the Indian revolutionaries in Europe, and no introductory letter for the authorities of any of the Central Powers. Still, like an explorer, he had launched himself into an endless voyage in an unchartered sea. Fate, however, smiled at the brave and a chance meeting at Geneva with Virendranath Chattopadhyay, the brother of Mrs. Sarojini Naidu and the head of the Indian Independence Committee at Berlin, determined the future course that he was to pursue.

Chattopadhyay assured him that he would be able to arrange an interview with the Kaiser himself and off they left for Berlin to reach there on 10, February, 1915.[6] On the 21st he called at the German Foreign Office and suggested that a mission might be sent to the Amir of Afghanistan to encourage him to attack Britain in India and to incite the frontier tribes to revolt.[7] The Indian Committee and the German Foreign Office were already toying with this idea, and now they grabbed the offer when a prince was willing to lead it. The so called Hentig-Pratap Mission left Berlin on 9th April 1915 for Istanbul by train.[8] While Hardayal, Birendranath Dasgupta, and Tirumal Achari accompanied them up to Istanbul, Maulvi Barkatullah was to be with it till the end. Dr.W.O.Von Hentig of the German Diplomatic Service was the secretary to the mission and 100,000 pounds were deposited in his favour with the Istanbul branch of the Deutsche Bank for the expenses of this mission.[9] Apart from official letters for the Sultan of Turkey and the Amir of Afghanistan they had with them the German Chancellor's letters for the King of Nepal and 26 other Indian princes asking them to overthrow the British yoke and assuring them of all possible German help.[10] At Istanbul, they were honourably received by the Sultan himself and they reached Kabul on 2 October 1915 after covering the entire distance from Baghdad on carts or on horse-back. Many of us are aware of this Hentig-Pratap Mission and details about it are now available to the German knowing readers through Hentig's Afghanistan, ein Jahrbuch der Weltpolitik, Ripart von Bluecher's Zeitenwende in Iran, and Dr.Ulrich Gehrke's masterly research work, Persien in der Deutschen Orientpolitik, in two volumes.

One should remember that things in Western Asia were then much different from what they are now, when one can comfortably cover the distance from Baghdad to Kabul in a luxury bus, in less than a week. Ninety years ago communication system there was primitive and it was wartime when Russian and British soldiers and their agents were in control of the area they were passing through. Often the mission had to fight through hostile elements and, more than once, had narrow escape with their lives. In short, the journey was not only very difficult, but was also very dangerous. However, ultimately they made it.

Here too the mission and, particularly the Raja himself, was very well received. The Amir met them on 24th October and asked the German officers with them to train the Afghan army on modern lines. Although Amir Habibullah was pro-British and a peace loving person, his brother Nasrullah and Crown Prince Inayatullah sympathized with the Central Powers. So Mahendra Pratap, on 2nd December 1915 announced the formation of the Provisional Government of free India. Though purely symbolic, such actions are of immense significance in a nation's struggle for freedom.[14] However, since there was no prospect of the German army approaching the Afghan frontier, the Amir refused to adopt any anti-British posture and the Germans in the Mission left for home in May 1916.[15] Mahendra Pratap and Barakatullah, however, decided to stay behind, and in the spring and autumn of 1916 made two attempts to contact the Russian authorities in Turkistan through emissaries. The Russians, as allies of the British, proved to be unresponsive. The same was the response of the Nepalese authorities when Kala Singh visited Kathmandu in June 1917.[16] Even in Turkistan the Government of Kerensky, which had come to power in Russia in March 1917, proved to be as unresponsive as their Czarist predecessors . However, some sort of an opportunity came, in early March 1917, when the new Bolshevik authorities, obviously in response to his earlier efforts, invited Mahendra Pratap to Russia. He immediately set out for Leningrad where, in the absence of Lenin, he had a meeting with the redoubtable Trotsky. The latter, however, was in no position to offer him anything beyond sympathy and Mahendra Pratap , though impressed with the ideals of communism, left for Germany and reached Berlin on 28th March, exactly three years after he had left for Kabul with high hopes.[17] In the meantime, he had come very close to the ruling family of Afghanistan and had been granted Afghan citizenship and passport, and Afghan officials all over the world were hereafter available to him with their help. But he was not the person to enjoy a comfortable life at Kabul or anywhere else. Something in him constantly impelled him to go ahead, to discover new pastures, and to do something for peace and the down-trodden.

For sometime, he even toyed with the idea of organizing an international socialist army comprising those of the Central Powers and Bolshevik Russia, and met the famous Envar Pasha of Turkey. When nothing matured in the desired direction, he left for Afghanistan in 1919 on hearing that Amir Amanullah had declared war on Britain. On his way he met Lenin and literally escorted the new Soviet Ambassador, Suritz, to Kabul.[18] The Afghans, however, lost the short war and early in 1920 the Raja once again set out in search of fresh opportunities. Enroute, at Tashkent he met the celebrated M.N.Roy and his old friend Barkatullah, and reached Berlin in January 1922.[19] By then he had seen enough of war, revolution and bloodshed and had slowly come to the conclusion that his ultimate aim should be to work for love, liberty and unity of mankind. Though physically an Indian by birth and legally a citizen of Afghanistan he had become at heart a citizen of the world, and his sole aim hereafter was the spread of his message of World Federation and to approach India with it for her overall liberation. So, after spending some time in Western Europe he went to Mexico and USA and then to Japan (where he met the celebrated revolutionary Rash Behari Bose), China, Mongolia and ultimately to his favourite Kabul. A year later he again set out from Afghanistan as the unofficial ambassador of Amir Amanullah to Japan and reached there on 14th June 1926 after spending nearly two years on the way preaching his message and collecting funds and followers especially from among the Indian settlers in California. This time he went much beyond Japan and reached the inner frontiers of Tibet, but no further. Thus he continued to cross high hills, oceans and deserts, never at rest and ever on the quest, preaching and searching like the peripatetic philosophers of the past.[20] He attended the first and second Pan-Asian Conferences in Japan in the summers of 1926[21] and 1927, and established an office of his pet dream of World Federation at Berlin, in September 1929. A few years later it was Tokyo with its Buddhist tradition that became the main centre of his World Federation movement and he took a prominent part in the Great Pan Asian Conference at Darien in Manchuria, in February 1934. Thus he continued moving across international borders with his message of love and unity as the unofficial emissary of humanity in search of hope. When Japan joined the war, in December 1941, he was there and it was no longer possible for him to move around war hit East Asia. Nor was he then liked in Japan drunk with the heady wine of war and domination. So, he remained confined there till the end of the war when the stormy patrol of years of bloodless battles could return to his now independent homeland, after a long and event packed self-exile of thirty two years. But the old war horse was apparently neither tired nor frustrated, and he continued till the end with the propagation of his ideas from his retreat at Dehra Dun.

A short note may be added here on what he really meant by his conception of the world federation. As I could gather from him personally and from A.M.Sahay, who had worked closely with him in Japan, it was not to be a replica or parallel organization of the League of Nations. It was to be a people's movement. His aim was to bring the people of different lands and faiths closer to one another through mutual love and understanding, so that the seeds of conflict are destroyed even before germination. Obviously, in terms of numbers and visible impact, his long years of struggle and suffering have not yet produced any significant result, and what is worse his is today a forgotten name. Those who matter in today's world know little about him and care even less. But such a man should be measured not by his worldly achievements but by what he had lived for and how. It is the cause and the commitment that make one a real good man, and we wait for the day when this world learns to place the good in the galleries of the great.

References

1. Mahendra Pratap, *My Life Story of Fifty-five Years* (Delhi, 1947), p. 1
2. *Ibid.*, p. 22
3. *Ibid.*, p. 23
4. *Ibid.*, p. 71
5. *Ibid.*, p. 28
6. *Ibid.*, p. 39 & 43
7. Gehrke, Ulrich, *Persien in der Deutsche Orientpolitik*, (Stuttgart, 1961).Vol. 1, p. 146
8. Gehrke, op. cit., pp. 36. Also, Dr. Becker's Diary, Foreign Political 1920 July 376, and statement of B. N. Dasgupta.
9. Gehrke, op.cit., Vol. II, p. 141
10. Pratap, pp. 141. Copies of these letters are there among MSS Eur. E. 209, in India Office Library, London.
11. Pratap, pp. 44, 45 & 48. Also, Gehrke, Vol. 1, pp. 148-49. Also Dr. Becker's Diary, op.cit.
12. Bose, A.C., *Indian Revolutionaries Abroad*, (Patna, 1971), pp. 108-09.
13. Pratap, pp. 49-51.Also, the *Summary of the Administration of Lord Hardinge of Penhurst.*, p. 98
14. Pratap, pp. 51-52
15. Bose, A.C., pp. 111-12
16. Pratap, pp. 55-57. Also, *Director Criminal Intelligence* of 27-

01-17 in Home Political 1917 Feb. 397-400 B

17. Pratap, pp. 57-58. Also, F.M. Bailey, *Mission to Taskhent*, (Lond, 1946), pp. 7-8
18. Pratap in Anand Gupta (Ed.), *India and Lenin,* (Delhi, 1960)., pp. 32-34. Also the *Times* (Lond.), dated 16-01-20, and 12-17-03, p. 20
19. Pratap, pp. 71-72
20. Ibid., pp. 74 to the end.
21. *Activities of Emissaries* in Home Political 8F 235/II/26 of 1926. Also, B.B. Bose, *Karmavir Rashbehari* (in Bengali), Calcutta, 1956, p. 199.

Raja Mahedra Pratap : A Zealous Revolutionary : 1919-46

Yuthika Mishra

Few people can match the revolutionary zeal and sacrifices of Raja Mahendra Pratap during the struggle for India's independence. Born into a royal family, the riches and attractions of royalty could not deter him from plunging into the inundating waves of the independence movement. In 1914, he left India and worked for the cause of freedom for the next thirty one years, in exile. He travelled around the world as a spokesman of India and interacted with many Governments as well as revolutionary groups. All through this Raja Mahendra Pratap stands out as a patriot devoted not only to the freedom of the country but also to its economic emancipation and revival as an abode of learning and education.

This paper attempts to trace his activities during the period (1919-1946) and has been divided into 3 sections. The first section (1919-24) deals with that phase of Mahendra Pratap's activities when, under socialist impact he tried to get the support of the left bloc for his anti-British efforts abroad, almost single handed. In the second phase (1925-30) of his work focus is on his direct involvement with the Ghader party, his main work interest, with its headquarters in the U.S.A. The year 1930 has been the breaking point because thereafter he got more and more attracted towards the ideology of world religion and brotherhood. The Gandhian impact was very obvious in his approach to the freedom of India after 1930. But his objective still remained the same i.e. the attainment of the country's freedom. In the third section (1931-47), his contribution to the National Movement has to be analysed in the background of the II World War and the role of the British Raj in India. As far as his method is concerned, it appeared to be less revolutionary and almost brinking on the philosophical.

It is not mere coincidence that most of these dates which mark a watershed in the life of Raja Mahendra Pratap also denote the occurence of a major event on the international and Indian political scene. The end of the I World War in 1918 changed the international scenario. While the European countries were already divided into Allied and Axis powers, now they were joined by Russia, U.S.A. and Japan. It was the newly established socialist ideology which had the greatest impact on the political creed of Raja Mahendra Pratap in the first phase. Oviously, the anti-British stance of the left block and of Axis powers influenced and shaped his political career in the next few years.

While the second phase saw an intensification of his revolutionary zeal, it is actually the third phase which has generated a lot of controversy about the nature of his work and thus calls for more research in the future. It is generally understood that during the third and fourth decades of the 20th century, also known for the II Word War and its disastrous impact, his ideology seemed to shift more towards religion, the concept of world federation and brotherhood. But here it would be sufficient to remark that his publication 'World Federation,' which was launched in September 1929, was found to be distinctly revolutionary and anti-British by the Indian authorities and prohibitory orders were issued against it in April 1931.[1] Another element which acted as a catalyst for increasing their apprehensions was that the paper was published in vernaculars like Urdu and Gurmukhi and also in foreign languages like Japanese and Chinese. As a result the British official attitude had hardened in view of the increased revolutionary threat to the British Empire from all quarters.

I

The Period between 1919 to 1924 saw a wave of revolutions all over Europe. Raja Mahendra Pratap himself saw the nationalist upheavals of 1919 in Hungary and Bavaria and witnessed their new birth as democratic republics. Kaiser Wilhelm II took refuge in Holland. Events took a favourable turn in Afghanistan. King Amanullah declared war on the British. This news rejuvenated the Raja's spirits and he immediately took off for Kabul breaking journey over Russia to meet Lenin to seek his cooperation. A combined Indo-Russian mission then proceeded to Afghanistan where he was made the head of the Afghan delegation and was assigned the job of visiting several countries namely Tibet, China, Japan, Siam (Thailand) U.S.A., Germany and Turkey However this enthusiasm was short lived as the Afghan Amir got all that he wanted from the British and ceased all hostilities against them. The mission was called back and once again Raja Mahendra Pratap was on his own.

Meanwhile it was felt that a stable base was necessary for any future activity. Consequently, he set up an office in Leipzig, Germany in 1922, from where he published and distributed thousands of pamphlets and propaganda material to the harassment of the British Government.[2] The early 1920's was the most active phase of Raja Mahendra Pratap's political career which not only shows the anxiety of the Raj about the activities of Raja Mahendra Pratap but is also a pointer to the fact that he had become a big menace for the British rule in India. He even carried a reward on his head and once again a proposal for attachment of his property was being mooted. It was stated that :

"...as he is still abroad (despite the war being over) and is closely connected with interests which are hostile to British Government, it is here noted that the government have offered a substantive reward for his apprehension....He is still a declared rebel, with a price on his head and no arrangement in regard to his estates can...be entertained..., that would offer any possibility of his receiving money from them." Subsequently his estates were forfeited and the share of his son, Prem Pratap, was transferred to him.[3]

As has already been pointed out, by 1922 he was once again settled in Germany. The same year is marked by a proliferation of seditious letters and literature all over India for example the British authorities intercepted a printed leaflet addressed to Rajas, Maharajas, etc. bearing a German address and signed by Raja Mahendra Pratap. This appeal, "in the interest of humanity," was an attempt to tell the Indian people about the dangers of the present rule and a call for the Indian rulers to stand up and work for their people in the spirit of service and dedication.[4]

An official extract from the Bengal Newspapers Report for July 1922 quoted "The Viswamitra" (Calcutta, June 18, 1922) as saying that Raja Mahendra Pratap has sent an appeal for publication in their newspaper. It remarked that while it was "lofty in matter and spirit" it could not be published due to legal contraints. While proscription of Raja Mahendra Pratap's writings was being strongly considered by the British government, another appeal was issued by him to the "Indian People." This pamphlet exhorted them not to waste another opportunity of getting rid of the British yoke as they had already lost one opportunity during the I World War. Here he asked the people to adopt the path of revolution instead of "sitting at 'Charkha' like old women when manly (and I shall also add womanly) duties require them to grasp the holy sword."[5]

In 1923 many articles were written by Raja Mahendra Pratap in Indian and Afghan newspapers. As many as nine of these were impounded by the C.I.D. The concern of the authorities with these writings was so great that "the desirability of initiating all possible steps to intercept letters and telegrams addressed to, or despatched by, Mahendra Pratap..." was being considered. Another step which was considered desirable was the "urgent necessity for regularizing the mutual positions of India and Afghanistan in respect of postal communications." It was felt that Raja Mahendra Pratap was able to use the postal facility as also the Indian press for anti-British propaganda leading to "the desirability to taking legal action...against the journals.[6]

These writings depict Raja Mahendra Pratap as a staunch patriot who was peace loving but was not averse to using force and armed rebellion to overthrow the British Empire. He was thoroughly influenced by socialist movement and thanked the British for confiscating his property and delivering him from the stigma of capitalism. He enjoined Hindus and Muslims to fight the British unitedly. Freedom of India was so sacred to his heart that he was ready to carry the fight against the British with whatever allies he could get.[7]

The threat of Raja Mahendra Pratap led the British to toy with the idea of his arrest in China. The official opinion was divided over the question whether his arrest would be worth the trouble or not, since it involved two main difficulties, that of extradition from another country and his having an Afghan passport and naturalization papers.[8] However, the former view prevailed as it was felt that "It would be a mistake to underestimate Mahendra Pratap's capacity for mischief." His connections with Rash Bihari Bose and other "Indian malcontents", his collusions with the socialist bloc and his seditious activities were indications enough to prosecute him.[9]

With the hostile authorities close on his heels and the possibility of a warrant against him, under the Fugitive offenders' Act 1881[10], Raja Mahendra Pratap launched extensive travel plans. In 1922, he did extensive propaganda work in Japan and opened his office there. In this he was helped mainly By R.B. Bose and a few other anti-British Japanese friends. In 1923 he first went to Peking and then returned to Kabul.

There is also evidence of a brief and secret visit by Mahendra Pratap to Moscow on his way to Kabul from China. In a telegram from the British Minister at Peking to the British Viceroy at Simla, dated July 4, 1923 it was stated that "he left train at Ulgan and started for Mongolia by motor car enroute presumably to Urga and Siberia. All trace to him has now been lost, as Chinese authority does not extend into Mongolia proper..."[11]. Another "very secret" document about the Indian Communist Party, dated 31.10.23, began thus :

"Further information has been obtained regarding the decision made at Moscow at the secret conference. Discussions were held regarding the progress of revolutionary activity in India, in the presence of several important members of the Russian Foreign Office...Shortly after these discussions Mahendra Pratap reached Moscow from China, and was approched by both Chicherin and Obeidullah. Pratap undertook to use his personal influence with the Amir, and he accordingly left for Kabul...It is now reported that Mahendra Pratap has succeeded in winning the sympathies of the Amir, has organized a center in Kabul, and has also sent Soviet funds to the Muhajirin on the frontier. In addition he has obtained permission from the Amir for Obeidullah, Dr. Nur Muhammad and Zafar Hassan to return to Kabul, where their presence would be welcomed."[12]

In Kabul, in 1924, all his activities were tapped and his next move, for going "to some other country", was being guessed in the British official circles.[13] "On September 16, Mahendra Pratap accompanied by Walther, Secretary of Russian Legation, left Kabul. Mahendra Pratap's intention, according to an informant in touch with him, is to visit Moscow, Berlin and thence proceed either to Angora or U.S.A. from either of which he will open communication with Swarajist Party in India."[14]

Thus he again launched a whirlwind tour of Russia via the difficult Hindu-Kush terrain where he was briefly arrested also on account of some misunderstanding and later released on the intervention of the Russian foreign office.[15] In October 1924, Raja Mahendra Pratap was in Russia as is evident from a secret communique of the British Foreign Office in Moscow to it's counterpart in India. This referred to a meeting of the Comintern, attended by "Indian Revolutionaries", held in Moscow, in which Raja Mahendra Pratap asked for help for the Indian cause. He said the timing was right as "the Gandhi agitation had created very favourable ground in India for the revolutionary work."

According to a report of December 29, 1924 Raja Mahendra Pratap went to Zurich and then to Paris. In a meeting with Madam Cama he expressed satisfaction over the progress of Indian agitation and showed "full confidence in Afghan and Russian help."[17]

He left Paris for New York on the 20th December, 1924. To meet his expenses in America he planned "to start some societies there to further his theories of Universal Brotherhood, and the Religion of Love". His other objective was "to advance the cause of Afghanistan" because "historically India and Afghanistan were not two separate countries".[18] It has been pointed out that the seeds of the present day collaboration between Russia and Afghanistan were sown by Raja Mahendra Pratap during his efforts to align them against the British.

II

On the first of January 1925 Raja Mahendra Pratap was in New York. At his juncture there is clear evidence that "he worked in cooperation with the Hindustan Ghadar Party in the U.S.A. which sent him to Tibet to organise a rebellion against the British".[19] The plan was to reach Nepal via Tibet and with the help of the Nepalese government attempt was to be made to set India free.[20] In the Ghadar centre in California, the Ghadaris gave him ten thousand dollars and seven volunteers for the mission. On April 28, 1925 they left America to reach Peking via Japan on June 26. Braving all natural and man-made adversities, this group could reach the Tibetan border only on October 16, 1925. But due to sour diplomatic relations between China and Tibet, with the British as the mediator, the scheme to cross Tibet could not materialise.[21]

The British restlessness was once again evident from the fact that they had not only pursued Raja Mahendra Pratap's whereabouts with marked regularity but had also started comtemplating about his arrest once again, either in Nepal or in

Tibet. It was felt that any attempt to arrest him in China would meet with the same fate as in 1923 because the situation in China in 1925 was "little better" than it was in 1923. Thus it was decided to refuse him entry into Tibet.[22]

The extent of the British discomfiture is very obvious from these remarks, "during the last two years Mahendra Pratap's influence and power of mischief have been steadily dwindling. Recently a good many of his letters and comunications to newpapers have been seen in the secret censorship,[23] and in their general character they are unpractical and even drivelling...they contain clear evidence of a certain softening of the brain". It was at this point that he adopted a new name, "Peter Pir Pratap, so that my Hindu name will not be an obstacle to preaching my "Prem Dharma" among Christians, Muslims and Hindus". Development of such traits led the British to conclude that he wasn't any more a cause for "real anxiety". But still they persisted with their efforts in trying to bring him to book.[24]

The authorities remained hot on Raja Mahendra Pratap's trail. In May 1925, he was in Japan, where he was being helped by the Japanese communists. It was "not possible nor desirable to attempt the arrest of Mahendra Pratap in Japan" but still it was thought advisable to aquaint the Japanese government (which was showing little encouragement to Raja Mahendra Pratap) with his antecedents and thus with his communist connection.[25] Definite arrangements were made to secure his arrest in China, by sorting out the naturalization problem with Afghanistan, should he go in China from Japan. But all this came to a nought as the Chinese ruled that "unless he was guilty of some act in contravention of Chinese law" his arrest was not feasible and he was allowed to have his way in China.[26]

Raja Mahendra Pratap reached north Tibet in November 1925. It was reported that "several Indians, one of whom styled himself "Rajah"..., had passed through Sining and Tankar on their way to Lhaasa, with the object of stirring up trouble there against the English and Moslems."[27] Very conveniently the communal element was infused here by the British, which was fought throughout by Raja Mahendra Pratap during his political career.

While his next move was still being guessed, Raja Mahendra Pratap had already met H.H. Dalai Lama and the Prime Minister and governors at Chamdo in Eastern Tibet.[28] The British had anticipated his arrest in Tibet at this juncture[29] but this was not to be, since he had Chinese backing and the British didn't want any tension on the frontier on account of Raja Mahendra Pratap and his mission despite the fact that in January-Febuary 1926, there were indications of hectic but secret moves to recruit soldiers in the province to help the anti-imperialists. The aim was now to tactfully stop the mission from advancing into Western Tibet. So at Chamdo they were turned back in February itself but no arrests were made in view of their Chinese passports, as it might incur friction with the Chinese.[30]

In order to formulate a new strategy for his next move Raja Mahendra Pratap planned to attend the Pan-Asiatic Congress held in Nagasaki on August 1, 1926. Here also, the British spies kept a track of his activities. He didn't have a Japanese visa so he was held up by the police. Rash Bihari Bose intervened and through his influence was able to get him off at Osaka. But again he was forced to leave for China from where he went to Moscow, Afghanistan, Switzerland, France and thence to America.[32]

The latter half of 1926 also saw the drifting apart of Raja Mahendra Pratap and Afghans. Although his name remained attached to Afghanistan and he kept on working for them, though unofficially, they denied all links with Raja Mahendra Pratap at this point.[33] This may be due to the fact that now hostilities between Britain and Afghanistan were over in view of the independence of the latter in 1922. This must have been the chief reason as to why Raja Mahendra Pratap was getting closer to other groups like the Ghadar party or the Pan-Asiatic League whose second meeting he attended in October 1927 at Shanghai.[34]

At this juncture Mahendra Pratap agreed to a proposal of Maulana Barkakullah to go over to Germany. This was the time when Jawahar Lal Nehru was staying in Switzerland and Raja

Mahendra Pratap visited him too[35]. From here they both proceeded to the U.S.A. in early 1927. This second visit to San Fransisco was an attempt to give an account of the aborted Tibetan mission of 1925.[36] Unfortunately, Barkatullah died here and Raja Mahendra Pratap launched his anti-imperialist attack once again through talks and seminars in the U.S.A. He declared in April 1927 that "I am now serving humanity in my private capacity. This is the object which has brought me to U.S.A. and to attain this end I will go to Japan."[37]

Later in 1928 Raja Mahendra Pratap again had a quick detour of Japan, China, Russia and Germany. In the Far East he set up an India League in Japan, spoke at several meetings and started a paper there.[38] He formed the Eastern Oppressed Peoples' Association under Sun Yat Sen's influence and also published a paper 'Ghadar Dhandora' with the aim of spreading the message of revolution.[39]

Athough it is said, "disappointed in his main political aims, he turned more and more to religion and to the establishement of a World Federation" it only proves that he was not only a patriot but also a leader with a message for humanity. Message of equality of races and nations was the essence of his idea of world federation.[40]

However, this ideal of world cooperation included an equal and just distribution of resources and freedom of people. It was enough to cause the British to get upset with. The publication, called World Federation, first came to their notice in September 1929 and in April 1931 prohibitory orders were issued against this "distinctly revolutionary and anti-British" paper.[41]

Another trip round the world in 1930 took him to Germany via Moscow. At Frankfurt the Anti-Imperialist League Conference was being held. Here, while some eyebrows were raised at his "internationalism", he was able to raise much needed funds for World Federation. This trip also took him to America once again with the aim of "inviting the American capital to Afghanistan".[42]

III

The year 1930-31 has been taken as the starting point of the third phase of our study because of convenience. This was also the year which saw him start another whirlwind tour of the world as on several other occasions before. This period could be further sub-divided into three sections namely, the years from 1930 to 1934, which saw the crystallisation of his ideas on World Federation and a massive effort to spread it at a global scale. The second phase between 1935 to 1939 was the beginning of his efforts to seek repatriation to India. And finally the period marked by intensified British counter offensive during the Second World War between 1939 and 1945, both in India, against the revolutionaries as well as against the Axis powers who were also the main allies of the disaffected groups outside India, culminating in his return to India in August 1946.

Mahendra Pratap's whirlwind tour of the world in 1930 took him to the U.S.A., Afghanistan, Russia, Germany, China and Japan. It was the beginning of his tryst with the East. For the next 16 years, first China and then Japan were his home. From the summer of 1930 to the spring of 1933 he established a formal office of World Federation at Tientung Khu near the Imperial Palace, Peiking. Here he opened a free school, gave lectures without fees, held World Federation club meetings and on Sundays held prayers according to the unity of religions and the Religion of Love. In 1934 due to the British pressure from Hongkong he was deported from Canton by the Cantonese Dictator, a General who was later ousted from his capital. Till 1934 he toured China, Japan and Mongolia several times to enlist support and volunteers for organising an Asiatic or a people's Army. In 1935-36 he rented a Japanese house for his stay instead of staying in a hotel as on earlier occasions.[43]

His experiment of the Asiatic Army could not take off due to official hinderances and unseen obstacles. The officers tried to put obstacles in his path through their agents. But his activities concerning the work of World Federation were not considered dangerous and therefore they went on unhindered. He went on holding meetings and publishing his monthly circular.[44] While his idea of World Federation had many takers it had an almost equal number of critics. One Mukutar Singh Chaudhury, Managing Agent of Daurala Sugar Works at Meerut wrote to him in 1937 saying that "I am not against the idea of World Federation but I feel it diverts our attention from the immediate need of our country. Besides who is going to hear a cosmopolitan idea from those who are passing a dependent life."[45]

That he was continously in touch with the National leaders is obvious from his corrospondence with them which is available with the National Archives of India. During this period the influence of Mahatma Gandhi was quite apparent on his thought. Mahatma Gandhi was very appretiative of his hard work abroad and said that "I know that you are doing all that you can for the country" and took comfort in his World Federation motto that "peace is to be attained by reconciliatin and service."[46] Similarly Nehru informed Mahendra Pratap about the Lahore Congress proceedings where the Independence Resolution of Purna Swaraj was passed and 26th January, 1930 was declared as the Indepence day. He also assured him that "the Congress is definitely and finally comitted to full independence of India. This is a great gain. In the course of the year there is likely to be a big struggle for independence."[47]

The period between 1935-39 is marked by efforts to bring him back to India, which were intensified at all levels. Right from Mahatma Gandhi onwards to the UP government to the individual Legislative Assembly members; like Sri Krishna Dutt Paliwal in 1934-6; Lala Jagdish Prasad in 1936, Brijlal Biyani in 1937, Badri Dutt Pande in 1938, A.N. Chattopadhyaya in 1941 and Sri Prakash in 1946; to his friends and well wishers; all those who could do anything towards this end did their best to repatriate him to his homeland. He was not the only one who was wanted back by the countrymen. A whole movement to bring back the great sons of India was on foot as is obvious from the British Records of those days.

That the British authorities were still fearful of his moves, and of course of the moves of other revolutionaries, is quite obvious from their concern issue of repatriation as is obvious from their official documents. For instance in a confidential enclosure to a despatch from Tokyo, dated 31st October 1934, concern was shown about the increasing alliance between the Indian revolutionaries led by Rash Behari Bose and the Japanese superpatriots like Mitsuru Toyama and Ryohei Uchida. An increasingly anti-British sentiment was discerned in the Japanese media, press, journals and publications of various political and cultural societies. Referring to the role of Mahendra Pratap, it was suggested that; "...one way of counteracting anti-British propaganda in this country (i.e. Japan) is to remove the distributors of it, and that to grant Pratap permission to return to India would be to ensure that an adequate watch was kept on his movements and activities."[48]

On the home front during 1935-37, Mahatma Gandhi made all possible efforts to bring him back. He also contacted Prof. Jugal Kishore to help Raja Mahendra Pratap abroad.[49] While advising him to work for his livelihood in Japan, Gandhiji asked him to be patient. He himself gave assurance to talk to Nehru and also expressed hope "that the UP Premier will do whatever is possible. The U.P. Education Minister, Sampurnanand expressed the U.P. governments's eagerness in having him back soon as it will provide an opportunity to get his invaluable experience abroad.[50] This was the time when he drew up a plan of founding World Federation centre near Tokyo at Kokubunji. He managed to collect some money, bought a piece of land and started building cottages in 1937. In September 1937 he could move into his cottage at World Federation centre. In 1936 and 1941 he paid short visits to China of about 2 months each but as he says in his "Reflections" ("Reflections of an Exile" is the original autobiography of Raja Mahendra Pratap written in 1946 and is now known as Reminiscenes) for 10 long years from 1936-46 my home was in Japan." From here he published his World Federation from 1933 to 42 regularly with only a couple of exceptions. Between 1940-45 he also wrote many books, pamphlets, stories and dramas and held meetings from time to time at his centre.[51] All these activities were carried out in the backdrop of his efforts to come back to India. This becomes more than obvious when he himself remarked "In 1939 when war broke out in Europe I became restless and tried to proceed to Europe but I could not."[52]

Although differences between him and his closest friends Rash Behari Bose and Anand Mohan Sahay kept on cropping up from time to time but they took care not to let those differences override them. Any tussle amongst them was quickly followed by a reconciliation. A.M. Sahay on his part kept on helping him financially also[53] On the delay in his return to India Sahay invited him several times over to stay in the India Lodge at Kobe, the office of the Indian National Association of Japan and even extended pecuniary help from time to time. But when Raja Mahendra Pratap gave credit to God more then the donors for the help Sahay used to openly protest. He remarked "If at all, the credit should go to the donors and also to me for sending the cheque to you...I do not think God's kindness or his greatness has any place in this transaction whatsoever. I do not believe in giving such undue credit to anyone."[54] R.B. Bose writing in 1938 said that "We are born friends and nothing worldly can separate us. I know well that we will always work together for the salvation of India. It is our destiny."[55]

During the last few years of the third phase of this study i.e. from 1940 to 47 one could see the frantic efforts at home to bring Raja Mahendra Pratap back as well as the hardening of British official stand on the issue. In 1940 Raja Mahendra Pratap along with his friends organised the Executive Board of India with the definite aim to free India. In this Raja Mahendra Pratap was the president, R.B. Bose was the Vice President, A.M. Sahay was the Chief Secretary. The fate of Executive Board dwindled immediately after its inception. R.B. Bose wrote down "it is not desirable to dissolve the Board, if we dissolve it, it will please the British and harm the cause of India freedom . I think it would be better to reorganize the Board with younger elements". Giving poor health of both Raja Mahendra Pratap and Rash Bihari Bose as the main reason for withdrawal he named Messrs. Sahay, Lahiri, Das and Deshpande, who should be given full authority to decide about the future reorganisation.[56] In 1941 Raja Mahendra Pratap also started his movement for the Aryan Army to spread the message of World Federation. but when the War broke out on the 8th December. that year in Japan, Japan started its own Indian Organisation. Raja Mahendra Pratap could not agree with the Japanese plans and was ordered to sit quiet at his centre, on 6th March 1942.

That was the beginning of his forced quiet life. In 1945 when the war ended he thought that he would be completely free to leave Japan but was instead arrested and locked up by the orders of the occupying army i.e. the Americans on 14th September 1945. For 5 months he was in American custody. In Febuary 1946 when he was released he tried again to get home to India but it took him another 5 months to get the required permission. He finally landed on the Indian soil on August 9, 1946 at Madras from Japan "amidst happy rejoicing and a grand welcome that awaited him here."[57]

During all the years of uncertainty during and after the war frantic efforts were being made at home by his countrymen to bring him back to his homeland in the Legislative Assembly as well outside it in the face of the still strong British official stand which kept on harping over the age old issue of his being an Afghan national and not an Indian. The other excuse, that was put forth was that he had not himself applied for a repatriation asking for pardon for past misdeeds and promising not to indulge in such activities in future. This of coures was not true as evidence is that he had on three occasions written letters to the authorities namely in 1935, 1937 and 1940.[58]

The actual fact that stands out from the Intelligence Reports is that the British were still quite afraid of his potential as a major threat to their authority in India which in any case was dwindling after the war. They also had to give way to the increasing demand for his return from all quarters. Frantic efforts by the British were on to stall the homecoming of Indian heroes by way of biennial intelligence reports in early 1940s and then half yearly reviwes of various cases from 1945 onwards. Finally in 1946 Febuary the authorities çould no longer hold the tide of Raja Mahendra Pratap supporters and had to give way under their increasing pressure.[59]

However the story of a great freedom fighter doesn't end here for he continued to inspire coming generations of Indians with his continued participation in public life as an MP from 1957-62 and later also till his demise in 1979. Indeed during the period from 1919 to 1946 a religio-philosophical streak was visible in the Raja's demeanour but it is very difficult to agree with a statement which highlights these years as a period marked by an increasing tendency for reform or religious zeal concomitent with setbacks in the political field. On the contrary he was still very much politically motivated. A "life-long revolutionary", he remained an enemy of British imperialism and high handedness throughout.[60]

There is a need to highlight his role in the overall freedom movement. His colossus contribution to the struggle for independence is second to none and in fact his concept and efforts of freedom through the armed struggle with foreign help preceded that of Azad Hind Fauj. That there is a remarkable parallel between Raja Mahendra Pratap and Subhash Chandra Bose is not a mere coincidence because the latter took heavily from the ideas of the former.[61]

Raja Mahendra Pratap continued to be active inspite of the waning influence of the Ghadar Party. He shifted his base to Japan and continued his activities from there. He was imprisoned by the Americans during the second world war for six months. With the efforts of the Indian National Congress and Mahatama Gandhi he was released and returned back to India in 1946. He served as an MP from 1957-62 before his demise in 1979. He was truly an illustrious son of our nation who should be given his long overdue and privileged place in the history of our freedon struggle.

References

1. Raja Mahendra Pratap papers, National Archivers of India (henceforth NAI), Home Political files (henceforth H.P.), 29/IV/1931, p. 3.
2. "Just an Outline of his career," Scrap book I, op.cit., p. 3, and Raja Mahendra Pratap, *Reminiscences of a Revolutionary* ed. by Dr. Vir Singh, 1999, Delhi, p. 27.
3. NAI, HP, 320/1924, pp. 1-2.
4. NAI, HP, 73/1922, pp. 1-3.
5. Ibid., pp. 3-4, 16-9.
6. NAI, HP, 5/II/1923, pp. 105-6.
7. NAI, HP, 5/II/1923, pp. 107-9.
8. NAI, HP, 5/II/1923, pp. 1-3.
9. Ibid., pp. 4-5
10. Ibid., pp. 8-14.
11. Ibid., p. 119.
12. Ibid., p. 102-3.
13. NAI, HP, 141/1924, p. 3.
14. NAI, HP, 141/II/1924, p. 38.
15. Braj Bihari Lal Sharma ed. *"Raja Mahendra Pratap Janam Shatabdi Smarika,"* Vrindavan, 1986, p. 5 and *Reminiscences of a Revolutionary,* p. 42-43.
16. NAI, HP, 21/I/1925, p. 7.
17. Ibid. p. 10-11.
18. Ibid.
19. *Dictionary of National Biography,* Vol. III, p. 10.
20. NAI, HP, 21/II/1925, p. 24.
21. For chalking out the details of his travels a combination of the article by Sh. J.P. Chaturvedi in the *"Smarika..."* op.cit., *Reminiscences of a Revolutionary,* 53-58, are used.
22. NAI, HP, 21/II/1925, pp. 1-5.
23. For a collection of such newspaper excerpts see HP, 141/II/1924.
24. NAI, HP, 21/II/1925, p. 6.
25. Ibid., p. 48 and 57.

26. Ibid., pp. 42, 44-5, 54-5.
27. NAI, HP, 19/1926, pp. 13-4.
28. *"Just an Outline...,"* op.cit. p.3.
29. NAI, HP, 92/II/1927, pp. 13, 17-9.
30. NAI, HP, 19/1926, pp. 5-11 and pp. 16-8.
31. Ibid., pp. 32-38.
32. Sh. J.P. Chaturvedi in *"Smarika"*, op.cit., p.7. See also HP, 92/1927, p.3.
33. NAI, HP, 19/1926, pp. 44 and HP, 92/1927, p.3.
34. NAI, HP, 92/II/1923, pp. 31.
35. *Reminiscences of a Revolutionary* p. 27.
36. Sh. J.P. Chaturvedi in *"Smarika"*, op.cit., p.7.
37. NAI, HP, 92/1927, p.9.
38. *"Just an Outline..."*, op.cit, p. 3.45.
39. PPS. NAI, RMP, Newspaper Cuttings, pp. 1-3.
40. DNB, Vol. III, p.10.
41. NAI, HP, 29/IV/1931, p.3, 17, 21.
42. *Reminiscenes of a Revolutionary* p. 69, 43.
43. *Reminiscences of a Revolutionary,* p. 78
44. Ibid. p. 122
45. RMP papers—Correspondence (henceforth Correspondence) S.No. 37, no. 61(1), Letter from Mukutar Singh Choudhary, dtd. 20th. June, 1937.
46. Ibid., S.No. 19, Letter from M.K. Gandhi, dated. 31st October, 1935.
47. Ibid., S.no. 5, Letter from Jawaharlal Nehru, dated. 4th February, 1930.
48. NAI, HP, 1/3/1935, pp. 30-36, 64-65.
49. Correspondence, S.No. 21, Letter from M.K. Gandhi to RMP dtd. July 1935.
50. Ibid., S.No. 32 and 39, letters from Mahadev Desai dtd. 11th Sept. 1936 and from Pyarelal dtd. 5th. Sept. 1937 (on behalf of Gandhiji) to RMP, S.No. 69 Letter from Ministry of Education United Provinces to RMP dtd. 16th Feb. 1939.
51. *Reminiscences of a Revolotuionary,* p. 78
52. *Reminiscences of a Revolotuionary,* p. 78.

53. Correspondence, S.no. 25, 41, 42, 45, 46.
54. Ibid. S.no. 38, Letter from A.M. Sahay to RMP dtd. 29th June, 1937.
55. Ibid., S.No. 61, Letter from Rash Behari Bose to RMP dtd. 18th Aug. 1938.
56. Correspondence, S.No. 85, Letter from Rash Behari Bose to RMP Dated 29th December 1940.
57. *Reminiscences of a Revolotuionary,* pp. 78-79.
58. NAI, H.P. (I), 17/33/1937.
59. NAI, H.P. (I), 1/1/1946.
60. *"Just an Outline..."* op.cit. p.3
61. Col. Amar Bahadur "A meeting of Raja Mahendra Pratap with Subhash Chandra Bose" in "Smarika", op.cit. pp. 29-31.

Raja Mahendra Pratap and the Executive Board of India at Tokyo

Vir Singh

Raja Mahendra Pratap is a legendry figure amongst the revolutionaries abroad. His first attempt to liberate India during the First World War has drawn attention of the scholars. The defeat of anti British forces and the peace treaty of Afghanistan with the British resulted in the end of Raja Mahendra Pratap's first Provisional Government of India at Kabul.

Then Raja Mahendra Pratap tried to wipe out imperialism from the map of the world through his concept of World Federation. Scholars have not taken note of his relentless anti-imperialist struggle in foreign lands between two world wars. Raja Mahendra Pratap realised that so long as imperialism existed in the world his cherished vision of federal world could not be fulfilled because only independent states could become members of the World Federation. It was very painful to him that even his own country was not free and he could not succeed in liberating it in his first attempt during the First World War. During the Second World War he tried again to utilize the war situation to achieve his cherished dream of independent India.

Here, an attempt has been to apprise the readers of the war convictions of Raja Mahendra Pratap. Raja tried his best to unite Japan, Korea, Manchuria, Mangolia, China and Tibet of Asiatic Group of Countries according to his concept of World Federation. But he could not succeed and he reached the conclusion in 1932 in Peking: *The World should know that in spite of the League of*

Nations, World Court, the Treaties of No War and...my proposal of cooperation among China, Japan and Tibet fell flat on rough ground due to robber instinct, aggressive elements and Imperialism in these nations and they clashed with one another. He apprehended that: *Another great world war is at our door.* He requested Indian Community in Yokohama, Japan, in 1933 *to prepare themselves for all eventualities. As soon as a general war starts India should make a desperate effort to break her chains. It will be a gloden opportunity when the task masters have their hands full.* He clarified: *I am not an enemy of the English Nation. I stand for the destruction of English Empire.*[1]

Raja Mahendra Pratap realized in 1938 that : *under the present conditions in the world we can only postpone a war. Wars are inevitable unless a just world government is established on the earth.*[2] He pronounced his strategy in case of world war at Kobe in Japan in 1938: *that the present technique of non-violence and fasting was unsuited to a war situation. I recommended cooperation with Iran, Afghanistan and Nepal and understanding with Japan, Italy and Germany in case of war. But we would not do anything to harm the great leadership of Mahatma Gandhi. Let him march forward and try to get what he can from the British. His victory is our victory. From outside we will do what we can to bring complete independence to India.*[3] Raja Mahendra Pratap, before the Indian students association in May 1939 at Kobe, Japan, made it plain: *that Mr. Sahay is my colleague in the Congress camp. Mr. Bose is my personal friend but I have my own plan for immediate action to free India. I honestly believe that with the cooperation of Iran, Afghanistan and Nepal, some of the Indian princes and the Congress volunteers India can be liberated at once, as soon as a general war comes.*[4] His brother had died due to the setback from the harsh attitude of the British and he was waiting for the opportune time to over throw the foreign rule from India.

Raja Mahendra Pratap recalls that his brother Kunwar Baldeo Singh *was to leave in March (1939) to meet me in Japan. Passport was refused to him. Then he hoped to see me back in India. This hope was also shattered by the government decsion. ...The letter of the government of India, is dated 25th of March, and just two days later, on the 27th of March my brother passed away. According to the confirmed news he was not sick. He died of heart failure, they say. Government is certainly responsible for the shock which he got.*[5]

Raja Mahendra Pratap met H. H. Maharaja of Kapurthala at Imperial Hotel in Tokyo in 1939. Maharaja, who was not aware of the denial letter of 25th March of the government, said *that he could now return to India.* The followig utterances of Raja Mahendra Pratap in June 1939 indicate his anguish at the denial of his entry to his motherland: *They or Maharaja Sahib are not anti-British government. But they can see that I, an open worker, believing in truth, can not possibly do any mischief in India. And my principle of Hindu-Muslim unity and my sympathetic attitude towards princes will bring unity and create a peaceful atmosphere. ....As I am not a blind follower of something I am also not a blind worker of humanity, I know what I must do under the different circumstances. My true friends perfectly understand that if I can return to India, when the present conditions prevail there, I shall honestly act as law abiding citizen.*[6]

Raja Mahendra Pratap was in touch with the Indian leaders through correspondence and with the public through his articles published in Indian newspapers. A reporter of *Akali* told him in 1924; *that Malviya ji thought, I must wait, home-rule was at hand, and when India was free I could return home with honour.*[7] After a gap of eleven years the British Government provided 'Provincial Autonomy' in the Government of India Act 1935 but the Veto power remained with the Viceroy. When new king Edward VIII pardoned some convicts of India, in the changed circumstances he appealed through his circular to the king to be allowed to return to India in 1936 to propagate world federation movement. But there was no response. In the hope of returning to India he gave up his Afghan passport in 1937 when Congress Government was formed in U.P.[8]

The efforts to bring him back home were intensified at all levels in India by Mahatma Gandhi, Pt. Jawahar Lal Nehru, U.P. Government and its legislative members and other respected Indians between 1935-39. There was a movement to bring back all the revolutionaries abroad at that time. The records of those days are preserved in the Home Political files of the British Government in National Archives of India.

After denial of his entry to India in 1939 Raja Mahendra Pratap said. *It further shows that such is the freedom which the English rulers herald that they have given to India. Still a man like me with the full backing of our Congress cannot enter the land of my birth.* Under such circumstances, he declared in one of the anti-British meetings in June 1939, in Japan: *If I am forced to remain abroad, I should surely batter the walls of the British fortress and enter the land of my birth with flying flags.*[9]

Without losing any time Raja Mahendra Pratap started his Pen War against the British through the War Number of World Federation in June, 1939. But not a single country responded to the plan of Raja Mahendra Pratap. He said: *some how our Japan too could not adopt my plan and could not utilize my services. But I continued to think loud, talk loud, through my monthly circular letter.*[10]

Three months later in September, 1939, when the Second World War broke out in Europe he became restless and tried to proceed to Europe but could not. Then Raja Mahendra Pratap and Anand Mohan Sahay in Japan : *started a war fund with the object to have some young men at our centre here to assist in our propaganda work and to send some emissaries abroad, the object, of course, is to supplement the movement of freedom in India. We mean to move coutiously but resolutely, so that, we may remain in touch with the forward march of our Congress at home and at the same time leave nothing undone, what is possible, to bring about the political salvation of India from abroad. We hope and wish that all the Indians in the Far East, Germany,* USSR, *Afganistan and* U.S. *will evolve a common plan of action. But there is no time to be lost, we must act quickly....Our Congress at home is fighting our war of freedom. From abroad we want to hasten the process...Do not lose this apportunity, do something to make India free.*[11]

Raja Mahendra Pratap carried on brisk activities to unite Indian people in Japan and China. His secular and liberal leadership brought different groups of Indian revolutionaries, members of the Indian National Congress in Japan, Pan-Asiatic Society and Eastern Oppressed People's Association on a common anti-British platform with a common goal of achieving freedom for India. Pleased with the response of Indian community, Raja Mahendra Pratap formed the *Executive Board of India* on 22nd June, 1940 in Kobe but its formal establishment was announced at a function on the 31st of August 1940 at Tokyo in Japan with himself as its President, Rash Behari Bose as Vice-President and Anand Mohan Sahay as Chief Secretary. (see Appendix-A) Its immediate aim was to make India free.[12]

With great difficulty he got the police travelling certificate to China. He was allowed to carry foreign currency worth five hundred yens only. On the night of the 7th April, 1941 he left Tokyo. On 11th of April, 1941 he reached Shanghai (4 weeks), then Nanking (6 days) and arrived on 16th of May, 1941 at Peking (12 days) and after exact 54 days he reached via Tokyo at his World Federation Centre in Kobe, Japan on 31 May, 1941. The details of this hectic propaganda tour are given in Campaign No. 2 of June 1941. To the Indian friends he said: *Without our endeavours the British Empire was dying. Germany was destroying it in the West. Japan was forcing it out of the East. Even supposing England was a father to modern India, who can keep, forever, the corpse of a dead father. Corpse must be burnt or burried and then the home be looked after by sons and daughters. I simply ask you to manage your own home. Any quarrel among ourselves at this juncture will prove disastrous...Brethern, be prepared to join our* ***Indian army*** *if we must have one, to bring peace to our land as the British step out...If by some miracle the British could survive and peace would be restored in the world in that case our Indian Congress* *should still be able to win our war. We do not lose in any case. Just have faith and work with faith, move forward in every case.*[13]

At the end of his compaign the following narration is sufficient to prove his commitment for war propaganda in spite of scarcity of funds during the Second World War. On 12th June 1941 Raja Mahendra Pratap handed over the manuscript of war number 'Campaign No. 2' to the press in Japan. He writes: *I was wondering what should come next? The lack of funds, difference of opinion* (regarding funds) *with some of my colleagues and uncertainty in the international situation all harassed me. Then a certain kindly gentleman at Berlin had kindly sent me five hundred yen through a friend of his at Tokyo....that all my sufferings, financial poverty, during all these years of well-nigh three decades, are mainly due to my cooperation with Germany and some day Germany would repay me thousand times in spite of all intrigues of British agents....I set out for Kobe on 9th July 1941. The question was, how would our Indian friends respond to my request for funds for the World Federation circular. It is begging, of course begging, and begging for my daily bread too,because my food is also included in the budget of our circular. ...Brethren, Hindus, Muslims, Sikhs, Sindhies, Punjabies, Gujraties and Parsees too, came forward to throw their mites in my begging bowl...I economise for every bit of cent. I lead very simple life, I cannot beg and enjoy life. I must follow the precepts of those who begged for their daily bread and served society, such as Lord Buddha.* In August 1941 he could not draw his little money from postal saving account at Koku Bunji post office without proper permit from the finance office. Then he went round begging. The first big man had not sufficient hard cash at hand and the banks on Saturday were closed at noon. Then he went to Yokohama where he knocked at five different doors of three different nationalities. One was out, other went swimming, another was still asleep. But he got much more than what he had wanted. After mailing his circular he had very little left and starvation must follow if he did not approach his friends again. After negotiating tremendous amount of hardship he got his certificate on 25th August 1941, that he is not a subject of any country and therefore the freezing law does not apply to him.[14] He reminds us again and again that he could bear all these sufferings on the precept of Buddha, his guiding star who had toiled in the cause of humanity.

It needs to be elaborated here that Raja Mahendra Pratap always cherished the idea of raising his own army in foreign lands to liberate India. We can trace back this idea in the first quarter of 1915 when he tried to raise an army from the Indians in prison in the World War Prisoners' camp near Berlin. He was also successful in raising his own army of Afridi tribals in Afganistan in the last quarter of 1915. In 1918, he again tried that Germany should agree with him to raise an International Socialist Army. But it could not materialise due to Germany's reservation about red Russia. In January & February 1934 he toured the whole of China and Japan to enlist volunteers for an Asiatic Army and opened three recruiting centres in China, Japan and Manchuria. In the Pan Asiatic Conference on 10-12 February. 1934 Raja Mahendra Pratap's movement of the Asiatic Army of World Federation was approved at Dairen in Manchuria. But it could not be developed due to official hinderances. Again on the 22nd November 1941, he started his movement of Aryan Army in Japan.[15]

The plan of war as spelt out by Raja Mahendra Pratap is as under: *I have suffered all these long years only on account of my cooperation with Germnay during the last World War... now Hitler wants to corner the lion in his den and kill him there in his own lair...I wanted to have the British Empire destroyed in India and thus pull out the teeth and nails of the lion, and making him thus quite harmless to let him live on bread and milk diet.* In a meeting in Tokyo before an Italian official Mr. Mirko Ardemagni Raja Mahendra Pratap told the gathering that Japan had concluded a treaty with Germany and Italy. Raja Mahendra Pratap requested Japanese to *start cleaning up the Far East of all the British influence, occupy Hongkong and Singapore. And we (Executive Board of India), with the cooperation of Japan, Italy and Germany want to free India from outside. Mahatma Gandhi has also started civil disobedience in India which will disrupt the British administration in India.*[16]

When Japanese joined the Second World War on 8th December 1941, the situation changed. Prime Minister, General Tojo asked Raja Mahendra Pratap, the president of the Executive Board of India, to accompany Japenese army to attack British India. Raja Mahendra Pratap knew that the Japanese had not honoured their word to make Manchu Kuo entirely free. They had not withdrawn their forces from Manchu Kuo. So, he did not agree to their plans which were in practice, on the lines of British Imperialism. He told General Tojo that: *Japanese army should not go into India. I shall have my own army to free India. It displeased General Tojo. I was asked to remain quiet at our centre on 6th March, 1942. Then started my forced quiet life.* Mahendra Pratap always stuck to his principles. Once he said: *I am glad that I remained true to my principles. It is true, I seek cooperation in every quarter. However, I insist on my own terms.*[17] It was not possible for such a person to follow the dictates of the imperial army of Japan.

As mentioned above not a single state adopted the plan of Raja Mahendra Pratap described in his war number of World Federation circular of 1939. Let us look at his Plan. He categorically declared : *that we are not anti any people, even the English. But the British Empire must end. India must be made free. Our Aryan District must be realized, from Iran to Assam. And then, the Far East, Aryan and West Asia will evolve selfgoverning Asia, which will cooperate with U.S.S.R., Europe and America to create new order in the world, may be, one federated World State. The first step to that end is to drive out the British empire from Asia. Your great army, the Imperial Army of Japan can clean the Far East. And we with your cooperation and with the cooperation of Itlay and Germany want to free India immediately. To work for this immediate goal we have formed the Executive Board of India, here at Tokyo.*[18]

The above cited plan has not been analysed so far. It is a

multi-dimensional plan. It aims at:

i) destruction of the British Empire.

ii) freedom of India.

iii) establishment of Aryan district from Iran to Assam.

iv) the ultimate formation of federated World State.

He wanted the Imperial army of Japan to clear the Far East of all the British influence. Then with the cooperation of Japan, Italy, Germany, Iran, Afghanistan, Nepal and Indian volunteers in foreign lands he planned to liberate India from abroad. He never wanted that the Imperial Army of Japan should attack British India alone.

No kingly state, which was not at war with England, could involve itself in liberating India. No Imperial or expansonist power could help him to create new world order. It was fatal to their own existence. No body cuts his feet with his own axe. His notion of World State and World Cooperative turned out to be worrisome to these kingly states and imperial powers. The British approved his *concept of Universal Brotherhood...without resorting to any revolutionary ideas in Indian politics and were against mixing national or racial politics into it.*[19] On the contrary his too much indulgence in the world fedration movement from purely nationalist activities might have created some differences among his Indian nationalist colleagues in Japan, who wanted to play a positive role with the help of Japan in liberating India during Second World War. But in what way? This was the burning question.

We are aware that during the first world war Raja Mahendra Pratap agreed to cooperate with the Germans *on complete assurance that the Germans had no imperialist designs on India and that their only interest in helping the Indian freedom movement was to better their trade relations with independent India.*[20] But in the second world war he was sceptic about Japanese motive. It is true that Indian communities in Japan and Japanese friends of R.B. Bose and A.M. Sahay were cooperating with him. But Japanese Imperial powers were suspicious about his links with the socialists, red Russia and his intimate friendship with the Chinese revolutionary personalities like Mme Sunyat Sen and Wang Chiang Wei. The Assistant Military Attache of the Japanese Legation suddenly called him back to his hotel in Peking from the Chinese revolutionary gathering in 1925. Japanese knew that the Chinese helped Raja Mahendra Pratap in his tour to Tibet in 1925. Marshal Feng Yu Shiang asked him to speak to his military officers in Kalgan and arranged two mouser pistals and five rifles with ammunitions and forwarded hard cash to the Tibetan border through a Chinese merchant. Marshal also provided him carts driven by four horses. Another Chinese General of Nigoha offered his 25 thousand troops for liberating India. General Machi of Sning Fu also helped him to buy pony, horses and other equipment for his journey to Tibet. Raja Mahendra Pratap attended second Pan Asiatic conference in 1927 at Shanghai. In one of the meetings the Japanese delegation proposed that China should hand over Manchuria to Japan. Raja Mahendra Pratap got irritated and said how a younger brother can demand the hand of a wife of his elder brother. The tone and the answer of Raja Mahendra Pratap disarmed the Japanese on the occasion. But later on the Japanese army forced its way into Manchuria. He observes: *Now the Tibetans are reported as attacking Szechuan and western Konsu. The world should know that inspite of League of Nations and No-War treaties English imperialism has been trying all along through Tibet what the Japanese imperialism is now hoping to achieve through Manchuo Kuo.*[21]

Moreover, Raja Mahendra Pratap was '*not a subject of any country*' and not much trusted by the Japanese. They had more confidence in Ras Behari Bose, the Vice President of the Executive Board of India, because he was legally a Japanese citizen and had married a Japanese girl Toshoko and had two sons form her. Raja Mahendra Pratap himself had admitted earlier that: *Mr. Bose had good connections in the land of rising sun.* Japanese accepted him as the representative of the Indian residents in Eastern Asia and tried to utilize him. Anand Mohand Sahay, the Secretary of the Executive Board under the Presidentship of

Raja Mahendra Pratap, was monitoring all revolutionary activities in Japan. He was also the President of Congress Committee at Kobe in Japan and later on became the Ambassador of free India in Japan. According to him though Ras Behari Bose was a hard-core revolutionary in his individual capacity, he was incapable of leading an army or heading a mass movement of the Indian Community in East Asia. The first attempt of the INA failed in June 1943 because of the above weaknesses of Ras Behari Bose. It was very much expected. Sahay who anticipated such a situation had secretly maintained a contact with Subhash Chandra Bose, who was then in Berlin through the German Embassy in Tokyo. Dr. Walesar, the Counsel General of the Embassy was familiar with Rajaji from the First World War. Raja had introduced Sahay to him. During the Second World War Subhash Chandra Bose also went to Germany and wanted to liberate India with their help. So, while waiting for Subhash Chandra Bose, Sahay accepted the leadership of Ras Behari Bose without any hesitation. Raja Mahendra Pratap also had no ambition or consideration for himself: *I repeat as I ever did before that I am interested in the independence of India, no matter to me who realises it and how. I am always prepared to withdraw myself.*[22]

Under such circumstances, he was ordered on 6th March, 1942 to sit quiet at his World Federation Centre Kokubunji in Tokyo. After the fall of Singapore, there was a public meeting of ex-Indian soldiers and Indian residents in Far East on 28-30th March 1942 in Tokyo but Japanese did not invite Raja Mahendra Pratap and Anand Mohan Sahay to attend it. The Japanese police also interfered in the free publication of World Federation and it was stopped in April, 1942.[23] But for fear of his large following in the Far East he was not put in prison. The Japanese Government sanctioned some monthly amount for his living in his confinement.

There is a remarkable resemblance between Raja Mahendra Pratap and Subhash Chandra Bose, which is not a mere coincidence because the latter took heavily from the ideas of the former. Raja Mahendra Pratap, the *world wanderer* at a crucial juncture of history during the war years knew no rest and strived for an anti-British front and upheld the morale of revolutionaries and patriots in high spirit. When the novel experiment of 'Provisional Government of India' by Raja Mahendra Praptap in Kabul during the First World War was repeated by Subhash Chandra Bose during the Second World War in the form of 'Azad Hind Government', these revolutionaries in foreign countries joined it in thousands and assisted it. Subhash Chandra Bose was aware of Rajas nationalist stand through the German embassy in Japan so he followed the policy of Raja Mahendra Pratap and could work on much larger scale. An eyewitness Col. Amar Bahadur of Indian National Army (INA) recollects that Netaji in the presence of General Tojo addressed these Indian revolutionaries and soldiers at municipal ground of Singapore on 6th July 1943. His message was loud and clear to the Indian soldiers as well as the Japanese authorities: "मैं जापान के प्रधानमन्त्री तोजो को यह बतला देना चाहता हूँ कि अगर उनकी सरकार या उनके स्वयं के गन में कहीं छुपी हुई यह भावना या विचार हो कि अंग्रेजी सल्तनत की हार के पश्चात भारत को स्वतन्त्र कराने में सहयोग प्रदान कर कहीं वे भारत में राज्य करने का स्वप्न देख रहे हों तो वे बड़ी गलती पर होंगे। भारत तो हमारे खून से स्वतन्त्र होगा, हम जापान के सहयोग का आभार मानेंगे और अगर वे अपने विचारों को कार्यरूप में परिणत कर राज्य करना चाहेंगे तो हम जापान की सरकार को कह देना चाहते हैं कि हमारी आजाद हिन्द फौज तथा सरकार की जो कुरबानी अंग्रेजी साम्राज्य को उखाड़ फेंकने में लगेगी उससे दुगनी शक्ति से हम जापान सरकार को भारत भूमि से उखाड़ फैंकेगे। इसमें लेशमात्र सन्देह करने की आवश्यकता नहीं।" INA of Subhash Chandra Bose also advised Japanese authorities not to harass Raja Mahendra Pratap. It was the victory of his principles.[24]

Raja Mahendra Pratap prepared the base, laid the foundation by his incessant efforts during 1922 to 1942 in the Asiatic countries and the castle of Azad Hind government in the Far East was skilfully built on 21st October 1943 by Subhash Chandra Bose. In philosophical terms the material prepared by Raja Mahendra Pratap is *Upadana Karana* and the leadership of Subhash Chandra Bose is *Nimitta Karana.* Both these *Karanas* have contributed greatly in the erection of a castle of second "Azad Hind Government" abroad.

After the Japanese surrender, Raja Mahendra Pratap was arrested on 14th of September, 1945 and lodged in Sugamo prison in Japan as war criminal alongwith General Tojo and revolutionary Toyama of Japan by the American Army. At that time he was the only Indian leader alive. Ras Behari Bose died in Tokyo hospital on 21st January, 1945 and Subhash Chandra Bose had also died on 18 August 1945. With the efforts of Congress, Mahatma Gandhi and his American friends though he was released from prison in February, 1946, yet it took five months more to get the required permission to return home (not as an Indian but as a stateless person, because he had given up his Afghan passport in 1937). On the 21st July 1946 he left the Japanese port Kurey and reached Madras on 9th of August, 1946 on quit India day.[25]

Raja Mahendra Pratap was truly an illustrious son of our motherland, a revolutionary and partiot with indomitable zeal for India's freedom. During second world war, his non-cooperation with the Japanese Military Government is a buring example of Raja Mahendra Pratap's indomitable courage and morale. Scholars have not taken note of his foresight in not cooperating with the only imperial power in Asia during Second World War. Japan defeated Russia, China and occupied many islands in Pacific and Indian Oceans during the period 1931 to 1942. The historical map of that period indicates that the whole Far East upto Imphal in North-East India was in the grip of military power of Japan. (See Appendix B) There is a difference between the cooperation by the Indian revolutionary with the Imperial power of Japan and the cooperation by the imperial power of Japan with the Indian revolutionary leader to liberate India from the clutches of another mighty imperial power–the British. To cooperate with another imperial power in order to replace the existing imperial power in India would have been a suicidal act for the lifelong nationalist revolutionary as well as for the cause of the freedom of India. His contribution to India's independence movement during first and second world wars is second to none. He established himself as foremost leader and pioneer in many respects amongst the Indian revolutionaries abroad.

Reference

1. *My Life Story,* (edited by Dr. Vir Singh, 2004), p. 227, 230, 231, 241, 245, 258
2. *My Life Story,* p. 103
3. *My Life Story,* p. 314
4. *My Life Story,* p. 321
5. *My Life Story,* p. 317
6. *My Life Story,* p. 321-324; also see *Aaj, Sainik,* Newspapers of 6th June 1939; *Aaj,* 6th August, 1939; and *Fiji Samachar* of Suva 14th July, 1939
7. *My Life Story,* p. 91
8. *My Life Story,* p. 303-304, 85
9. *My Life Story,* p. 324 and 323
10. *My Life Story,* p. 336
11. *My Life Story,* p. 325, 327; *Reminiscences of a Revolutionary,* (edited by Dr. Vir Singh, 1999), p. 78
12. *My Life Story,* p. 330, 332, 337; *Reminiscences of a Revolutionary*, p. 78; see also Appendix A
13. *My Life Story,* p. 338-346
14. *My Life Story,* p. 347-351
15. *My Life Story,* p. 57, 250, 264-66, 280; *Reminiscences of a Revolutionary,* p. 23, 24,77-78
16. *My Life Story,* p. 331, 335-337
17. *My Life Story*, p. 227, 230-231, 244, 251, 253; *Reminiscences of a Revolutionary,* p. 64, 78; *Short Life Story*, p. 7-8
18. *My Life Story,* p. 337
19. Raja Mahendra Pratap Papers, Microfilm, Acc. No. 490, N.A.I.
20. *My Life Story,* p. 174 and 94
21. *My Life Story,* p. 102-103, 230, 244, 227; *Reminiscences of Revolutionary*, p 60-64
22. Raja Mahendra Pratap, *Abhinandan Grantha* (1976), p. 221-25, 601-610; Smarika, Part I, p. 64; *My Life Story,* p. 77, 146
23. *Short Life Story,* p. 7-8; *Reminiscences of a Revolutionary,* p.78;

Abinandan Granth, 608

24. Raja Mahendra Pratap *Janm Shatabdi Samarika*, 1986, Vrindavan, edited by Brij Bihari Lal Sharma, Khanda II, p. 30; *Abhinandan Grantha*, p. 225, 611
25. *My Life Story,* p. 85; *Reminiscences of a Revolutionary*, p. 78-79; *Abhinandan Grantha*, p. 226-227, 611, 626, Home Political, F.No. 1/1/46 Poll. (I), & K.W., NAI.

Appendix - A
Executive Board for India

Object : The Object of the Board is to make India Free immediately.

The Board : The Board consists of the following, and it had the power to decide everything:

(1) Raja Mahendra Pratap, the President.
(2) Mr. Rash Bihari Bose, Vice-President.
(3) Mr. Anand Mohan Sahay, Chief Secretary.

More members of the Board may be co-opted when and if necessary.

Advisers : The Board shall have Japanese, German and Italian Advisers, as soon as possible, and they will be consulted on all important questions.

Finance : Funds for the activities of the Board shall be received from friends and sympathisers.

Secretariat : There will be a number of workers to carry on work of the secretariat.

Volunteers : There will be a number of volunteers to assist us in the work. President will have full control of this department.

Information Department :

It is to watch the action of our co-workers. Vice President will be incharge of this department. The procedures will be to find treacherous talks or actions of the co-workers. As soo as a man is found quilty the Vice-President will present the case to the President. The chief secretary will defend the quilty. Decision will be absolutely with the President.

Decision : Everything will be decided by the unanimous vote of the Board.

Duration : The Board shall continue to function until an independent Indian Government is established in India.

Oath : Every member of the Board and all the members of the secretariat will solemnly take oath to observe loyalty to this constitution. Anyone found guilty or irregularity will be warned by the President and if someone does not agree he shall have to leave.

Publication : No part of the constitution and of the activities of the Board shall be made public without the unanimous decision of the Board.

Other Matters : Matters not mentioned here will be decided by the Board unanimously.

Sd/- Mahendra Pratap (Raja)
President.

Sd/- Rash Bihari Bose
Vice-President.

Sd/- Anand Mohan Sahay
Chief- secretary.

Kokubunji (Tokyo)

Raja Mahendra Pratap's private papers. Item No. 17. Box. No. 6, pp. 1-7, N.A.I. New Delhi.

Appendix - B

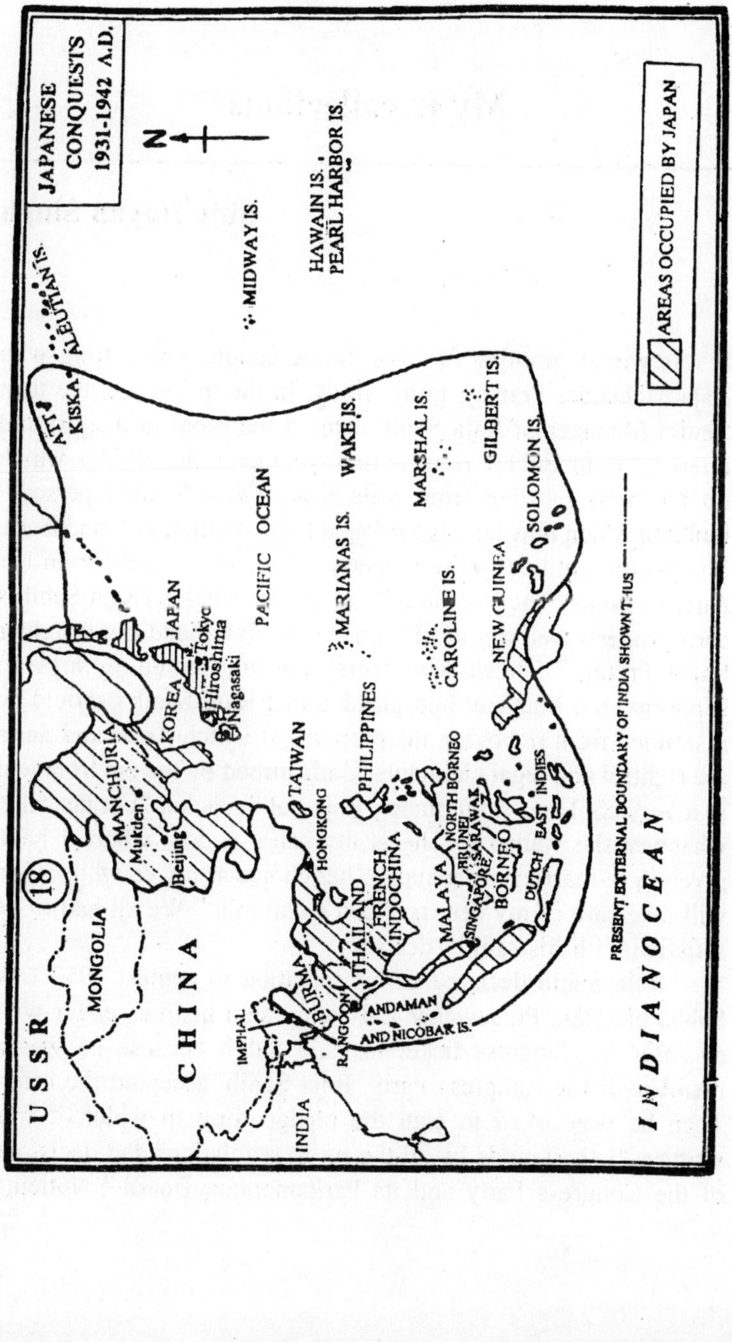
JAPANESE CONQUESTS 1931-1942 A.D.
18
N
U S S R
MONGOLIA
C H I N A
MANCHURIA
Mukden
Beijing
KOREA
JAPAN
Tokyo
Hiroshima
Nagasaki
TAIWAN
HONGKONG
PHILIPPINES
FRENCH INDOCHINA
THAILAND
BURMA
RANGOON
IMPHAL
INDIA
ANDAMAN AND NICOBAR IS.
MALAYA
SINGAPORE
SARAWAK
BRUNEI
NORTH BORNEO
BORNEO
DUTCH EAST INDIES
NEW GUINEA
CAROLINE IS.
MARIANAS IS.
PACIFIC OCEAN
WAKE IS.
MARSHAL IS.
GILBERT IS.
SOLOMON IS.
ATTU
KISKA
ALEUTIAN IS.
MIDWAY IS.
HAWAIN IS.
PEARL HARBOR IS.
AREAS OCCUPIED BY JAPAN
PRESENT EXTERNAL BOUNDARY OF INDIA SHOWN THUS
I N D I A N O C E A N

My Recollections

Shiv Dhyan Singh

It was winter morning of 1948. Some people were sitting with Raja Mahendra Pratapji in his study. In the meantime, the then Sindhi Manager of Raja Sahib entered the room in disgust and uttered, "Rani Baldev Kaur is removing even the articles which do not belong to her from Kala Kunj. (Raja Sahib's personal building which now houses Sri Pagal Baba Ashram in Vrindaban). She is only entitled to the property which she brought from her parent's home. The late Raja Prem Pratap Singh's (Raja Sahib's son) property belongs to his son Amar Pratap and his daughter Sarla Pratap." Those who were present, including myself, supported the Manager and pleaded that Rani Sahiba should be restrained from removing the property of which Amar and Sarla are rightful and legal claimants. Undisturbed by the environment in a very cool and calm maner, Raja Sahib spoke, "Let her take, whatever she wants to. She is my son's widow whom I have given in re-marriage to a man of her choice as my daughter. God will take care of my deceased son's children." We all had to be satisfied with his saintly decision.

Raja Sahib declared of his intention to contest 1952 Lok Sabha election. Pt. Jawahar Lal Nehru sent his messenger with an offer of Congress ticket to Raja Sahib because he was a member of the Congress Party. Raja Sahib, accepted the offer. Then he was asked to sign the pledge form in which it was written, "I shall abide by all the rules, regulations and decisions of the Congress Party and its Parliamentary Board." Noticing this, Raja Sahib, very firmly said, "No, I shall not sign this pledge. I shall act upon the voice of my innersoul." Thus he rejected the offer of the Congress Party and contested the election as an independent candidate.

I happened to be the organiser of Raja sahib's 1957 election compaign for the Lok Sabha. Prem Hotel at the Holi Gate in Mathura was the election's Head Office. Raja Sahib's trusted man Hafiz Mohd. Akbar Khan was the treasurer. On one morning of 1957, five vehicles were standing without petrol. Akbar Khan told me that he had no money to purchase petrol. All of our campaigners were sitting idle. At the same time, Raja Sahib came to the Hotel from Vrindaban. Noticing all present there in some what disappointing and woeful mood he asked me for the day's programme. I apprised him of the acute financial position. Unperturbed the least, joyfully and confidently, he replied, "Why do you worry? Let him be worried on whose command, we have taken up this task. If he wants to take work from us, he will also provide means for it." Raja Sahib had hardly completed the sentence, when a gentleman from Hathras happened to come there. During his talks with Akbar Khan Sahib, it was revealed that he was a tenant in one of the shops of Raja Sahib at Hathras city, and he wanted to purchase the shop. There and then an agreement was written for executing the sale deed of the shop and the man paid five thousand rupees as advance money. Immediately, all the vehicles and workers got moved with election work. What explanation can be advanced for this incident? Was it not a heavenly help extended at the call of a pious and great soul like Raja Sahib's?

Once it so happened that a naughty boy stole my money from my room while I was science teacher and Hostel superintendent in Prem Mahavidyalaya High School at Vrindaban. I asked the Hostlers in the evening roll call about the theft but of no avail. Next morning, I resorted to hunger strike and declared that I would not end the strike until the wrong doer returned the money and repented over what he had done. That incident was eared to Raja Sahib. He summoned a meeting of all the Hostlers.

When the incident was narrated to Raja Sahib, he narrated a similar happening occured with him while at Kabul. He told that his boy servant made away with some of his articles. He camplained to the Mullah who had engaged that boy as Raja Sahib's servant. The Mullah asked Raja Sahib, "Have you committed theft, Raja Sahib?" Raja Sahib clarified that the boy servant had committed theft in his room. The Mullah again repeated, "Have you committed theft Raja Sahib?" Thinking that the Mullah could perhaps not understand him, Raja Sahib again explained to him the incident of theft. At that the Mullah said, "Raja Sahib, you have not committed any sin. The boy has committed a sin by stealing your articles. You rest assure, the sinner would not escape God's fury, while your loss would be made good." After relating his own experience of such a happening. Raja Sahib urged upon the students that sinner would never escape God's eye he would be punished for his wrong action. He further told that if he repented for his sinful action and begged parden from the Almighty with the promise not to do it again, God was ever kind to forgive the sinner. Raja Sahib's advice had such an impact on the mind of the wrong doer that he slipped the stolen money wrapped in a paper inside my room which I found the next morning on opening the door of my room.

There was a man by the name of Prahlad Gujar resident of village Ujhani in tehsil Chhata of district Mathura, a part of Raja Sahib's erstwhile estate. Prahlad shouldered the blame of a boy's killing accidentally by Raja Sahib's son Raja Prem Pratap Singh during his hunting spree in the jungle of Ujhani. Raja Sahib was approached by prominent persons of the district and by his relatives to help in saving his son's life but he refused saying, "A guilty has to be punished according to law. In case he is not found guilty God will protect him." On the plea of confession, Prahlad was charge sheeted but for want of sufficient proof, he was acquitted by the trialent court. After the death of his son, Raja Sahib made Prahlad incharge of land and some buildings in Ujhani for their management. Once Prahlad came to Raja Sahib at Vrindaban. He gave three hundred ruppes to Raja Sahib as the sale price of *Sarkandas* and some trees removed from his land. Raja Sahib accepted rupees two hundred and returned rupees one hundred to him saying, "It is your remuneration for maintaining and looking after the land assigned to you." At that Raja Sahib was informed that Prahlad had not deposited full sale price which ran in at least two thousand rupees even than he was given one hundred rupees back. Raja Sahib, then remarked, "It is not even a drop in ocean. You know, this man put his life in danger in order to save my sons's life. What sacrifice can be greater than what he did?" Later on, Raja Sahib donated to him land, garden and a building in Ujhani.

Raja Mahendra Pratap

Hari Singh

Raja Mahendra Pratap had become a legend in the Freedom-Movement in India and abroad. I had often heard his name from my teachers and principals during my school and college days. I heard and saw Raja Sahib at Jhajjar in 1946 for the first time. His personality fascinated me. Like late Ch. Sir Chhotu Ram, I found him apostle of Hindu-Muslim Unity. He opposed the idea of partition on communal grounds as Anglo-American mischief against Indian Unity. On the other hand he wished creation of Aryan from Iran to Burmah. He warned against Chinese aggression if India did not go red. He proposed to strengthen Indian Defence after the British quitted India. There and then I decided to dedicate my life to the service of my great people as a social worker and teacher.

I went to Vrindaban in July 1947 and offered my services to Raja Sahab. The communal riots were the order of the day. He wanted me to work as principal of his Prem Mahavidyalaya which he had founded in 1909 on his return from his first world tour and called it his 'son'. During my stay as Principal of P.M.V. Vrindaban from 1947 to 1954, I found Raja Sahib a patriot, secularist, educationist, writer, orator and preacher in one. He thought, wrote, spoke and acted like a prophet of Religion of Love and World Federation. He was almost a mystic to be. The grabbing age could not understand and appreciate his saintly ways. His simplicity with aristocracy, humility with militancy, secularism with religion, nationalism with World Federation baffled all and made him a controversial and lonely figure. He was too great, too noble, too visionary to be understood and followed by the people lost in their petty pursuits for money, power and status. He towered over his contemporary politicians who indulged in their immediate calculations while he always looked around and beyond.

Raja Sahib believed in co-existence of castes, religions and social systems. He wanted to weave all the castes in India into national policy as spokes are fitted into a wheel. He was deadly against Karl Marx's ideology of class struggle. He started as a nationalist revolutionary and died as an utopian saint.

I kept regular correspondence with him up to the last. He was courteous to reply my queries and never minded my opposite stands on several issues. I saw him last in the meditation-room in P.M.V. Vrindaban on Feb. 22, 1979 on my return home from Trivendrum (Kerala). Though he was running through 93rd year of his life, yet his wanderlust was quite green. I said to him, "you will live up to 125 years!" He simply smiled, gave me *pera* sweets and walked upto the door to see me off. I did not know that would be my last *darshan* of that abode of Great Soul.

द्वितीय विश्व-युद्ध और राजा साहब

आनन्द मोहन सहाय

सन् 1938 के सितम्बर में जब द्वितीय महायुद्ध छिड़ गया तब राजा साहब जापान में ही थे। इस बीच जब-जब राजा साहब कोबे पधारे तब उस अवसर पर जापान स्थित भारतवासियों का देश के प्रति क्या कर्तव्य है, इस विषय पर हम दोनों के बीच विचार-विमर्श हुआ। साथ ही हमने तय किया कि एक संगठन बनाकर देश की सहायता की जाए।

उस समय कोबे स्थित जर्मन दूतावास के कोन्सिल जनरल, डॉ. वालसर साहब थे जो राजा साहब से प्रथम महायुद्ध के समय से परिचित थे। मेरा उनके साथ परिचय कराया गया जो आगे चलकर काफी लाभदायक सिद्ध हुआ। इस संगठन में टोकियो के क्रान्तिकारी रासबिहारी बोस जी को भी सम्मिलित किया गया और इस प्रकार राजा महेन्द्र प्रताप अध्यक्ष तथा रासबिहारी बोस उपाध्यक्ष और मैं मन्त्री बना। इस अधिशासी बोर्ड का जो विधान लिखा गया था उसकी मूल प्रति राजा साहब, स्वर्गीय रास बिहारी बोस और मेरे मूल हस्ताक्षरों के साथ भारतीय अभिलेखागार में सुरक्षित है।

जापान की युद्ध-घोषणा के बाद इसी अधिशासी बोर्ड ने आई.एन.ए. का रूप ले लिया परन्तु उस समय परिस्थिति वश राजा साहब ने इसमें आगे भाग लेने से इन्कार कर दिया। युद्ध के दौरान राजा साहब अपने कोकुंबुजी के आश्रम में ही रहने लगे और युद्ध के राजनीतिक कार्यक्रम से एक प्रकार से संन्यास ही ले लिया। इसके कारण नीचे दिए जा रहे हैं–

जापान के द्वितीय विश्व-युद्ध में शामिल होने से पहले हमारा क्रान्तिकारी काम राजा साहब की अध्यक्षता में चलता था यद्यपि योजना तैयार करना, धन एकत्रित करना, जापानियों से सम्पर्क स्थापित करना जैसे सब काम तब भी मैं ही करता था, परन्तु 8 दिसम्बर 41 को जापान के इस युद्ध में शामिल होने से स्थिति बदल गई। जापान के युद्ध में कूद पड़ने पर यह आवश्यक हो गया कि

हम लोग भी गुप्त कार्यवाहियाँ समाप्त करके प्रत्यक्ष संघर्ष में लगें और जापानी फौज तथा हुकूमत से घनिष्ठ सहयोग करें, परन्तु जापान सरकार न तो राजा साहब पर ही पूर्ण विश्वास करती थी और न मैं ही उसका विश्वास भाजन बनने का दावा कर सकता था। वास्तव में जापान सरकार के हम सबसे अधिक निकट श्री रासबिहारी बोस जी थे। वह जापान के नागरिक थे, जापान की एक लड़की से ही उन्होंने शादी की थी। वह हमसे पहले से वहाँ रह रहे थे और जापानी नागरिकों में और सरकारी अधिकारियों में उनका दबदबा भी था। ऐसी दशा मे स्वभावतः सरकार रासबिहारी बाबू पर पूरा विश्वास करती थी और उन्हीं के नेतृत्व में वह हमारी सहायता करना पसन्द करती थी, पर यह स्थिति राजा साहब के स्वाभिमान को ठेस पहुँचाती थी, क्योंकि वह स्वयं प्रथम महायुद्ध में भारत की प्रथम राष्ट्रीय सरकार के सभापति व नेता रह चुके थे और उन्होंने एक सेनापति के रूप में डटकर अँग्रेजों के विरुद्ध संघर्ष किया था।

दूसरा कारण जिसने राजा साहब को नेतृत्व से संन्यास लेने को विवश किया वह उनकी स्वतन्त्र विचारधारा थी। उनके लिए यह सम्भव नहीं था कि वे जापानी फौजी हुकूमत द्वारा बनाए गए कार्यक्रम का साथ दें और उसके निर्णयों के अनुसार काम करें। यह ठीक नहीं है कि जापानी युद्ध-क्षेत्र में बहुत वीरता से लड़ते हैं, परन्तु भारत की स्वतन्त्रता के युद्ध में उनका नेतृत्व हमारे हित में कदापि नहीं होता। वे भारतीय विचारधारा को और हमारी आवश्यकताओं को समझने की शक्ति नहीं रखते थे। यही कारण थे कि राजा साहब ने समय की स्थिति को समझकर रास बिहारी जी बोस का ही उस समय नेतृत्व करना ठीक मानकर, स्वयं संन्यास ले लिया।

परन्तु मेरी स्थिति उस समय राजा साहब से भिन्न थी, इसलिए मैं तब भी रास बिहारी जी के साथ बराबर काम करता रहा। मैं यह जानता था कि श्री रासबिहारी उस जमाने के क्रान्तिकारी थे जब क्रान्ति गुप्त रूप से कुछ अँग्रेजी शासकों की हत्या व तोड़-फोड़ तक ही सीमित थी। इन कामों में बोस जी प्रवीण थे, परन्तु जनता के सामूहिक आन्दोलन को चलाने से उनका कोई सम्पर्क नहीं था, न उन्हें ऐसे नेतृत्व का अनुभव था। महायुद्ध के समय एक फौजी संस्था अथवा पूर्वी एशिया में रहनेवाले भारतवासियों के जनसमूह का नेतृत्व करना रास बिहारी बाबू के लिए सम्भव नहीं था। पहली आई.एन.ए. की असफलता का भी यही कारण था और रास बिहारी जी के नेतृत्व में हम इस प्रयास की असफलता भी अनिवार्य मानते थे, परन्तु इस परिस्थिति को भाँप कर मैं पहले से ही टोकियो स्थित जर्मन दूतावास के द्वारा सुभाष बाबू से सम्पर्क बनाए हुए था। मैं उन्हें पूर्वी एशिया में लाकर इस संघर्ष का नेतृत्व सौंपने का प्रयास गुप्त रूप से कर रहा

था। इसलिए सुभाष बाबू की प्रतीक्षा के कारण मैंने बिना किसी संकोच के रास बिहारी के तत्कालीन नेतृत्व को कबूल कर लिया था, परन्तु राजा साहब की निर्भीकता ने उन्हें संन्यास लेने को ही बाध्य कर दिया।

यह संन्यास भी राजा साहब के चरित्र-बल तथा सिद्धान्त में अटल विश्वास का प्रतीक था। युद्ध के दौरान जापान में रहकर भी जापान के फौजी शासकों से असहयोग करना क्रान्तिकारी मनोबल तथा अगाध साहस का कितना ज्वलन्त उदाहरण था, यह वही समझ सकता है, जो जापान की उस समय की परिस्थिति से परिचित हो। मैं इसका साक्षी हूँ। राजा साहब जानते थे कि उस असहयोग के उनके लिए गम्भीर परिणाम हो सकते थे, परन्तु उन्होंने इसकी तनिक भी चिन्ता न करके युद्ध की राजनीति से संन्यास ले लिया। यह पूर्वी एशिया में रहनेवाली भारतीय जनता के राजा जी के प्रति श्रद्धा तथा प्रेम का फल था कि जापानी शासक राजा साहब का बाल भी बाँका न कर सके। इतना ही नहीं, जापानी सरकार की ओर से राजा जी के भरण-पोषण के लिए माहवारी के रूप में कुछ रकम भी तय कर दी गई। नेता जी की आजाद हिन्द सरकार ने भी जापानी शासकों को यही सलाह दी कि राजा साहब को कोई कष्ट न दिया जाए। यह राजा साहब के सिद्धान्तों की विजय थी। ऐसे दृढ़ निश्चयी भारत माता के सपूत को भारत वर्ष की जनता सदा गौरव और सम्मान के साथ याद रखेगी इसमें तनिक भी सन्देह नहीं है।

राजा महेन्द्र प्रताप–जीवन दर्शन की एक झाँकी

रमेश वर्मा

राजा महेन्द्र प्रताप का जीवन-दर्शन क्या है? उनके जीवन वृत्त में विरोधाभास है, उनका समाधान क्या है? और भी इस तरह के सवाल हैं, जो राजा साहब के सम्बन्ध में विचार करते हुए समाने आ जाते हैं।–आधुनिक भारत के निर्माताओं में उनका स्थान कहाँ है? स्वतन्त्रता प्राप्ति की एक क्रान्तिकारी (सशक्त) विचारधारा में है? या दूसरी गाँधी-वादी अहिंसा धारा में। राजा साहब को दोनों ही मार्गों का पथिक कहा जाता है। महात्मा गाँधी के 'अहिंसाधर्म' और राजा साहब के 'प्रेमधर्म' के तत्त्व एक ही हैं। उसमें पृथकता कहाँ है? इसी तरह गाँधी के ग्राम्य स्वराज्य और राजा साहब के पंचायती राज में भी। सरकारी पंचायत राज व्यवस्था में दोनों से ही अन्तर है। महात्मा गाँधी का 'सत्य का प्रयोग' राजा महेन्द्र प्रताप का, जनता जनार्दन के लिए 'प्रेम-धर्म' बन गया। संसार-संघ की कल्पना और उसे साकार रूप देने का आह्वान सर्व प्रथम राजा महेन्द्र प्रताप के जापान के आश्रम से हुआ, संयुक्त राष्ट्र संघ की स्थापना में जिसका प्रतिबिम्ब चमका है। राजा साहब संसार-संघ के उपासक रहे और जाति प्रथा को भी मानते थे, उनके आर्यान देश की मौलिकता और धर्म में राष्ट्रीयता की आधुनिकता में क्या तालमेल है?–आदि। ये प्रश्न ऐसे हैं, जिन पर राजा के विचारों का मनोवैज्ञानिक अध्ययन होना चाहिए। यह एक शोध ग्रन्थ (थीसिस) होगा क्योंकि राजा साहब का एक दर्शन है, जिसमें अथ और इति का कोई अन्तर नहीं हो सकता।

प्रथम अनुभूति

मेरा राजा साहब से निजी सम्पर्क नहीं रहा। मैं उनके विचारों का ही पाठक रहा हूँ। आपका सबसे पहले एक पत्र मुझे तब पढ़ने को मिला जब राजा साहब जापान आकर रूस गए थे। और उनके पत्र भारतीय समाचार-पत्रों–दैनिक 'आज' (काशी), साप्ताहिक 'प्रताप' (कानपुर) आदि में छपने लगे थे। साप्ताहिक 'सैनिक' के लिए

उनका पहला पत्र आया। मैं सैनिक के सम्पादकीय विभाग में कार्य करता था। ये पत्र सरकारी सैंसर द्वारा पढ़े जाकर छपने को प्राप्त हो जाते थे। राजा साहब के सम्बन्ध में इतनी ढिलाई अंग्रेज सरकार के रुख में आ गई थी।

यहीं से राजा साहब के सम्बन्ध में मेरा अध्ययन शुरू हो गया। पहला प्रश्न है–(1) राजा साहब ने ऐसी सरकार के विरुद्ध बगावत का झण्डा बुलन्द किया, जो विश्व की अद्वितीय शक्ति थी। क्या यह दुस्साहसिक प्रयास था जिसे उस समय के विचारों का अनुमोदन प्राप्त नहीं था? (2) दुश्मन का दुश्मन मित्र होता है, इसको मानते हुए भी क्या राजा साहब देश की स्वतन्त्रता के लिए युद्धजनित परिस्थिति में विदेशी सहायता पर अवलम्बित हो गये थे? (3) क्या उन्होंने निराश होकर ही जापान में अपना आश्रम बनाया था, जहाँ से उनके विचारों में परिवर्तन आ गया?

इस लेख में इतना ही विचार हो सकता है। वह विचार भी स्वातन्त्र्य के सन्दर्भ में ही।

प्रथम प्रश्न

राजा साहब के देश से बाहर जाने के समय तक, अर्थात् प्रथम महायुद्ध से पूर्व, उपनिवेशिक देशों की स्वतन्त्रता का मार्ग सशक्त संघर्ष से ही था। अमेरिका की स्वाधीनता के संघर्ष ने इसका मार्ग प्रशस्त कर दिया था। भारत की स्वतन्त्रता के लिए प्रथम सशक्त संगठन 'गदर पार्टी' के नाम से अमेरिका में गठित हुआ, ये लोग साम्राज्यवादी दासता में पंजाब से गए थे। 1857 के प्रथम स्वतन्त्रता संघर्ष को भी गदर नाम दिया गया था।

इसका अंश गाँधी युग के 30 वर्ष के स्वतन्त्रता संघर्ष में भी जीवन्त रहा। यूरोप में जनक्रान्ति की लहरें उठ रही थीं। ब्रिटेन के पड़ोसी आयरिश स्वतन्त्रता का सिनफीन आन्दोलन, इटली की स्वतन्त्रता का संघर्ष, फ्राँस की राज क्रान्ति की चिनगारियाँ–जार्ज वाशिंगटन, डी वेलेरा, गेजनी-गैरी-वाल डी, स्वतन्त्रता की मशाल जलाने वाले नाम विश्वविख्यात हो गए थे। फ्राँस की राजक्रान्ति और ब्रिटेन में राजशाही के विरुद्ध विद्रोह के पीछे लोकतान्त्रिक अधिकरों की माँग थी। जनमताधिकार स्वीकार हो जाने पर इन देशों में संवेधानिक मार्ग अपना लिया गया। उपनिवेशिक आन्दोलन में दो तरह के तत्त्व काम करते थे–जिनमें एक शासन सुधारवादी पक्ष था, जिसे आशंका बनी हुई थी कि यदि ब्रिटेन छत्रछाया सिर से उठ गई तो दूसरी शक्तियाँ आ धमकेंगी, क्योंकि साम्राज्यवादी शक्तियों में आपस में झगड़े थे। भारत में फ्राँस और पुर्तगाल के भी उपनिवेश थे।

किन्तु दूसरा पक्ष पूँजीवाद और साम्राज्यवाद के विकल्प का पक्षधर था, जिसका मार्ग सशस्त्र क्रान्ति का था। इसे बौद्धिक समर्थन प्राप्त था। सावरकर बन्धु,

लाला हरदयाल, एम.एन. राय और अरविन्दघोष जैसे दिग्गज बुद्धिजीवी सशस्त्र क्रान्ति के लिए सक्रिय हो गए थे। भूमिगत सशस्त्र क्रान्ति की चिनगारियाँ फूट रही थीं और उसमें नौजवानों की आहुतियाँ लग रही थीं। क्रान्तिकारियों को काले पानी, फाँसी की सजा और दमन की कहानियाँ कानों कान जनता तक पहुँच जाती थीं। बंगभंग आन्दोलन से विदेशी सत्ता को यह आभास हो गया था कि क्रान्ति की चिनगारियाँ जनता तक पहुँच चुकी हैं। सन् 1905 के लार्ड कर्जन के बंगभंग को 1911 में वापस ले लिया गया, जब दिल्ली दरबार में वाइसराय के ऊपर बम फूटा था। बंगाल और पंजाब क्रान्तिकारी आन्दोलन के अग्रणीय क्षेत्र रहे हैं। 1947 की स्वतन्त्रता में बंगाल और पंजाब का ही विभाजन हुआ था। दो अवस्थाओं का यह कितना बड़ा अन्तर है? अतः सशस्त्र क्रान्ति की जड़ें भारत से लेकर लन्दन और अमेरिका तक फैल गई थीं। महायुद्ध छिड़ने पर जन मनोवृत्तियों में असाधारण परिवर्तन होता है। प्रथम महायुद्ध के समय में भी भारतीय जनसाधारण तक में जर्मनी के युद्ध चमत्कारों की चर्चा और ब्रिटेन की पराजय पर खुशी होती थी। यह मनोवैज्ञानिक पृष्ठभूमि और क्रान्ति की पूर्वावस्था का वातावरण था, जिसके लिए एक शंख फूंकने की आवश्कयता थी जिससे देश से बाहर क्रान्ति की बिखरी हुई शक्तियों को एक जुट किया जा सके और देश में सक्रिय ताकतों के साथ उसका सम्बन्ध जोड़ा जा सके। इसके लिए एक केन्द्रीय नेतृत्व की आवश्यकता थी। इस परिस्थिति में राजा साहब ने देश को छोड़ा और काबुल में आजाद हिन्द सरकार की स्थापना की जिसमें हिन्दू-मुस्लिम-सिख एक राष्ट्रीय क्रान्ति के सूत्र में बँध गए थे। यह भी स्मरण रखना चाहिए कि राजा साहब के नेतृत्व में बनी सरकार के समय ही राजा साहब ने यह घोषित कर दिया था कि इस सरकार का अस्तित्व तभी तक रहेगा, जब तक देश में राष्ट्रीय सरकार बनने की परिस्थितियाँ पैदा होती हैं।

द्वितीय प्रश्न

अर्थात् विदेशी सहायता अर्जन करना और देश की शक्तियों का मूल्यांकन। इसमें राजा साहब जैसे राजवंशी पुरुष को जोड़ बाकी का अंङ्क गणित लगाने की जरूरत नहीं थी। भगत सिंह ने विस्फोट किया था, उसमें भावना वेग ही प्रबल था और क्रान्तिकारियों का यही पथ रहा है। देश की स्वतन्त्रता में सरदार भगतसिंह, चन्द्रशेखर आजाद, सुभाष चन्द्र बोस, आजाद हिन्द फौज और क्रान्तिकारी बलिदानों का कितना योगदान रहा है, इसका गणित करने की जरूरत नहीं है। जहाँ तक सफलता असफलता का सम्बन्ध है, तो सिकन्दर महान और नेपोलियन का अन्त भी कैसे हुआ? इससे उनके ऐतिहासिक गौरव और पौरुषत्व पर क्या असर पड़ा? राजा साहब

के बाद छब्बीस वर्ष पीछे महात्मा गाँधी के जन आन्दोलन की लहर में भी सुभाष बाबू ने महेन्द्रप्रताप का अनुसरण किया। दोनों स्थितियों में अन्तर आ गया था, किन्तु स्वतन्त्रता के लिए मार्ग अपनाने में स्थिति समान थी। आज भी दक्षिण अफ्रीका और नामीबिया के लिए जन-आन्दोलन के साथ सशस्त्र संघर्ष भी अनिवार्य हो गया है। रोडेशिया (जिम्बाबे) की स्वतन्त्रता और अंगोला, वियतनाम के सशस्त्र संघर्ष ताजा उदाहरण हैं। अतः युद्ध के दबाव और जर्मनी, टर्की, काबुल व रूस की सहायता की राजा साहब की दृष्टि में एक सीमा तक ही अपेक्षा थी। यह देश युद्ध में फंसे हुए थे और काबुल में न इतनी शक्ति थी और न ही मनोबल था कि वह भारत पर आक्रमण करने का खतरा ले सके। राजा साहब भी जिसके लिए तैयार नहीं थे। यह भी इतिहास है कि जब जापान की सेना अण्डमान में मौजूद थी, तब नेताजी सुभाष की आजाद सेना ने देश की स्वतन्त्रता के लिए मार्च करते हुए जापानी सेना की सहायता नहीं ली थी। राजा साहब विदेशों से हथियार और युद्ध साधनों की सहायता ले सकते थे। स्वतन्त्रता का युद्ध उन्हें भारतीय शक्ति से ही लड़ना था। देश में क्रान्तिकारी दलों की सक्रियता के साथ राजा साहब को भारतीय सेना, रजवाड़ों की शक्ति जिसमें अभी स्वतन्त्र होने की भावना के चिह्न अवशिष्ट थे तथा खासकर युद्ध की परिस्थिति में जनता के अन्दर विप्लव की भावना उदय होने का विश्वास था। इस पर उनका आत्मविश्वास और अदम्य साहस काम करता था जिसके साथ पंजाब के इतिहास और वहाँ की जंगजू कौमीयत का अहसास था, राजा साहब की धर्मपत्नी जींद के राजघराने की सुपुत्री थीं। पंजाब के सिक्ख जाट राजघरानों में राजा साहब की प्रतिष्ठा तथा जनता में भी मान्यता थी। सीमा के पठानों ने अंग्रेजों की आधीनता स्वीकार नहीं की जो महायुद्ध के अवसर पर और भी सक्रिय हो गए थे। इसलिए पश्चिमी दिशा का खैबर दर्रा राजा साहब के लिए ऐसा ही मोर्चा बना हुआ था, जैसा कि दूसरे महायुद्ध में पूर्वी सीमा पर इम्फाल का मोर्चा जमा था। ऐतिहासिक घटनाओं का मूल्यांकन उसके परिणामों से ही होता है। महात्मा गाँधी के नेतृत्व में 1920 के असहयोग आन्दोलन और 1930 से 32 के सत्याग्रह संग्राम मंजिल के पड़ाव ही सिद्ध हुए हैं।

दो युगों का सन्धि-काल

यहाँ हमें प्रथम महायुद्ध और द्वितीय महायुद्ध की परिस्थितियों पर भी एक दृष्टिपात कर लेना चाहिए। द्वितीय महायुद्ध काल में भारत में अंग्रेजी सेना के साथ अमेरिकन सैनिकों की भी छावनी बन गई थीं। युद्ध का आंतक छाया हुआ था। स्वतन्त्रता का आन्दोलन भी चल रहा था जिसके साथ दो नारे काम कर रहे थे।–(1) भारत छोड़ो और (2) 'करो-मारो'। इसमें दो शक्तियाँ कार्यरत थीं। पहले नारे का

प्रतिनिधित्व कांग्रेस कर रही थी जिसका अर्थ पूर्ण स्वतन्त्रता प्राप्ति का था। पर इसका असर प्रतीक रूप में ही रह गया था। क्योंकि अंग्रेजों से समझौता करने की बातचीत भी चल रही थी, किन्तु दूसरे नारे को प्रयोग में लाने की शक्तियाँ भी काम कर रही थीं जो तोड़-फोड़ और गुरिल्ला युद्ध का रूप बन गया था। जब यह आन्दोलन शुरू हुआ था, तो उसके सामने रूस जैसी क्रान्ति पैदा होने का आदर्श था, जो महायुद्ध के दौरान ही हुई थी। इस क्रान्तिकारी शक्ति के बाद में कम्युनिस्ट दल अलग हो गया था। पर क्रान्ति के बुनियादी और नैमित्तिक कारण मौजूद थे। युद्ध समाप्त होने पर इसका विस्फोट भी हुआ। जब भारतीय सेना के एक अंग ने विद्राह कर दिया और कम्युनिस्ट पार्टी तक ने तेलंगाना में रूस की-सी क्रान्ति करने का दुस्साहसिक और असामयिक असफल प्रयास किया। किन्तु स्थिति बदल चुकी थी, क्योंकि भारत की मुख्य राष्ट्रीय-शक्ति कांग्रेस और अंग्रेजों में आजादी का सौदा हो चुका था। भारत के लिए सत्ता का हस्तान्तरण हुआ जिसके लिए महात्मा गाँधी जी का भी समर्थन प्राप्त नहीं था। यदि भारत ने शक्ति के बल पर स्वतन्त्रता प्राप्त की होती, तो देश का इतिहास कुछ और ही होता।

देश का विभाजन हो गया। स्वतन्त्रता मिली जिसका जनता को अपने रक्त से इतना मूल्य चुकाना पड़ा जैसा कि इससे पहले किसी देश में नहीं हुआ था। ख्याल रखना होगा कि द्वितीय महायुद्ध के अवसान पर देश में राष्ट्रीय शक्तियाँ कार्य कर रही थीं। प्रथम महायुद्ध के दौरान तो कांग्रेस भी मित्र-राष्ट्रों की विजय के गीत गाती थी। गाँधी जी भी रंगरूट भर्ती करते थे। मित्र-राष्ट्रों की विजय हो गई थी, रूस में क्रान्ति हो गई। राजा साहब की रूस की यात्रा और लेनिन व रूसी सेना के सिपह-सालार ट्राटस्की से भेंट राजा साहब का देश की स्वतन्त्रता के लिए अन्तिम प्रयास था। रूस की सहानुभूति राजा साहब के साथ थी पर क्रान्ति का निर्यात नहीं होता, वह देश के अन्दर ही पैदा होती है। इसलिए राजा साहब सफल नहीं हो सके। यहाँ से उनके विचारों में मौलिक परिवर्तन हो गया।

तीसरा प्रश्न

महायुद्ध के परिणाम स्वरूप विश्व की काया पलट हो गई। विश्व स्तर का ऐसा महायुद्ध इससे पहले कभी नहीं लड़ा गया जिसका असर हर देश के कोने-कोने पर हुआ। साम्राज्यवाद की शक्ति क्षीण हो गई और उसकी प्रहार शक्ति निस्तेज हो गई। दोनों ही महायुद्धों में अमेरिका की भूमिका निर्णायक रही है, जो स्वयं साम्राज्यवाद के विरुद्ध अपनी शक्ति के प्रयोग से स्वतन्त्र हुआ था। अतः दोनों महायुद्धों में मित्र राष्ट्रों की युद्ध घोषणा में स्वतन्त्रता और न्याय के उद्देश्य शामिल थे। इससे साम्राज्यवाद का दूसरे देशों पर शासन करने का नैतिक बल भी क्षीण

हो गया था। जन आन्दोलन को दमन करने का उनके पास कानूनी बल भी नहीं रहा। लोकमान्य तिलक का यह उद्घोष कि स्वराज हमारा जन्म सिद्ध अधिकार है विश्व का नारा बन गया। राज के विरुद्ध बगावत को देश द्रोह का नाम देकर उन्हें फाँसी, काले पानी के दण्ड दिए गए वह देश के विरुद्ध विदेशी सत्ताधारियों का अपराध बन गया। भारत में आजाद हिन्द सैनिकों पर जब मामले चलाए गए तो उसका फैसला साम्राज्यवादियों के विरुद्ध गया क्योंकि आजाद हिन्द सेना को विदेशी सत्ता से अपने देश को स्वतन्त्र करने का जन्म सिद्ध अधिकार था और वह शस्त्र बल के द्वारा भी। 18वीं और 19वीं शताब्दी के यूरोपियन राजनैतिक विचारकों के कथन साकार बन कर सामने आ गए। उसमें पूँजीवादी सत्ता के विरुद्ध शोषित जनता के वर्ग संघर्ष ने राष्ट्रीय स्वतन्त्रता के जन संघर्ष का रूप ले लिया जिसका सबसे बड़ा प्रयोग भारत में हुआ। महायुद्ध समाप्त होते ही देश में जन आन्दोलन की जैसी लहर पैदा हुई वह अपना लक्ष्य प्राप्त करके ही थमी थी। उसने विश्व का भी पथ प्रदर्शन किया। परिणामतः आधी शताब्दी से कम समय में ही दुनिया में साम्राज्यवाद के भग्नावशेष ही शेष रह गए।

यह युग-परिवर्तन था, जिसमें विचार-क्रान्ति के साथ उनका व्यावहारिक प्रयोग भी सफल हुआ। यहीं से राजा साहब के विचारों में परिवर्तन हुआ। प्रथम महायुद्ध में अंग्रेजों का साथ देने वाले गाँधी ने कहा था कि–"मैं देश में अराजकता पसन्द कर लूँगा बशर्ते कि अंग्रेज भारत छोड़कर चला जाय।" स्मरण किया जाय कि काबुल में स्वतन्त्र सरकार की स्थापना करते समय राजा साहब के जो विचार थे, उसी के अनुसार भारत में राष्ट्रीय सरकार बनने की परिस्थितियाँ पैदा हो गई थीं। काबुल में जो बीज बोया वह दिल्ली में हरा-भरा हो गया। द्वितीय महायुद्ध में जापान धुरी राष्ट्रों में शामिल था। प्रथम महायुद्ध से अधिक भारत में अंग्रेजी सत्ता पर दबाव था, जिसमें जापान ने उसकी पूँछ को भी पकड़ लिया था। पर राजा साहब अपने विचारों पर अटल रहे। उनकी यह स्थिति राजर्षि विश्वामित्र की-सी थी, जिन्होंने स्वयं शस्त्र ग्रहण नहीं किया लेकिन राम के द्वारा 'असुर-निकंदन' के प्रति उनकी आस्था रही और अपने राम का प्रशिक्षण भी किया। उनका राष्ट्रीय दृष्टिकोण विशाल होकर विश्व की सीमाओं तक फैल गया। महात्मा गाँधी का 'सत्य का प्रयोग' राजा महेन्द्र प्रताप का जनता जनार्दन के लिए 'प्रेम-धर्म' बन गया। 'संसार-संघ' की कल्पना और उसे साकार रूप देने का आह्वान सर्व प्रथम राजा महेन्द्र प्रताप के जापान के आश्रम से हुआ। संयुक्त राष्ट्र संघ की स्थापना में जिसका प्रतिबिम्ब चमका है। परतन्त्र भारत की बेड़ियों को काटने का संकल्प लेकर गए हुए पथिक ने स्वतन्त्र भारत की भूमि में पदार्पण किया। यह उनके संकल्प की विजय है। प्राचीन ऋषियों की मूर्ति में उन्होंने बत्तीस वर्ष तक तपस्या की। स्वतन्त्र

भारत की भूमि पर पैर रखते ही भारतीय जनता ने सजल नेत्रों से, उनका ऐसा ही स्वागत किया जैसा भरत और अयोध्या की जनता ने राम के बनवास से लौटने पर किया था। महात्मा गाँधी के राम राज्य में जो कल्पना है वही राजा महेन्द्र प्रताप के प्रेम-धर्म में है। जो भारतीय संस्कृति के 'विश्व बन्धुत्व' और 'वसुधैव कुटुम्बकम्' की अभिव्यक्ति है। राजा साहब के व्यक्तित्व का विराट के साथ समागम हो गया। राष्ट्रीय धारा के प्रांगण में राजा महेन्द्र प्रताप के व्यक्तित्व की अलग छाप है। सात्विक और राजस्व गुणों का समत्व महेन्द्र प्रताप का जीवन है।

राजा महेन्द्र प्रताप–उनकी जिन्दगी का मिशन और सन्देश

अकबर खान

राजा साहब जहाँ भारत की आजादी की लड़ाई के एक बहुत बड़े और मशहूर जनरल हुए हैं, उनकी बेमिसाल कुर्बानियाँ एक नमूना है, इसके साथ-साथ ही वे एक बहुत ऊँचे दर्जे के विचारक फिलासफर, रिफोर्मर, इन्सान-दोस्त, खुदापरस्त, मानवता की एकता और उसके सुख और शान्ति के लिए दुनिया की एक सरकार यानि वर्ल्ड फैडरेशन के जबरदस्त हिमायती थे। उन्होंने कई बार पूरी दुनिया के चक्कर लगाए और सबसे ज्यादा दुनिया देखने वाले लोगों में उनका दर्जा पंडित जवाहरलाल नेहरू के बराबर कहा जा सकता है। दीन-धर्म के बारे में उनकी जानकारी, समझ-बूझ और लगाव भी बहुत ज्यादा था और प्रेम धर्म के नाम से दिए गए उनके विचार सदा अमर और रोशन रहेंगे।

1946 में बत्तीस बरस की जिलावतनी के बाद राजा साहब के भारत लौटने के वक्त से 26 बरस तक उनकी सेवा करने और खिदमत में हाजिर रहकर उनकी आज्ञाओं का पालन करने का मुझे सौभाग्य मिला है। इस पर फक्र करने का मुझे पूरा हक है। मुझ पर उनकी बड़ी इनायत और मेहरबानियाँ रही हैं और यह कहना गलत ना होगा कि मेरे से ज्यादा शायद ही किसी ने उनसे, इस कद्र सीखने और रोशनी हासिल करने का मौका पाया हो। इसलिए उनके बारे में, मैं जो कुछ भी कह रहा हूँ उसमें शब्दों का सही इस्तेमाल किया गया है और किसी भी बात को बढ़ा-चढ़ाकर नहीं कहा गया है।

राजा साहब यकुम दिसम्बर 1886 को मुरसान में पैदा हुए, हाथरस राज के खानदान में गोद लिए गए और सर सैय्यद के जमाने में अलीगढ़ में तालिम पाई और रियासत जीन्द में हिज़ हाईनेस के यहाँ शादी हुई। 1906 में कांग्रेस के कलकत्ता सैशन के मौके पर शामिल हुए उस वक्त उनकी उम्र 20 साल की थी।

स्वदेशी लिबास पहना, छुआछूत के खिलाफ प्रचार शुरू किया और आगरा में एक भंगी के साथ बैठकर खाना खाया, उस वक्त से लेकर आखिरी दम तक कमजोरों गरीबों और पिछड़े वर्ग के लिए सहायता का काम किया। तमाम भारत वर्ष का दौरा किया और धर्मों के मशहूर मकामात का दौरा किया। कॉलेज की छुट्टियों के जमाने में ही यह तमाम सफर कर डाले। 1907 में दुनिया का पहला सफर कर डाला। 1909 में वृन्दावन का महल और बुलन्दशहर के पाँच गाँव दान देकर वृन्दावन में प्रेम महाविद्यालय कायम किया। इसका उद्देश्य पढ़ने के साथ-साथ दस्तकारी और इंजीनियरिंग की तालीम देना भी शामिल था। पं. मदन मोहन मालवीय भी उद्घाटन में शरीक हुए। डॉ. सम्पूर्णानन्द और आचार्य जुगलकिशोर जैसी हस्तियाँ भी प्रेम महाविद्यालय में पढ़ा चुके हैं। राजा साहब देहरादून से *निर्बल सेवक* नाम की पत्रिका भी निकालते थे, जिससे उनके सोचने का पता चलता है।

1914 में 29 साल की उम्र में बीवी बच्चों को छोड़कर और जानमाल की बाजी लगाकर अंग्रेजी के खिलाफ जंग आजादी का झण्डा ऊँचा करने और हिन्दुस्तानियों के दिलो-दिमाग में एक नई रूह और हौसला डालने के लिए जर्मनी चले गए और वहाँ के बादशाह कैसर विलियम से मिलकर अपने मुल्क की आजादी के लिए एक मनसूबा तैयार किया। और इस मनसूबे को लेकर तुर्की पहुँचे और मुसलमानों के खलिफा से मुलाकात की और उनकी हिमायत हासिल की और फिर वहाँ से काबुल पहुँचकर एक दिसम्बर 1915 में पहली आजाद हिन्दी हकुमत कायम करी, जिसके वो सदर और मौलाना बरकतुल्ला भोपाली बजीरेआजम थे।

राजा साहब की कोशिशों, कुर्बानियों और हौसले की कहानी एक मजमून में बयान करना और पूरी तस्वीर पेश करना करीब-करीब ना मुमकिन है। किसी शायर का ये शेर उन पर पूरी तरह फिट बैठता है :

कुछ बुलबुलों को याद है कुछ कुमारियों को हिब्ज़
आलम में टुकड़े-टुकड़े मेरी दास्तान कहें,

जनाब राजा महेन्द्र प्रताप की हस्ती और अजीम शखशियत एक बहुत विशाल म्यूजियम की तरह थी जिसको कोई भी पूरी तरह ना देख सका, एक फिल्मी गाना है "मेरे महबूब में क्या नहीं क्या नहीं।" दरअसल राजा साहब पर जबरदस्त रिसर्च करने की जरूरत है, तभी उनका मोतियों और हीरे जवाहरात से भरा दामन हमारे सामने आ सकता है। राजा साहब ने जो दुनिया देखी और जिस कदर देखी है और जिस नजर और दिलो दिमाग से देखी और उसको जिन हालातों में पाया है उसे किसने देखा और जाना है? राजा साहब के खिलाफ कुछ लोगों में गलतफहमियाँ पैदा हुई और वो एक खास किस्म और फिक्र के लोगों की नुक्ताचीनी

का निशाना भी बनें। राजा साहब ने आजाद भारत में भी तरह-तरह की ज्यादतियाँ सहने, सख्तियाँ झेलना और मुश्किलात का सामना करना पड़ा था। अपने घर मकान से लेकर मैदानों तक नागवार वाकियात से दो-चार होना पड़ा। मगर कभी भी इस मर्देखुदा के माथे पर किसी ने बल पड़ा हुआ नहीं देखा, हमेशा उनके चेहरे पर मुस्कुराहट ही रही। वे अपने बदतरीन दुश्मन से भी नफरत नहीं करते थे। उनके खिलाफ 420 का मुकद्दमा भी चलाया गया और दूसरे केस में जेल की सजा भी सुनाई गई, रिश्वत भी तलब की गई। एम.पी. जैसी मामूली चीज के लिए उन्हें तीन बार चुनाव भी हराया गया, मगर मैंने उनको शिकायत करते या किसी को बुरा कहते नहीं सुना, किसी को इल्जाम देते नहीं सुना और कभी गलत बयानी करते नहीं सुना।

राजा साहब बादशाहों, नवाबों, राजाओं, जमींदारों, मिल मालिकों और खुशहाल लोगों के साथ बेइन्साफी करने, उनको परेशान करने, उनसे नफरत करने को गलत समझते थे और उनकी तरफ से मजदूरों, किसानों, गरीबों मिडल-क्लास के लोगों को लूटने या सताने के भी सख्त खिलाफ थे। वे मजहबी संस्थाओं को मिटाने या मुल्ला-मौलवी, पण्डित और पादरियों की इज्जत न करने को भी पसन्द नहीं करते थे। दीन धर्म की अच्छी बातों के खिलाफ आलोचना और उसमें ऐब निकालना भी उन्हें पसन्द नहीं था। उनका एक मूल मन्त्र था कि सबको सभी की भलाई में लगाकर सभी को सुखी बनाना है। उनका कहना था हममें से हर एक को समाज में अपना-अपना स्थान समझना चाहिए और अपना-अपना काम करना चाहिए।

राजा साहब कभी भी मुँह देखी या चिकनी चुपड़ी बातें करना नहीं जानते थे और न उनके मुँह पर सच्ची बात कहने से कतराते थे, वो हमेशा सीधी-साधी जनता की भाषा बोलते थे और उन्हीं के लिए बोलते थे। वो लच्छेदार तकरीर या तहरीर के आदी नहीं थे। अगर वो मॉस्को में लेनिन से मिले तो उन्होंने कम्युनिज्म की तारीफ या बड़ाई नहीं की और सरमायादारों और राजाओं से कम्युनिज्म और सोशलिज्म के ऐब बयान नहीं किए।

राजा साहब की जिन्दगी और उनके ख्यालात की झलकियाँ चन्द अहम वाकियात और रोजमर्रा की बातें अगर आप सुनना चाहें तो मैं उनको जबानी सुना सकता हूँ और इस मजमून को यही खत्म करता हूँ।

उत्कर्षमूलक राजनीति के सूत्रधार : राजा महेन्द्र प्रताप

शिव कुमार

राजा महेन्द्र प्रताप अद्‌भुत प्रतिभावान, विरोधी विचार धाराओं के कल्पनातीत समन्वय केन्द्र, सर्वधर्म-समभाव-आविष्कर्ता, महान् विचारक कर्मयोगी, समष्टि-पोषक, संघर्ष विहीन सदाचारी समाज की संकल्पना वाले युग पुरुष तथा परमहंस थे। सार्वभौम कल्याणक तथा पोषक विचारों को पुष्ट करने के लिए उन्होंने जगत की परिक्रमाएँ करके मानव-कल्याणक सिद्धान्त खोजा जिसका ध्येय मनुष्य जाति का संयुक्त सुखी कुटुम्ब बनाना है। राजा जी ने आधुनिक राजनीति में प्रचलित प्रजातन्त्र, समाजवाद तथा समाजवादी राजप्रणालियों के गोरखधन्धों को भली-भाँति समझा तथा इनसे ऊपर उठकर सर्व सुखदा राजप्रणाली व्यवस्था का अन्वेषण किया। प्रभुसत्ता सम्पन्न ग्रामराज, नगरराज की कल्पना और कम खर्चीली तथा सुलझी राजनीति व्यवस्था की रूपरेखा देकर आधुनिक राजनीतिक दुखदा परिस्थितियों को निर्मूल करके राजनीतिज्ञों के विचारों को सर्व सुखी समाज निर्माण की ओर मोड़ दिया। सन् 1914 में स्वतन्त्र भारत की कल्पना करना उन राजनीतिज्ञों को भौंचक्का करनेवाला था जो केवल आंगल शासकों से माँग कर समाज को ऊपर उठाने की ही सोचते थे। अत: देशवासियों की माँगने की प्रवृत्ति की कीचड़ में उगा यह सुविकसित कमल स्वेच्छा से प्रवासी बना तथा भारत की स्वतन्त्रता का समर्थक बनाने के लिए विश्व की राजनीति को झकझोरा।

इस युग पुरुष का आविर्भाव, 1 दिसम्बर 1986 को ब्रज पूर्वांचल में स्थित, जनपद अलीगढ़ में मुरसान के राजा घनश्याम सिंह के तृतीय पुत्र के रूप में, माता रानी दानकौर की कोख से हुआ। बालक को जन्म देने के अल्पकाल बाद माता जी स्वर्ग सिधार गईं। बच्चे को 3 वर्ष की अल्प आयु में हाथरस के राजा हरनारायन सिंह ने दत्तक पुत्र बना लिया। राजा महेन्द्र प्रताप के प्रिय पितामह राजा दयाराम ने हाथरस के गढ़ को विकसित करके भारत के सुदृढ़त्तम गढ़ों की संज्ञा दिलाई। 1817 में इस गढ़ को जीतने आंग्लो ने भारी तैयारी करके भारी-से-भारी तोप सेना

जैसी कि भारत में उससे पहले कभी नहीं देखी गई थी इकट्ठी कीं तथा गढ़ को घेर लिया। तोपंदाजी में राजा ने अंग्रेजों को पीछे धकेल दिया। उन्होंने धोखाधड़ी से किले की बारूद में आग लगवा दी तथा राजा हाथरस छोड़कर चला गया। 1818 में हाथरस राज्य समाप्त हो गया। इसी प्रतिशोध की अग्नि ने इस नवयुवक राजकुमार को गर्म रखा तथा आंग्लों को उखाड़ फैंकने की बेचैनी से बाट जोही।

राजकुमार ने गढ़ से निकलकर झांका तो दरिद्रता का नंगा नाच देखा। मजदूर किसान की दयनीय स्थिति देख राजा को महल के भोग-विलास चुभने लगे। **'निर्बल सेवक'** पत्र निकाला तथा स्वयम् सम्पादन किया। जाति-पाति, छुआ-छूत विरोधी राजा ने भंगी तथा टमटाओं के साथ सहभोज किया। आंग्लों के विरुद्ध प्रचार करने सवैतनिक प्रचारक रखे। गाँधी जी के ऊपर गोरों के अत्याचार देख, सहायतार्थ अफ्रीका जाने की ठानी। तुरन्त गोखले से मिलने दक्षिण भारत पहुँचे। युवक का उत्साह देख उन्होंने कहा : "मुझे यह पता नहीं था कि आप जैसे व्यक्तित्व भी उत्तरी भारत में पाए जाते हैं।" उन्होंने समझा बुझाकर अफ्रीका जाने से रोक दिया तथा एक सहस्त्र रूपए सहायतार्थ भेजने स्वीकार किए। एक बार प्रेम महाविद्यालय वृन्दावन में राजा साहब के तैलचित्र का अनावरण करते हुए महात्मा गाँधी ने कहा था : "आप मुझे सबसे बड़ा मानते हैं ये मुझसे भी बड़े हैं।" दूसरी बार कहा : "राजा साहब जैसा व्यक्तित्व भारत में दूसरा कोई नहीं।"

इस चमत्कारी राजकुमार का विवाह सिक्ख राजघराने की कन्या महाराज रणबीर सिंह की अनुजा राजकुमारी बलबीर कौर के साथ हुआ। तरुण रानी के साथ विश्वभ्रमण किया तो पाया कि भारत तथा पाश्चात्य देशों की आर्थिक स्थिति में आकाश-पाताल का अन्तर है। हमारे देश के कुशल कारीगरों को अंगभंग करके आंग्ल सरकार ने निर्दयता से यहाँ के देशी उद्योग-धन्धों को नष्ट करके हमें खेल-खिलौने तथा सुई धागों तक के लिए विदेशों पर निर्भर कर दिया। हमारी दरिद्रता का प्रमुख कारण इसे मानकर पाश्चात्य ढंग के उद्योग-धन्धों को भारत में लाने के लिए युवारानी के आकर्षण तथा राजमहल के भोग विलासों को त्यागने का दृढ़ संकल्प लिया। निमन्त्रण पत्र भेजे : "श्रावण मास की हरियाली तीजों के महोत्सव पर वृन्दावन में मेरे पुत्र का समारोह पूर्वक नामकरण संस्कार सम्पन्न होगा...पधारें।" पण्डित मदन मोहन मालवीय जी को आग्रह पूर्वक बुलाया गया। यज्ञ सम्पन्न होने के पश्चात् परमत्यागी विचारक ने घोषणा की : "मैं पाश्चात्य प्रणाली का उद्योग धन्धों का महाविद्यालय खोलने अपनी सम्पूर्ण चल-अचल सम्पत्ति को दान देता हूँ। यही मेरा बिना हाड़-माँस का बेटा है।"

मामा रोईं रनबासों में, हाय राम क्या होगा।
राजा से हम रंक बन गये, भूकों मरना होगा ॥

समझाया फिर राजकुमार को, आधा दान दीजिये।
राजनियम का पालन कीजै, अग्रिम काम कीजिये ॥

उक्त घटना 1908 की है। 1909 में वृन्दावन के राजभवन तथा आधी रियासत दान कर प्रेम महाविद्यालय खोला जहाँ पर यूरोपीय कारखानों के समकक्ष वस्तुओं का निर्माण हुआ तथा यूरोपीय प्रदर्शनियों में पारितोषिक प्राप्त किए। सन् 1914 में इसी प्रेम महाविद्यालय के प्रांगण में वार्षिकोत्सव के अवसर पर मथुरा के आंग्ल जिलाधीश तथा आगरे के आंग्ल कमिश्नर की किंचित् चिन्ता न करके प्रतिभा तथा सत्साहस के पुंज राजाजी ओजस्वी स्वर में बोले : "मैं अन्याय को राजगद्दी से हटाकर न्याय को पदासीन करूँगा।" कमिश्नर चौकन्ना हो गया तथा दूसरे दिन निर्भीकता की प्रतिमूर्ति को डराने धमकाने लगा। तन में स्फूर्ति संचारित होने से दाहिना पैर ऊपर उठा तथा भूमि पर गिरा, तथा मन-ही-मन में भीष्म प्रतिज्ञा ली, "मैं भारत में अंग्रेजी साम्राज्य को कुचल कर भुरता बना दूंगा।"

संयोग से उसी समय जर्मन सम्राट विलहैल्म द्वितीय ने आंग्ल सम्राट के विरुद्ध युद्ध की घोषणा कर दी तथा अपनी वायु सेना के भरोसे जीतने की स्थिति बना ली। मामा फूफी के दो भाइयों की लड़ाई से लाभ उठाकर भारत स्वतन्त्रता के स्वप्नद्रष्टा राजा महेन्द्र प्रताप ने सशस्त्र क्रान्ति द्वारा स्वदेश को स्वतन्त्र करने की योजना बना कर जर्मनी जाने की पूरी तैयारी कर ली तथा 20 दिसम्बर, 1914 को रात के दस बजे रानी से विदा लेने **'धर्म'** नाम के अपने भवन में आए। मार्ग में भृत्यगण जल कलश लिए कतारबद्ध होकर खड़े थे। विदेश गमन की सुनकर रानी भौंचक्की रह गई–

खाय पछार गिरी धरती पर, सिसक सिसक कर रोई।
प्राणनाथ बन को जाते हैं, तन की सुधि बुधि खोई ॥
भार्या का सुख राजभोग सुख उनको कहाँ सुहाये।
पर दुःख कातरता जिनके डर, उद्वेलित हो जाये ॥
बहुतेरी समझाई रानी, कैसे समझ सुहाती।
चिर वियोग की ज्वाला भड़की सब तन तत्त्व जलाती ॥
विद्युत प्रकाश मन्द पड़ गया, सोते बच्चे, चूमे।
स्वतन्त्र भारत ध्येय पूर्ति हित, जग प्रांगण में घूमे ॥

जर्मनी की राजधानी बर्लिन पहुँचे तो वहाँ की सरकार ने आपको आतिथ्य देने को कहा परन्तु कुशल विचारक राजनीतिज्ञ को डर था कि कहीं कोई अंग्रेजों को निकालकर स्वयं देश पर हावी हो गया तो खेल बिगड़ जाएगा। अतः कुछ समय रुककर जब जर्मनी के जनरलों को भारतीय स्वतन्त्रता का पक्षधर पाया तब

वहाँ की सरकार का आतिथ्य स्वीकार किया। जर्मन सरकार ने नौकर-चाकर तथा सुरक्षा कर्मी सेवा में रख दिए। सम्राट एक बड़े हौल के बीच में खड़ा आप से मिलने की बाट देख रहा था। जैसे ही आप दरवाजे में दिखाई दिए सम्राट ने आगे बढ़कर हाथ मिलाया तथा काबुल के बादशाह से मिलकर तुर्की तथा जर्मनी की सहायता से भारत पर आक्रमण की योजना बनाई। जर्मन सरकार ने उनको सर्वोच्च भारतीय माना तथा सन्धि की कि राजा महेन्द्र प्रताप की सहायता को जर्मन की जल सेना भारत जाएगी। रेगिस्तानी मार्गों के विशेषज्ञ डॉ. वर्नर ओतो फान हेटिश को यात्रा का प्रबन्धक बनाया गया। मौलाना बकर्तुल्लाह जर्मनी से साथ आए। मार्ग में टर्की के सुल्तान ने दल का स्वागत किया तथा सहायता का वचन देकर केप्टन काज़िम बेग को साथ भेजा। प्रथम विश्व युद्ध की बरसती आग में होकर यह यात्रा करनी पड़ी।

वीयना के होटल में मिश्र के शासक ने आपको शाही भोज दिया। अंग्रेजों के दुःखदायी व्यवहार से वे बेचैन थे। रास्ते में आपने एक हंगरी के ज्योतिषी की भविष्यवाणी सुनी : "वह व्यक्ति जिसका नाम 'म' से प्रारम्भ होता है तथा भारत की ओर बढ़ता जा रहा है। अंग्रेजों की शक्ति को उसी प्रकार कुचल देगा जैसे आदमी साँप को मारता है।" रूसी सीमा में प्रवेश से पहले केप्टन नीडर मायर (जर्मनी) ने दल को तीन टुकड़ियों में बाँटा तथा बीच में टुकड़ी में राजा साहब को रखा। शत्रु के जासूसी जाल की सूचना पर पाँच सौ रूसी घुड़सवार सैनिक तथा ढाई सौ आंग्ल घुड़सवार सैनिक दो ओर से पकड़ने झपटे। एक दल पकड़ा गया। दो सुरक्षित निकल गए। अफगानिस्तान पहुँचने पर हिरात के गवर्नर ने स्वागत किया तथा काबुल तक की यात्रा का प्रबन्ध कर दिया।

2 अक्टूबर, 1915 को भारतीय योद्धा ने काबुल में प्रवेश किया। अफगान सेना ने तोपें दाग कर तथा नागरिकों ने ताली बजाकर अपने अतिथि का सत्कार किया तथा बागे-बाबर राज महल में रहने का प्रबन्ध किया। 1 दिसम्बर, 1915 को इण्डो-जर्मन-तुर्को मिशन ने अस्थाई हिन्द सरकार का गठन किया जिसके राष्ट्रपति राजा महेन्द्र प्रताप तथा प्रधानमन्त्री मौलाना बर्कतुल्ला बने। मौलाना उबैदुल्ला गृहमन्त्री थे। बहुत से भारतीय सचिवालय के सचिव रहे। सरकार का अपना सैनिक संगठन था तथा अमरीका में गठित गदर पार्टी सहयोगी संस्था थी। जो राष्ट्र अंग्रेजों के विरुद्ध थे उन्होंने तुरन्त मान्यता दी। रूस को अंग्रेजी जाल से बचाने अस्थाई सरकार के राष्ट्रपति राजा महेन्द्र प्रताप ने सोने की पोस्ट कार्ड के आकार की तख्ती पर पत्र लिखकर उसको एक निपुण तुर्क से खुदवाया तथा सीलबन्द करके अपने दो राजदूतों के हाथ जार को भिजवाया। जार ने पत्र रख लिया तथा सोना-चाँदी जो भेंट भेजे थे वापिस कर दिए तथा अंग्रेजों का साथ नहीं

छोड़ने की कहकर दूतों को लौटा दिया। इस बीच में लन्दन सरकार ने मास्को स्थित अपने राजदूत को कहा कि "राजा महेन्द्र प्रताप तथा मौलाना बर्कतुल्ला बड़े खतरनाक हैं। किसी भी प्रकार से इनके दूतों को पकड़वा लो।" जार सरकार ने ऐसा करने से इन्कार कर दिया। रूस में किरैंस्की सरकार आने पर पुनः पत्र भेजा। पुनः वही उत्तर मिला तथा एक जनरल ने दूतों को पकड़कर लन्दन सरकार को सौंप दिया। जब हिन्द सरकार के राष्ट्रपति दूतों की खोज में रूस पहुँचे तो उस जनरल की पत्नी ने बताया, "आप यहाँ से चले जाइए। मेरे पति ने आपके दूत पकड़ लिए थे। वे आंग्ल सरकार को सौंप दिए।"

राजा साहब लेनिन की क्रान्ति सफल होते ही रूसी तुर्किस्तान के कमिश्नर ने आपको विधिवत् निमन्त्रण भेजा। रेलगाड़ी के रिजर्व यान द्वारा ताशकंद आए तथा वहाँ से स्पेशल रेलगाड़ी से पैत्रोग्राद पहुँचे। 1918 का मार्च का महीना था। कमिश्नर ने बुलाकर ट्राटस्की से अनौपचारिक भेंट कराई। रूस में अकाल था तथा गेहूँ की भारी कमी थी। राजा जी ने रूस को पेट्रौल के बदले अफगानिस्तान से गेहूँ दिलवाया। सन् 1919 में हिन्दी सरकार की मन्त्रणा से अफगान शाह अमानुल्ला खाँ ने अंग्रेजों के विरुद्ध युद्ध की घोषणा कर दी। युद्ध में अंग्रेजों को दब कर सन्धि करनी पड़ी।

1919 में आपने लेनिन से भेंट की। जैसे ही दरवाजे पर दिखाई दिए लेनिन दौड़कर एक कोने से आपको बैठने के लिए कुर्सी लाया। लेनिन ने प्रेम धर्म को तालस्तायवाद बताया तथा शान्तिपूर्वक अपने अतिथि की बातें ध्यान से सुनीं। लाल रूस का राजदूत काबुल की सरकार में रखवा कर दोनों देशों के राजनयिक सम्बन्ध कराए। लेनिन सरकार ने भारत के स्वतन्त्रता संग्राम के लिए सोना भेंट किया। हिन्द सरकार के राष्ट्रपति के नाते राजा महेन्द्र प्रताप भारतीय राजा, महाराजा तथा नवाबों को पीली रेशम के रूमाल पर पत्र लिखकर दूतों से भिजवाते थे। वे दूत उन्हें कपड़ों की सीमनों में या जूतों की तलियों में रखकर लाते थे। जर्मन सम्राट तथा प्रधानमन्त्री से जो पत्र लाए थे, वे यथास्थान पहुँचाए। तुर्क सुलतान, अफगान अमीर तथा नेपाल सम्राट के पत्रों पर जर्मन सम्राट के हस्ताक्षर थे। शेष पर प्रधानमन्त्री के थे, लिखा था : "स्वतन्त्रता संग्राम में राजा महेन्द्र प्रताप की सहायता करो।" महाराजा नेपाल को सम्बोधन में 'हिज मैजेस्टि' राजा साहब ने कह कर लिखवाया था। अब अंग्रेजों को इसका पता चला तो वे भी 'हिज मैजेस्टि' लिखने लगे थे। देश-विदेश के विद्वानों ने 'पीत रेशम-पत्र षड्यन्त्र' पर शोध की है।

प्रथम विश्व युद्ध में अमरीका की सहायता से आंग्ल विजय प्राप्त कर सके। इसके पश्चात् हिन्द सरकार तितर-बितर होने लगी। जलियाँ वाले बाग के हत्याकाण्ड से क्रोध से उद्वेलित हिन्द सरकार ने पोस्टर छपवाकर सीमावर्ती क्षेत्रों के नगरों में एक रात में ही योजनाबद्ध विधि से चिपकवाये। लिखा था, "जलियाँवाले बाग के

हत्यकाण्ड का बदला लेने वाले आ रहे हैं।" प्रथम विश्व युद्ध से द्वितीय विश्वयुद्ध तक राजा महेन्द्र प्रताप ने उत्साह वर्धन के साथ विश्व राजनीति को भारतीय स्वतन्त्रता का पक्षधर बनाने का घोर प्रयत्न किया। भारत के सीमावर्ती राज्यों को आंग्लों, के विरुद्ध उकसाया। संयुक्त राज्य अमेरिका के स्टाकटन नगर के गुरुद्वारे में राजाजी को डालर भेंट किए गए। जिनको इन्होंने यूरोप में रह रहे मित्रों में बाँटा तथा सिक्ख जाटों का दल लेकर चीन के रास्ते तिब्बत पहुँचे। तिब्बत के शासक दलाईलामा ने सोना-चाँदी भेंट किए तथा पत्र लिखकर आपको जीवित 'बुद्ध' कहा तथा लहासा में न आने की प्रार्थना की क्योंकि उसे आंग्लों के प्रकोप का भय था। स्टाकटन के गुरुद्वारे में अब भी राजा साहब का चित्र टंगा है तथा उनका साहित्य रखा है। स्वर्ण की फोटोस्टैट कापी तथा साहित्य लेनिन लाइब्रेरी मास्को में है। नेशनल आरकाईव्ज लन्दन में एक 500 पृष्ठ की छपी पुस्तक राजा साहब के चित्रों सहित रखी है। इसमें आंग्ल गुप्तचरों की राजा जी के प्रवास काल की सूचनाएँ छपी हैं। जब बाबू आनन्द मोहन सहाय भारत के राजदूत बनकर टोकियो गए तो वहाँ से राजाजी का साहित्य लाकर आर्काइव्ज दिल्ली में रख दिया गया।

जापान में प्रवास के समय राजा महेन्द्र प्रताप ने 'एक्जीक्यूटिव बोर्ड ऑफ इण्डिया' नाम से भारत को तुरन्त स्वतन्त्र कराने के लिए एक संस्था बनाई। स्वयं अध्यक्ष, बाबू रास बिहारी बोस उपाध्यक्ष तथा बाबू आनन्द मोहन सहाय महामन्त्री थे। इस संस्था ने विदेशों की सहायता से देश को स्वतन्त्र करने का प्रयत्न किया। द्वितीय विश्व युद्ध में अमरीका के जनरल मैकार्थर ने गोले वर्षा कर जापान को बर्बाद कर दिया तथा जापान सरकार जनरल के हाथ की कठपुतली बन गई तथा जापानी पुलिस ने षड्यन्त्र रचकर राजा साहब को, अमरीका की जापान में सुगातो युद्ध अपराधियों की जेल में बन्द करा दिया। ऐसा इसलिए हुआ कि युद्ध में जापान सरकार की फौज ने भारी संख्या में हिन्दुस्तानी सिपाही पकड़ लिए। उनके रहन-सहन का व्यय जापान सरकार के सिर-दर्द का कारण बना। तत्कालीन प्रधानमन्त्री तोजो ने राजा साहब को बुलाकर कहा कि इन सिपाहियों से कहकर हमारी सेना के साथ अंग्रेजों से लड़ने को कह दें। उत्तर मिला, "यह कभी नहीं हो सकता।" मैं सरकार बनाऊँगा। अपनी सेना बनाऊँगा। आप मेरी सहायता करें। मैं अंग्रेजों को निकाल कर भारत में आपके शासन के विरुद्ध हूँ। मैं भारत को स्वतन्त्र करूँगा।" राजा जी से सन्धिवार्ता भंग हो जाने पर जापान सरकार ने स्विटजरलैण्ड से नेताजी सुभाष बोस को बुलाया। जब वे भी नहीं माने तो विवश होकर उन्होंने हिन्दुस्तानी सिपाही बाबू सुभाष को सौंप दिए।

युद्ध की समाप्ति पर शान्ति-दूत को युद्ध भड़काने वाला समझा गया। वे टोकियो के कोकूबुञ्जी नगर में अपना घर बनाकर रहते थे। इसका नाम 'वर्ल्ड

फैडरेशन सेन्टर फॉर जापान' था। एक दिन वे अपने घर से किसी मित्र के यहाँ भोज पर जाने के लिए कोकूबुञ्जी रेवले स्टेशन पर पहुँचे तो एक कार बड़ी तेजी से दौड़ी आई। उसमें से एक बड़ा पुलिस् ऑफिसर निकला तथा राजा साहब को सैल्यूट देकर कार में बैठने का इशारा किया। उन्होंने समझा कि जिस मित्र के यहाँ भोज है उन्होंने कार भेजी है। अत: वे उस कार में सहर्ष बैठ गए। जब कार टोकियो से बाहर निकलने लगी तो पूछा, ''Where are you going'' (तुम कहाँ जा रहे हो?) ऑफिसर बोला, ''You are under arrest''. जेल का बड़ा फाटक खुला तथा अन्दर करके राजा साहब की जेबों की अशर्फियाँ निकाल कर उन्हें जेल की कोठरी में बन्द कर दिया। महामानव के बन्द होने की सूचना संसार में विद्युत वेग से फैल गई। इस कारागार में अमेरिका द्वारा विजित देशों के राष्ट्राध्यक्ष तथा प्रधानमन्त्री बन्द थे। जेल अधिकारियों को आपका विशेष ध्यान रखना पड़ा। केवल राजा साहब के कमरे को गर्म रखने के लिए दरवाजे पर स्टोव जलाया गया। औरों से काम लिए गए। किसी से फर्श धुलवाया तो किसी से बर्तन साफ कराए गए। भोजन सभी को प्रथम श्रेणी के भोजनालय का जैसा दिया गया। राजा साहब से कोई काम नहीं लिया गया। भारत के जाट महासभा अध्यक्ष चौ. छोटूराम तथा महात्मा गाँधी ने राजा साहब की प्रशस्ति में पत्र लिखा। अमेरिका तथा यूरोप से पत्र आए। और तो और इंग्लैण्ड के प्रधानमन्त्री मजदूर दल के नेता लार्ड एटली ने राजा जी को निर्दोष बताया तथा 'वर्ल्ड फैडरेशन' पत्रों की फाइलों ने रामवाण औषधि का काम किया। विश्व एकता के उद्‌बोधक को युद्ध भड़काने वाला कौन सिद्ध करता। फाँसी लगने वाले दिन से एक दिन पहले पादरी उपदेश करने आया तो हँसते हुए किवाड़ खोलकर पादरी से कहा, "पादरी साहब आप यहाँ बौद्धों को ईसाई बनाने आए हो पहले अमरीका के ईसाइयों को तो ईसाई बना लो।" पादरी ने कहा, "आप छूटने वाले हैं।" उसने भी राजा साहब को निर्दोष बताया था। और सबको फाँसी हुई तथा आपको 14 फरवरी, सन् 1945 को कारागार से मुक्त कर दिया गया। इसी दिन अमरीका में बड़े दिन का पर्व मनाया जाता है। जेबें खाली थीं। टोकियों में उन दिनों विदेशियों से आने जाने का किराया नहीं लिया जाता था। अपने घर आए तो पाया कि जिस प्रकार ताले की सील कर गए थे वैसा ही पाया। अन्त में इस विश्व-विजयी महारथी के सामने इंग्लैण्ड की सरकार नतमस्तक हो गई तथा भारत लौटने का आदेश देना पड़ा। जब टोकियों स्थित ब्रिटिश राजदूत के पास पारपत्र बनवाने पहुँचे तो वहाँ एक और अंग्रेज भी बैठा था। उसने कहा, ''You are sending him to India. He is very dangerous man.'' आप इन्हें भारत भेज रहे हैं। ये बहुत खतरनाक हैं," राजदूत ने उत्तर में कहा, "भारत की राजनैतिक स्थिति इतनी अधिक बिगड़ चुकी है कि उमसें कुछ भी बढ़ोत्तरी नहीं कर पाएँगे। आप अगस्त

1914 में आंग्ल कमिश्नर के सामने अन्याय को मिटाने की घोषणा करके गए तथा 9 अगस्त सन् 1946 को अपने जलपोत से मद्रास के अंग्रेज गवर्नर के सामने विजेता के स्वरूप में उतरे। जनता की अपार भीड़ के जयघोषों के मध्य आप ने सरदार बल्लभ भाई पटेल की कार में प्रवेश किया तथा उनकी लड़की कार चलाकर वार्धा लाईं। वहाँ पं. नेहरू, मौ. अब्दुल कलाम आजाद तथा पटेल आदि नेता गले मिले तथा सीधे कांग्रेस की कार्यकारिणी सभा में ले गए। शाम की सभा में महात्मा जी ने अपना प्रवचन न देकर आपसे ही प्रेम धर्म का भजन कराया।

> विजय जलूसों का अंधड़ तब, पूरे भारत पर छाया था।
> जयति जयति राजा महेन्द्र, मुक्त कण्ठ से दुहराया था।
> ब्रज का लाल अनोखा आया, आंग्ल देखकर भाग जाएँगे।
> परमवीर योद्धा के साके, भारत वासी नित गाएँगे।

इंग्लैण्ड की मजदूर सरकार ने घोषणा की कि जून सन् 1948 में भारत के किसी संगठन को शासन की बागडोर सौंप दी जाएगी। राजा महेन्द्र प्रताप ने मार्च सन् 1947 में तुरन्त स्वन्तत्रता प्राप्त करने हेतु भारतीय फौजों को सशस्त्र क्रान्ति के लिए तैयार करने के लिए 'फौजी कौमी संघ' के निर्माण की प्रेम महाविद्यालय के उसी प्रांगण में घोषणा की जहाँ 1914 में अन्याय को मिटाने की थी। फौजी कौमों से कहा, "देश की सेना की रीढ़ फौजी कौमें हैं। वे ही स्वतन्त्रता की रक्षा कर सकती है। अतः एक साथ मिलकर उन्हें कांग्रेस के नेतृत्व में शासन अपने हाथ में लेना चाहिए। नहीं चेते तो राज, जमींदारियाँ, खेती, वैभव तथा आत्म सम्मान सबकुछ खो बैठोगे। देश की सेना में तथा जनता में क्रोध की अग्नि जलने लगी तथा अंग्रेजों को 15 अगस्त, 1947 को शासन सत्ता कांग्रेस तथा मुस्लिम लीग को सौंपनी पड़ी। चौ. छोटूराम ने महात्मा गाँधी तथा जिन्ना को देश की अखण्डता बनाए रखने के लिए चुनाव युद्ध को ललकारा। देश का दुर्भाग्य कि चौधरी साहब स्वर्ग सिधार गए। देश बँट गया। राजा महेन्द्र प्रताप ने जर्मन सरकार से कहकर पाकिस्तान समर्थक मुसलमानों को जर्मनी की सीमा से बाहर खदेड़वा दिया था। चौ. छोटूराम ने 24 घण्टे की चेतावनी देकर जिन्ना को लाहौर से भगा दिया था। आंग्ल प्रशासन, कांग्रेस तथा मुस्लिम लीग की साँठ-गाँठ सफल रही। कुछ को गद्दियाँ मिलीं। शेष खिसियानी बिल्ली की तरह मुँह ताकते रहे। राजा महेन्द्र प्रताप अपनी जकड़ देश की जनता पर शीघ्रता से नहीं जमा पाए।

जिस महारथी को आंग्ल सरकार चोटी से एड़ी तक पसीना बहाकर भी नहीं पकड़ पाई। तीन बार भयंकर विष पान कराए जाने तथा साँपों की बामी में सोए जाने पर भी काल कवलित नहीं हो सके, वे 29 अप्रैल, सन् 1979 को भारत

की राजधानी दिल्ली से स्वेच्छा से स्वर्ग चले गए। सरकारी संरक्षण में उनका शव प्रेम महाविद्यालय प्रांगण में मध्य रात्री में ठीक 12 बजे पहुँचा जहाँ से राजनीति का खेल खेलना प्रारम्भ किया था, वहीं समाप्त कर दिया। अब विद्यालय के सामने बगीची में, कालिन्दी तट पर चिर विश्रामरत हैं, राजा महेन्द्र प्रताप।

त्रिपंथ-पिटक-सिद्धान्त

एक दिन लेखक पद्मासन पर बैठा था। मन में विचार उपजा, "राज महेन्द्र प्रताप जन कल्याणी त्रिपंथ-पिटक-सिद्धान्त के अन्वेषक हैं। तुरन्त उठकर शब्द कोष देखा तो पाया कि यही सिद्धान्त भगवान बुद्ध का था। स्मरण हुआ आज से पाँच सहस्त्र वर्ष पूर्व भगवान कृष्ण ने गीता में कहा, "जब-जब धर्म की हानि होती है मैं आता हूँ।" उनके ठीक ढाई सहस्त्र वर्ष बाद आए बुद्ध भगवान तथा उनमें ढाई सहस्त्र वर्ष बाद आए राजा महेन्द्र प्रताप जिन्होंने कृष्ण तथा बुद्ध दर्शन को युगानुकूल स्वरूप दिया। भगवान ईसा, हजरत मुहम्मद, गुरु नानक आदि इसी धर्म शृंखला की एक कड़ी हैं। त्रिपंथ-पिटक सिद्धान्त सबको सबके लाभ में लगाकर सबको सुखी बनाने के लिए अचूक है। जिन खोजा तिन पाईयाँ गहरे पानी पैठ।

1. प्रेम-धर्म

काबुल में 1916 की रामनवमी का सूर्य उगने ही वाला था कि राजा महेन्द्र प्रताप शाही महल बागे-बाबर से निकलकर उद्यान के खुले वातावरण में आए जहाँ पवन सुरभित सुमनों की सुगन्ध को वायु मण्डल में फैला रही थी तथा पक्षीगान आत्मोल्लास का जागरण कर रहा था। मखमली घास पर पल्थी मारकर बैठकर लिखने लगे। यह प्रेमधर्म की भूमिका बन गई। उधर विश्व युद्ध में अंग्रेज जीत गए तो बादशाह ने सोचा कि राजा साहब का काबुल में रहना अंग्रेजों को खटकेगा। अतः उनको अफगानिस्तान के धार्मिक नगर मजारे-शरीफ में वहाँ के गवर्नर की देख-रेख में रख लिया। अफगान सरकार उस समय आप पर तथा आपकी सुरक्षा पर 1600 रु. प्रतिदिन व्यय करती थी। इसी नगर में प्रेमधर्म की पुस्तक 1916 में दीपावली पर्व पर पूरी हुई तथा प्रवर्तक ने दीप जलाकर मानव जाति की धार्मिक सेवा के लिए पुस्तक को उर्दू भाषा में प्रकाशित कराया। कुछ मुसलमान बादशाह से मिले और कहा, "हुजूर राजा महेन्द्र प्रताप ने 'दीने मुहब्बत' नया दीन निकाला है। इस्लाम के नियमानुसार नया दीन निकालने वाले को पत्थर से मार देना चाहिए।" उत्तर मिला, "यह हरगिज नहीं हो सकता। वे हमारे मेहमाने मुहतरम (प्रतिष्ठित अतिथि) हैं। मैं उनको बुलाकर पूछूँगा कि प्रेमधर्म क्या है?" जब 'दीने मुहब्बत' जाना तो कहा, "इसमें इस्लाम के विरुद्ध कुछ भी नहीं है।" बादशाह ने प्रभावित

होकर काबुल में हिन्दुओं पर लगी पाबन्दियाँ जैसे रंगीन पगड़ी नहीं बाँधना तथा घोड़े पर चढ़कर नगर में नहीं घूमना' आदि को तुरन्त हटा दिया। गो-वध पर पाबन्दी लगी तथा मुल्लाओं ने भारत को फतवे भिजवाये कि बकरीद के अवसर पर गोवध आवश्यक नहीं। एक बार बादशाह ने राजा साहब को भोज पर बुलाया। ऐसे अवसरों पर राजा साहब बादशाह के दाहिने बैठते थे। तथा एक ओर काबुल सरकार के प्रधानमन्त्री तथा उच्चाधिकारी तथा दूसरी ओर हिन्द सरकार के प्रधानमन्त्री आदि। राजा साहब को जानकारी नहीं थी कि फिर भी किसी ने बादशाह से कहा, "हुजूर राजा महेन्द्र प्रताप चाहते हैं कि हिन्दुओं पर से रंगीन पगड़ी नहीं बाँधने की पाबन्दी हटा दी जाय।" तड़क के साथ उत्तर मिला, यह हरगिज नहीं हो सकता। मुसलमान-मुसलमान से सलाम वालेकुम बोल सकता है। पगड़ी का पाबन्दी हटने से हिन्दू तथा मुसलमान की पहचान न हो पाएगी।" यद्यपि राजा साहब ने नहीं कहा था फिर भी बोले, "आप नहीं हटाएँगे तो आपके बाद गद्दी पर बैठने वाला हटा देगा। हिन्दू और मुसलमान धर्म एक है। हिन्दू जिसे ब्रह्म कहते हैं। मुसलमान अब्राहम कहते हैं। फारसी भाषा के नियमानुसार 'अ' जोड़ दिया है।" और भी शब्द बताए तो अमीर चुप हो गया। पाबन्दी हट गई। आठ ब्राह्मणों को बादशाह से कह कर राजा साहब ने फाँसी के तख्ते से बचाया था। बादशाह का युवराज ज्येष्ठ पुत्र शाहजादा इनायतुल्ला खाँ पीले रेशमी रूमाल पर राजा साहब से उपदेश लिखवा कर उन्हें चौखटे में मढ़वाकर कलमे के साथ रखता था। जर्मनी के प्रसिद्ध पत्रकार डॉ. रोजन वर्जन कौच जर्मन भाषा में एक पत्रिका निकालते थे। उन्होंने एक पन्ने पर गोल घेरे में सभी धर्म प्रवर्तकों के चित्र छापे। इस्लाम में मुहम्मद साहब का चित्र छापने की मना है, अतः उनका नाम लिख दिया था। सबसे ऊपर प्रेमधर्म प्रवर्त्तक राजा महेन्द्र प्रताप का चित्र था। लेखक एक दिन दरबार में बैठा था। तब राजा साहब के सौजन्य से पत्रिका देखने का सौभाग्य प्राप्त हुआ। यूरोप में प्रवास के समय प्रेमधर्म का प्रचार नियोजित हुआ। प्रेमधर्म प्रवर्तक से दीक्षा लेकर अनुयाई बने तथा प्रचार-कार्य में जुडे ईसाइयों ने प्रेमधर्म प्रवर्तक के लिए मन्दिर बनाकर बिठाने को कहा तो राजा साहब ने नहीं स्वीकारा। पूजा नहीं ज्ञान प्रकाश फैलाना उनके जीवन् का उद्देश्य था। रोम में ईसाइयों की सबसे प्राचीन तथा बड़ी मौनस्टैरी (Monastery) मठ में प्रेमधर्म का प्रचार करते हुए जब राजा महेन्द्र प्रताप पहुँचे तो उन्हें वही कमरा तथा पलंग दिया गया जहाँ ईसाई जगत का सर्वोच्च पादरी रहता तथा सोता था। अंग्रेजी में सबसे पहली पुस्तक (Religion of Love) जर्मनी में छपी।

जापान तथा चीन में प्रवास के समय जापानी तथा चीनी में वहाँ के अनुयाइयों ने प्रेमधर्म पुस्तक के अनुवाद छापे। तिब्बत के शासक दलाईलामा ने प्रेमधर्म प्रवर्त्तक

को जीवित बुद्ध लिखा तथा बहुत से बौद्ध आपको ऐसा ही समझते थे। एक जापानी प्रेमधर्म का अनुयाई जब स्वर्ग जा रहा था तो राजा साहब को उसी भाव से याद कर रहा था जिससे भगवान को किया जाता है। यह सूचना उसकी पत्नी ने पत्र लिखकर दी।

संयुक्त राज्य अमरीका के श्री के. हाइड, जो राष्ट्रपति निकसन के चुनाव अधिकारी थे, प्रेमधर्म प्रवर्तक का चित्र गले में लटकाकर अमरीका में प्रचार करते थे। कनाडा की बीबी पीसपिलग्रिम ने भी यही किया। न्यूजीलैण्ड की आंट हेसिल अनुयाई बनीं।

सभी धर्मों ने प्रेम धर्म पवर्तक को माना तथा सराहा। कम्यूनिस्टों ने राजा साहब को कामरेड राजा कहकर पुकारा इसलिए उनके नाम पीटर पीर प्रताप सिंह, मौजैज आदि पड़े। चीनी तथा जापानी भाषाओं में भ्री नाम हैं। प्रेम धर्म पुस्तक हिन्दी, उर्दू तथा अंग्रेजी भाषा में राजा महेन्द्र प्रताप मिशन, वृन्दावन में प्राप्य हैं।

2. संसार-संघ

राजनीति के भीष्म पितामह राजा महेन्द्र प्रताप की राजनीति व्यक्ति से लेकर परिवार, ग्राम, नगर, देश तथा संसार संघ तक धीरे-धीरे विकसित होकर पहुँची।

क्षेत्र में सर्वाधिक शक्तिसम्पन्न अपने परिवार का वैभव छल से गिराने वाले आंग्लो के सामने वे कभी झुके नहीं, सदैव सीना ताने रहे। जैसे-जैसे विचारों का विकास होता गया तैसे-तैसे राजनीति का कार्य क्षेत्र बढ़ता गया। राष्ट्र की परतन्त्रता मिटाने की प्रतिज्ञा ली तथा उसे पूरा करके दिखाया। एशिया मुक्ति का अभियान चलाने के कारण एशिया पुत्र कहलाए। इंग्लैण्ड के कवि हैफन्डन ने 'एशिया पुत्र' (Son of Asia) नाम से प्रशंसा में लम्बी कविता लिखी। प्रथम विश्व युद्ध की विनाश लीला देख हृदय तिलमिला उठा था तथा जर्मनी की राजधानी बर्लिन में बैठकर संसारसंघ राज की योजना बनाकर सितम्बर 1929 से आजीवन **'वर्ल्ड फैडरेशन'** मासिक पत्र निकाला। उद्देश्य मात्र इतना था कि सभी देशों को मिलकर राष्ट्रसंघ को संसारसंघराज में बदल देना चाहिए। सेना केवल संसारसंघराज रखेगा। देश अपनी आन्तरिक सुरक्षा के लिए पुलिस रखेंगे संसार संघ का न्यायालय देशों के आपसी झगड़ों को तय करेगा।

जब आर्यान पेशवा राजा महेन्द्र प्रताप वृन्दावन में होते थे, तो लेखक शाम को उनके दर्शनार्थ तथा उपदेश सुनने दरबार में जाया करता था। एक दिन कहा, "देखिए अमुक सज्जन आए थे उन्होंने मुझसे कहा कि 'वर्ल्ड फैडरेशन' राष्ट्रसंघ के पुस्तकालय में भेजा करो।" वाया डाक अखबार जाने लगा। एक दिन पुनः बताया कि मुझे सूचना मिली है कि संयुक्त राष्ट्र ने 'वर्ल्ड फैडरेशन' विभाग अलग से

खोल दिया है। राजा साहब की इस राजनैतिक सूझबूझ ने संसार के अस्सी प्रतिशत राजनीतिज्ञों को अपनी ओर खींचा तथा आजकल तो समस्त विश्व ही इसे सिद्धान्त रूप में स्वीकारता है। संसारसंघराज की स्थापना ही संसार को अणु आयुधों की अग्नि में भस्म होने से बचा सकती है। समय की दीवार पर बड़े-बड़े अक्षरों में लिखा है, "या तो संसारसंघराज बनेगा या संसार भस्म होगा।" जो ईश्वर संसार को अब तक चलाता लाया है आगे भी ले जाएगा। हमें चिन्ता नहीं करनी चाहिए। संसारसंघराज की स्थापना के लिए प्रयत्न करना अपना ईश्वर प्रदत्त कर्तव्य स्वीकार कर आगे बढ़ना चाहिए। संसार ईश्वर का बाग है। हम सब उसके माली हैं। माली का कर्तव्य है कि बाग को हरा-भरा रखे। राजा महेन्द्र प्रताप ने भारत लौट आने पर हिन्दी में संसारसंघ तथा उर्दू में इत्तिहादे दुनिया निकाले। इन सबकी फ़ायलें राजा महेन्द्र प्रताप मिशन के कार्यालय में प्राप्य हैं। 'वर्ल्ड फैडरेशन' पुस्तक भी है।

3. नवीन विचार विज्ञान

"मैं मनुष्य मात्र के लाभार्थ विचार देता हूँ, पर मनुष्य उन्हें समझते नहीं। इसका कारण नासमझी है, जो मनुष्य के विकास में बाधक है। विचार शक्ति बड़ी प्रबल है। विचार ही मनुष्य को महान तथा तुच्छ बनाते हैं। मैंने समाजोत्थान की योजनाएँ खोजी हैं। उनसे तभी लाभ हो सकता है जब उनके अनुकूल आचरण बनाया जाए। यदि कोई दिन के प्रकाश में आँखें बन्द करके चले तथा चट्टान से टकराकर सिर तोड़ ले तो इसमें सूर्य भगवान का क्या दोष!" यह सोच थी, योगिराज आर्यान पेशवा राजा महेन्द्र प्रताप की। उन्होंने अच्छे-से-अच्छे विचार देकर स्वर्गलोक जाने की इच्छा व्यक्त की तो एक विचार मन में यह आया कि अभी एक काम और करना है। मनुष्य की सोच को ऊपर उठाकर उसे समाज का उपयोगी अंग बनाना है, जिससे वह इतनी योग्यता प्राप्त कर सके कि प्रेमधर्म से संसार संघ तक की यात्रा पूरी करके अपना तथा मनुष्य जाति का कल्याण करने वाली अश्वमेघ महायज्ञ में पूर्ण आहुति दे सके। अपनी आयु के चौथे पन में आठ पुस्तकें नवीन विचार विज्ञान' पर लिखी जो मनुष्य के मन-मस्तक की बुराई को धोने की क्रियाएँ उजागर करती हैं। इस विज्ञान की कक्षाओं का विद्यार्थी लेखक भी रहा है जिसने महामानव के उपदेश सुनकर अपने को परिमार्जित करने में आशातीत सफलता प्राप्त की और यहाँ तक विकास किया कि स्वयम् नरपुंगव भगवान के स्वरूप राजा महेन्द्र प्रताप लेखक को अपना प्रतिनिधि नियुक्त कर स्वर्ग सिधार गए। तदुपरानत लेखक ने कुशलता पूर्वक अपने कर्तव्य का निर्वहन करके समाज के मनीषी शुभचिन्तक महामानवों को अपनी ओर आकृष्ट किया है।

नवीन विचार विज्ञान की प्रयोगशाला में मनुष्य तथा पुस्तकों के विचारों का विश्लेषण करके उपयोगी तथा हानिकारक विचारों को अलग-अलग छाँटकर प्रथम को मन में जमाया जाता है। तथा द्वितीय को निकाला जाता है। इस तरह शुद्ध किया हुआ मस्तक संसार संघी बन जाता है और कहने लगता है, "सब जगह तू ही तू है। प्रेम ही समस्त धर्म है।" सर्वत्र एक ही एक दिखाई देने लगता है। दुई का नाम मिटने से भी सभी प्रकार के संघर्ष समाप्त होकर मनुष्य समाज विकासोन्मुख होता है। जो सोचते हैं और सोचते हैं कि छिक जाते हैं, जो सोचकर आगे बढ़ते हैं यात्रा पूरी करते हैं।

राजा महेन्द्र प्रताप मिशन

राजा साहब मेरा मिशन, मेरा मिशन कहा करते थे। उनके स्वर्गारोहण के पश्चात् उनके प्रिय शिष्य श्री शिवकुमार ने 'मेरे' के स्थान पर राजा साहब का नाम लिखकर संस्था रजिस्टर्ड कराई। उद्देश्य राजा महेन्द्र प्रताप के संसार में फैले शिष्य एक जुट होकर उनके सन्देश को उसी प्रकार फैलाएँ जैसे भगवान् बुद्ध के शिष्यों ने दुर्गम पहाड़, समुद्र और खाइयाँ पार करके फैलाए। जब तो आजकल जैसे प्रचार साधन भी नहीं थे।

मिशन में जहाँ बड़े-बड़े विचारक, कवि, योगी, राजनीतिज्ञ तथा धार्मिक सज्जनों ने सहयोग दिया वहाँ कूपमंडूक विचारकों ने रोड़े अटकाने में कमी नहीं रखी। भला ईश्वर की पुकार को कौन रोकेगा। काम आगे बढ़ा। पुराना साहित्य रक्षित किया नए साहित्य का विपुल मात्रा में प्रकाशन किया। अब मैं वृद्ध हो गया हूँ।

प्रेम केन्द्र में प्रेमधर्म की दीक्षा दी जाती है। संसारसंघ का प्रकाशन होता रहता है। प्राकृतिक चिकित्सा द्वारा मनुष्य को स्वस्थ तथा निरोग करके अपने तथा समाज के लिए उपयोगी बनाया जाता है। विचार टकसाल विचारों की परख की जाती है। विपुल साहित्य भण्डार है। जानकारी के लिए लिखें या मिलें। श्री शिवकुमार, राजा महेन्द्र प्रताप मिशन, वृन्दावन। निवास स्थान : प्रेम विहार, केशीघाट, वृन्दावन।

प्रेम-धर्म

साध्वी महानन्दमयी माँ

बल, बुद्धि दो प्रभु काम करेंगे, जगती के उद्धार का।
जन जन में जागरण भरेंगे, प्रेम पगे व्यवहार का ॥
जग सेवा भारत की सेवा, और जाति उद्धार करें।
रीते भरें भरों में वृद्धि, ज्योतिर्मय उपकार करें ॥

त्रि-पंथ-पिटक-सिद्धान्त प्रेमधर्म, संसारसंघ एवं विचार विज्ञान कर्मयोग का संसार रूपी सागर का तरंगित तथा विकासक जल है जो संसार उद्यान को निरन्तर हरा-भरा रखने का ज्योतिर्मय अभियान है। यह भरों से छीनकर तथा लूटकर निर्धनों को धनी बनाने का मत प्राप्त करने को कोरा षड्यन्त्र नहीं जो सबको दरिद्र बनाता है। रीतों को भरना तथा भरों में वृद्धि करना इस सिद्धान्त का दर्शन सूत्र है। इसका प्रथम सोपान प्रेम धर्म विनाश से बचाने तथा विकास को गति देने का रामबाण सु-नियोजित प्रेम प्रकाश है जो धर्मान्धता को दूर कर जन-जन में प्रेम जगाकर संघर्ष विहीन समृद्धि तथा विकास प्रवीण समाज के निर्माण की प्रेरणा देता है। यह एक जीवन्त धर्म क्रान्ति का उद्घोष है जो सभी धर्मों में ऐसे स्वयं सेवक खोजता है जो सब धर्मो में मेल कराकर समस्त भलाई को इकट्ठी करके समस्त बुराई के विरुद्ध महाभारत रचने के लिए दीर्घ शंखनाद करता है। इसके जनक राजा महेन्द्र प्रताप ने संसार के कोने-कोने को अपने अडिग पगों से नापा तथा संसार सागर को ज्ञान की मथानी से मथ कर तीन ज्ञान रत्न प्राप्त किए-प्रेमधर्म, संसार संघ तथा नवीन विचार विज्ञान।

जब संसार के प्रगति के पैर दासता की बेड़ियों में जकड़े देखे तो जगत नियन्ता ने स्वतन्त्रता का अलख जगाने राजा महेन्द्र प्रताप को भू-माता पर उतारा तथा वे अपने जग उद्धारक त्रि-पंथ-पिटक-सिद्धान्त देकर ज्ञान मार्तण्ड के अज्ञान अँधकार को मिटाने का अचूक साधन दे गए। मैं अपने इस लेख के पाठकों को

बताऊँगी कि प्रेमधर्म ने कैसे-कैसे चमत्कारिक विचार दिए जिनके कारण सदियों से चली आ रही घृणा द्वेष की रूढ़ियाँ समाप्त हुई तथा विभिन्न धर्मों के अनुयायी परस्पर प्रेम पूर्ण व्यवहार करने लगे।

पाठक गण, मुझे विश्वास हो गया है कि जो नियमित सवेरे तथा सन्ध्या में प्रेम धर्म के भजन को दुहराएँगे उनमें अभूतपूर्व आत्म जागरण की लहरें उत्पन्न होकर उनके जीवन को आल्हादित करेंगी। वे समाज को जोड़ने वाली शृंखला की सुदृढ़ कड़ी बनकर संसार के दुःखों के कारणों का शमन करेंगे। मैं प्रेम धर्म के भजन को अपने लेख से जोड़कर पाठकों में नव चेतना तथा धार्मिक क्रान्ति के बीज बोना चाहती हूँ। मैं अपने श्री कालेश्वर महादेव मठ में प्रतिदिन प्रातः सायं प्रेम धर्म की सामूहिक प्रार्थना सभा भगवान शिव की आरती के पश्चात् कराती हूँ। एतदर्थ आश्रम वासियों में चेतना जगी है तथा वे जहाँ आश्रम के वातावरण को स्वच्छ रखने में चमत्कारिक गतिशीलता आई है वहाँ विभिन्न धर्मों के अनुयाइयों को आश्रम की ओर खींचा है। मक्का के इमाम स्वयं आश्रम में पधारे तथा पवित्र शिवलिंग के दर्शन किए तथा उजागर किया कि यहीं पवित्र लिंग तथा ऐसा ही मठ मक्का शरीफ में है जो चद्दर से ढका रहता है। आज भी मुसलमान चद्दर उठाकर सिजदा करते तथा दुआ माँगते हैं।

मैंने एक खोजपूर्ण धर्म ग्रन्थ लिखा है। धर्म के उदय काल में सभी महाद्वीपों में शिव लिंग पूजा का प्रचलन था। द्वितीय स्थिति में मूर्ति पूजा आई। धर्म का विकास ही पूर्वजों की पूजा से हुआ है। तृतीय चरण में भगवान बुद्ध ने प्रबुद्ध धार्मिक संसार की रचना की। तत्पश्चात् देश काल तथा जलवायु के अनुकूल धार्मिक भावनाएँ भगवान ईसा, हजरत मुहम्मद तथा गुरु नानक ने फैलाई। जब इन धर्मों के कूप मंडूक विचारक धर्म विरोधी भावनाओं में फंसकर लड़ने लगे तो भगवान राजा महेन्द्र प्रताप प्रेम धर्म का ज्ञान देने प्रगट हुए।

यह धर्म आधुनिक युग की बुराइयों को मिटाकर सामाजिक जीवन को जोड़ने वाली स्वस्थ परम्पराओं का विकास करता है। आइए आपका सीधा साक्षात्कार प्रेम धर्म से कराती हूँ–

प्रेम-धर्म

'प्रेम-धर्म' इस युग का धर्म है। इसके प्रवर्तक राजा महेन्द्र प्रताप ने विश्व के कोने-कोन को सच्चे ज्ञान-प्रकाश से भरने हेतु इसका आविष्कार किया। सन् 1916 में राम नवमी के पर्व पर अरुणोदय काल में एक वृक्ष के नीचे मखमली घास पर पलथी बैठकर सुरभित भवन तथा पक्षीगान के मध्य बाग बाबर राज भवन काबुल में लिखना प्रारम्भ किया। यही प्रेम धर्म की भूमिका बनी। ईश-प्रेरणा से लिखते

रहे जैसे-जैसे विचार आते रहे। उसी वर्ष प्रकाश के पर्व दीपावली पर अफगानिस्तान के एक दूसरे नगर मजारे-शरीफ में लिखना पूरा किया। यही लिखित प्रेम धर्म की पुस्तक बनी। प्रेम धर्म इस वैज्ञानिक युग को सुख शान्ति का सीधा सच्चा मार्ग दिखाता है। मानव मात्र को मोक्ष दिलाता है।

चमत्कार

प्रेम धर्म के प्रकट होते ही अफगानिस्तान के कट्टर मुसलमानी बादशाही परिवार पर गहरा प्रेम रंग चढ़ा। धार्मिक सहिष्णुता यहाँ तक आई कि हिन्दुओं पर से बहुत रोकें हटाई गईं। उदाहरणार्थ रंगीन पगड़ी जिसे बाँधने का उन्हें कानूनन अधिकार नहीं था वह मिला। युवराज शहजादा इनायतुल्ला खान इतना प्रभावित हुआ कि रेशमी कपड़े पर लिखे राजा साहब के विचारों को शीशे के चौखटे में मढ़वाकर कुरान के कलमें के साथ रखा। गोवध पर रोक लगी। ब्राह्मण फाँसी से मुक्त हुए। अफगानिस्तान के मुल्लाओं ने भारतीय मुसलमानों को फतवा भेजा कि ईद पर गौकशी जरूरी नहीं है। कट्टर मुसलमानी देश में गौवध पर रोक लगी। प्रेम की बंशी बजी।

प्रेम धर्म प्रवर्तक राजा महेन्द्र प्रताप ने जापान तथा चीन में आवास काल में बौद्ध-धर्म के चोटी के अनेकों अनुयाइयों ने प्रेम धर्म की दीक्षा ली। प्रेम धर्म पुस्तक को जापानी तथा चीनी भाषाओं में अनुवाद करके छापा। बौद्ध धर्मी सरकारों ने उच्च आदर दिया। तिब्बत के धार्मिक शासक दलाईलामा की ओर से हार्दिक स्वागत किया गया। सोना चाँदी भेंट में मिला। इन बौद्ध धर्मी देशों ने राजा साहब को जीवित बुद्ध कहा। ईश्वर के जगत में प्रेम-रंग वर्षा थी।

रोम के पास ईसाइयों की सबसे बड़ी तथा पहली मौनेस्ट्री है। वहाँ प्रेम-धर्म प्रवर्तक को रहने वही कक्ष तथा पलंग दिया गया जहाँ ईसाइयों के सबसे बड़े पोप ठहरते थे। मध्य यूरोप के ईसाइयों ने आपको मन्दिर में बिठाकर देवता के रूप में पूजने की योजना बनाई। उसको राजा साहब ने अस्वीकार कर दिया था। राजा साहब पुजने नहीं ईश्वर के जग को साफ सुथरा करने आए थे। यूरोप महाद्वीप के बहुत से ईसाइयों ने प्रेम धर्म की दीक्षा ली। कट्टर ईसाई श्री के. हाइड जो राष्ट्रपति निक्सन के चुनाव अधिकारी रहे थे, आधुनिक समय में प्रेम-धर्म का प्रचार अपनी छाती पर राजा साहब का चित्र लटका करते थे। वे राजा साहब से अन्तिम समय तक सम्पर्क बनाए रहे।

धर्म की लहर चली। भ्रमित भावना हुई भली ॥

हिन्दू धर्म के महानतम सन्तों ने जगत् गुरु शंकराचार्य से लेकर स्वामी शिवानन्द तक और अन्यों ने परम आदर मान दिया। हिमालय की गोद में तपस्या

रत साधुओं से लेकर वृन्दावन धाम के बड़े-बड़े सन्तों ने सराहा। एक बोले : आप आधुनिक कृष्ण हैं। दूसरे बोले : राम केवल 14 वर्ष बनवास में रहे। आप 32 वर्ष रहे औरे बोले भगवान बुद्ध अपनी पत्नी तथा बच्चे को सोता छोड़ गए। आप पृथ्वी पर पछाड़ खाकर गिरी पत्नी को बिलखती ही छोड़ गए। भारत विख्यात सन्त देवरहा बोले : राजर्षि राजा महेन्द्र प्रताप।

सार्वभौम सम्मान पाया। ऐसा प्रेम धर्म अपनाया ॥

प्रेम धर्म में हिन्दुओं के पण्डित, सिखों के ग्रन्थी, ईसाइयों के पादरी, बौद्धों के भिक्षु, मुसलमानों के हाजिम व मुल्ला तथा आर्य समाज के चोटी के नेताओं ने सम्मिलित होकर सच्चा आल्हाद और उल्लास पाया है।

सब धर्मो को मिली भलाई। सभी बुराई अति घबड़ाई ॥

धर्म विरोधी कम्यूनिस्ट दौड़े आए। राजा साहब से हाथ मिलाए। भेंट वार्ता के समय उनके बैठने के लिए साथी लेनिन स्वयं कुर्सी लाए। हाथ मिलाकर बैठने की प्रार्थना की। प्रेम धर्म को टौल्सटौयबाद बताया। सोना तथा सर्वोच्च सम्मान दिया। कम्यूनिरट चीन के सर्वोच्च नेताओं ने परम आदर दिया। उनके प्रिय 'साथी राजा।'

प्रेम धर्म अपने अनुयाइयों को अपने पुराने धर्मों तथा विश्वासों से दूर नहीं करता है। केवल बुराई को जड़ से खोदकर निकालता है और सभी धर्मों के अनुयाइयों में एक-दूसरे से मिलकर रहने की उत्कट इच्छा पैदा करता है। सबको मिलाकर सबको लाभ में लगाकर सबको सुखी बनाता है। बुराई से लड़ता है। भलाई बढ़ाता है। समस्त धर्मों की सम्पूर्ण भलाई को मिलाकर सम्पूर्ण बुराई से महाभारत करता है। ऐसा प्रयत्न पहले कभी नहीं किया गया।

राजा महेन्द्र प्रताप मिशन, वृन्दावन : राजा महेन्द्र प्रताप ने जन्म से निर्वाण तक घोर तपस्या एकाग्रचित्त से की। मानव मोक्ष के लिए त्रि-पन्थ-पिटिक-सिद्धान्त अर्थात प्रेम धर्म, संसार संघ तथा नवीन विचार विज्ञान का आविर्भाव किया। यह मनुष्य जाति के लिए सर्वाधिक उपयोगी तथा आधुनिक विचारों की त्रिवेणी है। इसमें गोते लगाते ही मानव जीवन सुविकसित गुलाब सुमन की भाँति सत्यम् शिवम् सुन्दरम् स्वरूप प्राप्त कर खिल उठता है। अत: महेन्द्र विनय-पिटक अर्थात् राजा महेन्द्र प्रताप के शाश्वत, मानसिक तथा सामाजिक अनुशासन सम्बन्धी नियमों को जन-जन को सिखाने के लिए जगत पिता ईश्वर ने राजा साहब के स्वर्गारोहण के तुरन्त बाद राजा महेन्द्र प्रताप मिशन, वृन्दावन नाम से उनके एक प्रिय शिष्य श्री शिवकुमार द्वारा संस्था स्थापित कराई, जो समाज कल्याण की भावनाओं से ओत-प्रोत सज्जनों का आकर्षण केन्द्र बनी। यह ईश्वरीय परिवार अद्‌भुत गति से समाज सेवा पथ

पर अग्रसर है। ईश्वर कृपा से संस्था में सम्मिलित उच्च विचारक बुराई को प्रभावी ढंग से दबाकर भलाई का शंखनाद मिलकर कर रहे हैं। राजा साहब की तपस्या का लाभ जन-जीवन को दे रहे हैं। पाँच-पाँच सौ रुपए के संरक्षक तथा सौ-सौ रुपए के सदस्य आत्म प्रेरणा से बन रहे हैं। ज्ञान का सूर्य उग रहा है। जग का एक संयुक्त कुटुम्ब बनेगा। समाज का संघर्ष मिटेगा। दलबन्दी नहीं रहेगी। सर्व धर्म की जय होगी। आओ मिलकर काम करेंगे। जग का नव निर्माण करेंगे।

मिशन में सभी धर्मों, जातियों, सम्प्रदायों, दलों आदि के महानुभाव प्राकृतिक खिंचाव से खिचे चले आ रहे हैं। वैचारिक क्रान्ति का उद्घोष है। जिसका ईश्वर पालन-हारा। उसका होगा जग रखवारा। समाज के दुःख दर्द मिटेंगे। मानव-मानव एक रहेंगे।

विभिन्न जन समुदायों में मिशनरी प्रेम शंख बजा रहे हैं। सबको एक बना रहे हैं। घृणा द्वेष को मिटा रहे हैं। प्रेम की गंगा बहा रहे हैं।

सेवा : जन साधारण के लाभार्थ हम प्रेम धर्म के भजन की विधि को यहाँ दुहराते हैं। जहाँ आप अपने धर्मों के भजनों को दुहराते हैं वहाँ इस भजन को भी दुहराएँ तथा इसके अनुसार अपने दैनिक जीवन को ढालने का प्रयत्न करें। इससे आपके जीवन को एक नई दिशा मिलेगी। मानव जन्य क्लेश नष्ट होंगे तथा सुखी सम्पन्न और प्रसन्न जीवन बनेगा। यदि आपका हृदय जागे तो आप प्रेम धर्म पुस्तक का भी पाठ किया करें।

प्रेम धर्म पुस्तक में सात ईश्वरीय आदेश तथा एक सौ एक प्रश्नोत्तर हैं। यहाँ केवल प्रेम धर्म का भजन तथा प्रथम पाँच प्रश्नोत्तर ही दिए जाते हैं। प्रेम धर्म पुस्तक सच्चा और सीधा ज्ञान मार्ग दिखाती है। मन को प्रसन्न तथा उजागर करती है। मोक्ष दाता गंगा है। प्रातः साँय प्रेम धर्म का भजन दुहराने से आत्म शुद्धि होती है।

प्रेम धर्म का भजन

'प्रेम धर्म' कहता है, प्रतिदिन सबेरे शाम भजन करो। समय का हिसाब दो, कैसे समय बिताया। व्यर्थ तो नहीं बिताया है। व्यर्थ बिताया है तो ईश्वर से क्षमा मांगो। आगे व्यर्थ समय नहीं बिताओगे–ऐसे संकल्प करो और जो अच्छा समय बिताता है उसके लिए ईश्वर को धन्यवाद अर्पण करो।

फिर से कहो–ॐ, देवा, प्रेम, अल्लाह, जिहोवा सब जगह तू ही तू है। जो कुछ दीखता या बे दीखता है वह सब तेरा ही शरीर है, तेरी ही आत्मा, तेरा ही चमत्कार। सब केवल एक ही हैं।

मैं मुझ में हूँ। सभी तुझ में हैं। हम सब में ही ऐसा प्रेम होना चाहिए जैसे

शरीर के एक भाग का दूसरे से है। केवल प्रेम ही समस्त धर्म है।

हे अनन्त प्रेम मुझे इस ज्ञान से अलग न होने दे। घमण्ड न करूँ मैं। व्यभिचार के जाल में न फँसू, न झूठा मोह करूँ। न मान और धन की लालसा करूँ। न कदापि झूठ बोलूँ और न अनुचित क्रोध करूँ मैं।

अमर प्रेम धर्मानुसार कार्य करता हुआ बिल्कुल निडर रहूँ। न्याय सच्चाई, दया, क्षमा मेरे मन को रोशन रखें। मैं सदा मनुष्य जाति की सेवा करता रहूँ और सभी मनुष्य, मनुष्य जाति की सेवा करते रहें।

फिर ध्यान करो कि तुम ईश्वर में हो। सभी मनुष्य ईश्वर में हैं। सभी से प्रेम रखना तुम्हारा कर्तव्य है। सोचो आज धर्म के विरुद्ध कोई काम तो नहीं किया है। किया तो ईश्वर से क्षमा माँगो, संकल्प करो कि यह बुराई आगे नहीं करोगे। जो आज अच्छे काम किए हैं उनके लिए ईश्वर को धन्यवाद दो।

अन्त में अपने को प्रसन्न अनुभव करो। जब तुम प्रसन्न हो ईश्वर प्रसन्न है। ईश्वर ने यह वचन दिया है कि ऐसा भजन करेगा सदा प्रसन्न रहेगा।

(1) प्रश्न–मनुष्य क्या है?

उत्तर–ब्रह्माण्ड की एक लहर।

(2) प्रश्न–ब्रह्माण्ड क्या है?

उत्तर–जो कुछ दीखता या बे दीखता है यह सब ब्रह्माण्ड है।

(3) प्रश्न–ब्रह्माण्ड को किसने बनाया?

उत्तर–एकमात्र परमात्मा ने।

(4) प्रश्न–परमात्मा ने ब्रह्माण्ड को क्यों बनाया?

उत्तर–अपने आनन्द के लिए।

(5) प्रश्न–परमात्मा ने किससे ब्रह्माण्ड को बनाया?

उत्तर–परमात्मा ने अपने में ही से यह रूप बनाया। ब्रह्माण्ड ईश्वर का ही स्वरूप है।

मानव कल्याण सोपान : संसार संघ

योग महर्षि स्वामी महानन्द महाराज

त्रि-पंथ-पिटक-सिद्धान्त है, उत्कर्षक सोपान।
संकट मोचक ज्ञान है, सीधा मोक्ष-विधान ॥

क्रमिक विकास

राजा महेन्द्र प्रताप का जन्म असाधारण था। विकराल परिस्थितियों के समक्ष घुटना टेकना उनके स्वभाव के विपरीत था। मुँह में चाँदी की चम्मच लिए राजघराने में उद्‌भव होना तथा दलित तथा दरिद्रों से प्रेम होना भी असाधारण था। राजसी ठाट-बाट तथा सेवकों की भरमार और वैभव की चकाचौंध उनके लिए काँटों की शैय्या के समान थे। सर्वाधिक अशक्त तथा सताए हुए दलित, भंगी तथा टमटाओं के साथ भोजन करना उनकी दीनबन्धुता की पराकाष्ठा थी। उस समय उच्च वर्ण वाले उनकी छाया पड़ने मात्र से 'अपवित्र' होते थे। यदि कोई जाति पूछता था तो अपनी जाति भंगी बताते राजा साहब। दम्भी, पाखण्डी उच्च वर्ण वालों के कड़े विरोध की चिन्ता न करते 'अछूत' भाइयों को गले लगाना उनके साहस की विलक्षण झलक थी। वे किसी जाति विशेष के लिए नहीं, सम्पूर्ण मानवता के प्रति समर्पित थे। वर्ष 1908 में उन्होंने सम्पूर्ण चल अचल सम्पत्ति दान कर दी। दरिद्रों तथा बेकारों को तकनीकी शिक्षा दीक्षा देने की उनकी ऐसी सूझबूझ थी जिसने औद्योगिक विकास की पाश्चात्य रीति नीतियों के अनुकूल शिक्षा की नींव डालकर भारत के उज्ज्वल भविष्य की नींव डाल राष्ट्र को विकास का मार्ग दिखाया। समस्त विश्व को युद्धों की ज्वाला से बचाने संसार संघ के राज की 1929 में कल्पना कर अणु युद्धों से संसार को भस्म होने से बचाने की साकार योजना बनाई।

जब बचपन में अपने परिवार तथा राष्ट्र के वैभवशाली अतीत की कहानियाँ सुनी तो उनको स्वाभिमान जगाने के अवसर मिले और भारत में जन्म लेने को अहोभाग्य की संज्ञा दी। दास तथा प्रताड़ित राष्ट्र के दुःख सहन न कर पाने के

कारण सन् 1914 में अन्यायी राज्य को समूल उखाड़ फेंकने की भीष्म प्रतिज्ञा ले स्वेच्छा से बनवास लिया। भारत की स्वतन्त्रता के लिए जब विदेशी सरकार के विरुद्ध युद्धरत थे तो एशिया भूखण्ड को स्वतन्त्र कराने हेतु योजना बद्ध काम किया। शत्रु की आँखों की किरकिरी बने रहे। तदुपरान्त पूरे विश्व को संघ राज में गूँथने का प्रयत्न किया। 9 अगस्त सन् 1946 को विजेता स्वरूप में भारत में आ धमके। शत्रु उँगली भी नहीं उठा सका। राष्ट्र संघ द्वारा वर्ल्ड फैडरेशन डिपार्टमेंट (संसार संघ विभाग) खोलना उनकी सूझबूझ का ही परिणाम था। अपना 'वर्ल्ड फैडरेशन' पत्र राष्ट्र संघ के पुस्तकालय को भेजा करते थे। आज संसार के शत प्रतिशत राजनीतिज्ञ इसी सिद्धान्त पर चल रहे हैं। समय की दीवार पर लिखा है, संसार संघ राज बनेगा या समूचा विश्व अणु युद्ध से भस्म होगा। रचनाकार अपनी रचना की रक्षा अवश्य करेगा। अतः आज नहीं तो कल संघ राज बनके रहेगा। युद्ध समाप्त होंगे। पृथ्वी पर स्वर्ग उतर आएगा। सर्व संघ की जय होगी।

संसार संघ राज की स्थापना के प्रयत्न

इसकी कहानी मैं राजा महेन्द्र प्रताप द्वारा लेखनी बद्ध किए आंग्ल भाषा के लेख का हिन्दी रूपानतर करके लिखता हूँ। श्री संजीव चौधरी एडवोकेट राजा साहब के अनुयाई थे। उन्होंने कलकत्ता में 'दा वर्ल्ड कांग्रेस फॉर वर्ल्ड फैडरेशन' की ऐतिहासिक सभा बुलाई। इसमें देश-विदेश के प्रतिनिधि तथा दर्शक आए। राजा साहब ने अपने अध्यक्षीय भाषण में कहा–

"दा वर्ल्ड कांग्रेस फॉर वर्ल्ड फैडरेशन के प्रतिनिधि तथा दर्शको, मैं आपका स्वागत करता हूँ। मित्रो, मुझे बड़ी प्रसन्नता है कि आप कृपा करके वर्ल्ड कांग्रेस फैडरेशन के उत्सव में भाग लेने पधारे हो। सन् 1929 से मैं मासिक पत्र वर्ल्ड फैडरेशन का प्रकाशन करता आया हूँ। मैंने बर्लिन, जर्मनी में सितम्बर 1929 में इसे प्रकाशित करना आरम्भ किया था। 1930 में संयुक्त राज्य अमेरीका में प्रकाशन किया। ठीक इसी वर्ष मैं जापान में आ गया तथा अपने 'वर्ल्ड फैडरेशन' को वहाँ से प्रकाशित किया। वर्ष 1930 से 1942 तक जापान तथा चीन में प्रकाशित होता रहा, परन्तु सूर्योदय के देश से ही अधिक प्रकाशित हुआ। द्वितीय विश्व-युद्ध में जापान सरकार अपने पड़ौसी राज्यों से ही भिड़ बैठी। उसके आक्रामक रुख को मैंने विराम देना चाहा। अतः दोनों में मतभेद के कारण चार वर्ष तक युद्ध काल में मेरा पत्र बन्द रहा। जापान सरकार मेरे विचारों के प्रचार-प्रसार को अपने लिए अहितकर मानती थी। युद्ध में जापान को अमरीका के जनरल मैकार्थर ने गोले वर्षा कर तबाह कर दिया था। तथा जापान सरकार अमरीका की कठपुतली सरकार बन गई। जापानी पुलिस की सरारत से मुझे सुगानों की युद्ध अपराधियों की अमेरिकन

जेल में बन्द कर दिया गया। संसार की राजनीति में उथल-पुथल मची। यूरोप, अमरीका तथा एशिया से राजनेताओं ने मुझे निर्दोष बताते हुए छोड़ देने को पत्र लिखे। लन्दन से लार्ड एटली तथा भारत से महात्मा गाँधी तथा चौ. छोटूराम ने मेरे बचाव में पत्र लिखे। मेरे वर्ल्ड फैडरेशन की फाइलें अदालत में पेश हुई तथा मुझे फरवरी सन् 1946 को अमेरिकियों ने बड़े दिन के त्यौहार पर छोड़ दिया। आंग्ल सरकार झुकी तथा 9 अगस्त सन् 1946 को इकत्तीस साल सात माह बाद में पुनः अपने देश में आ गया। लम्बे बनवास के बाद मैंने भारत में आते ही अपना पत्र प्रकाशित करना प्रारम्भ कर दिया। अब यह इंग्लिश, हिन्दी तथा उर्दू प्रत्येक माह एक, ग्यारह तथा इक्कीस तारीखों में तीन बार प्रकाशित होता है। तीनों पत्र स्वतन्त्र हैं। वे एक-दूसरे के अनुवाद मात्र नहीं हैं। अपना-अपना स्वतन्त्र उपदेश पाठकों को देते हैं।

मेरे जीवन का लक्ष्य ऐसे संघीय संसार संघ राज की स्थापना करना है जिसमें सभी धर्म मिलकर रहें तथा आर्थिक व्यवस्था का स्वरूप संयुक्त परिवार प्रणाली हो। मैं यह प्रस्ताव रखता हूँ कि प्रत्येक गाँव तथा नगर और देश एक ही संयुक्त परिवार घोषित किए जाएँ। बूढ़ों का सम्मान हो। बच्चों का पालन-पोषण लाड चाव से हो तथा सभी की निःशुल्क शिक्षा की व्यवस्था हो। प्रत्येक पाठशाला तथा महाविद्यालय के पास खेत तथा कारखाने हों जिनके साथ-साथ दुधारू पशु भी रखे जाएँ। विद्यार्थी प्रतिदिन तीन घण्टे पढ़ें तथा पाँच घण्टे काम करके अपनी आवश्यकता की वस्तुओं का उत्पादन करें। शिक्षा प्राप्त करने के पश्चात् उन्हें पाठशाला की सम्पत्ति का संयुक्त स्वामित्व प्रदान किया जाए। उनके जीवन का उद्देश्य सरकार की सेवा करना नहीं होना चाहिए। सरकारी उच्च पद प्राप्त करना अथवा व्यापार करके स्वयं को धनी बनाना जीवन का उद्देश्य नहीं है। सब सबके लाभ में लगकर सबको सुखी बनाएँ ऐसा ही विधि का विधान है। जीवन का लक्ष्य स्वस्थ तथा सुखी रहना है।

मुझे विश्वास है कि समय तथा स्थान की आवश्यकता धर्म की जननी है, जिसका उद्देश्य मनुष्य समाज में शान्ति स्थापित करके जीवन को उच्च आदर्शों में मण्डित करना है। जंगली जानवरों जैसा स्वभाव दबाकर रखना चाहिए। विभिन्न स्थानों पर राज्यों की स्थापना दुःखी मनुष्यों के जीवन को सुख शान्ति प्रदान करने के लिए हुई जो सम्पूर्ण समाज को सच्चे न्याय के द्वारा सहज लब्ध सुख देती है।

आज कल चार बड़े राज्य हैं : संयुक्त राज्य अमरीका, सोवियत संघ, ब्रिटेन तथा फ्रांस। दूसरे सभी राज्य किसी-न-किसी कारण से इन पर निर्भर हैं अथवा कम शक्तिशाली या छोटे हैं। इसी प्रकार चार बड़े-बड़े धर्म हैं : ईसाई, बुद्ध, इस्लाम तथा हिन्दू। और सभी धर्म किसी-न-किसी प्रकार इनसे सम्बन्धित हैं। या कह सकते

हैं उनके अनुयाई कम हैं अथवा वे छोटे-छोटे धर्म हैं।

आज संसार के राज्यों को ऐसी समझदारी की बड़ी आवश्यकता है कि वे आपस में लड़कर एक-दूसरे को तबाह नहीं कर दें। मनुष्य रक्त धारा तथा समाज से प्राप्त शिक्षाओं के अनुरूप अपनी जीवन की गतिविधियों को ढालता है। धर्मों को नास्तिकता के अभिशाप से अपनी रक्षा करने के लिए एक हो जाना चाहिए। अधर्म की आँधी को रोकने धर्मों की ईंटों से सुदृढ़ धर्म दीवार बना ली जाय। सभी धर्म मिलकर बुराई से लड़ें। भलाई को बढ़ाएँ।

मैं आपसे प्रार्थना करता हूँ, दलगत भावनाओं तथा विचारों से ऊपर उठकर काम करें। जो कुछ बचपन से अब तक आपने सीखा है उसमें रक्त धारा तथा विचार धारा ही आपको चलाती आई है। जो कुछ हमारे मस्तकों में भर दिया जाता है, ग्रामोफोन की पट्टी की भाँति हम उसे दुहराते रहते हैं। हमारी रक्तधारा हमें उपद्रवी, जिद्दी, शान्ति प्रिय अथवा सहनशील बनाती है।

मुझमें आप यह न कहें कि आपका यह विचार अथवा विश्वास है, जैसा विचार तथा विश्वास आपके मस्तक में भर दिया गया है उसी को आप अपना कहते हैं। आपको इससे उत्तेजित तथा क्रोधित नहीं होना चाहिए। रक्त धारा का यह गुण है। मनुष्य विचारों का चलाया उसी प्रकार चलता है जैसे कुम्हार गधे के गले में रस्सी बाँधकर खींचता है, हर हालत में मनुष्य दास है, इस या उस विचार का।

मैं कट्टर हिन्दू परिवार में पैदा हुआ तथा मुसलमानी महाविद्यालय में शिक्षा पाई तथा शादी हुई सिक्ख राजघराने में। मैंने संसार की पाँच बार परिक्रमा लगाई, मैं इटली में रोमन कैथोलिक मौनेस्ट्री का अतिथि रहा। मुझे रहने को वही कमरा मिला जो उनके सबसे बड़े पादरी का था। उन्हीं के पलंग पर सोया। मैं कुछ महीने तिब्बत की बुद्ध लामासरी में रहा, दलाईलामा ने मुझे जीवित बुद्ध पत्र में लिखा। मैं छः वर्ष से अधिक अफगानिस्तान में रहा। मैं दस बार लाल मास्को गया। साथी लेनिन से मिला। लाल रूस तथा शाही अफगानिस्तान का राजनयिक सम्बन्ध कराया। लेनिन के साथ रूस की स्वतन्त्रता का उत्सव मनाया। मैं संयुक्त राज्य अमेरीका में रहा। मैं चीन, मंगोलिया, कोरिया, श्याम, वर्मा, लंका तथा फिलीपीन्स की यात्राओं पर गया, मैंने फ्रांस, इटली, मिश्र, तुर्किस्तान, फारस इराक, मैक्सिको, कनाडा तथा इंग्लैण्ड में रहकर देखा। कैसर की जर्मनी में बहुत रहा, स्विटजरलैण्ड, बैल्जियम, पोलेण्ड, आस्ट्रिया, हंगरी, रूमानिया तथा ग्रीस में रहा। मैंने मध्य एशिया में यात्राएँ की तथा तीन बार दुनिया की छत पामीर में रहा। पन्द्रह वर्ष से अधिक जापान में रहा। लिस्बन तथा क्यूबा गया। मैं जर्मन, तुर्की, अफगानी, रूसी तथा चीनी सरकारों का सम्मानित अतिथि रहा। मेरी इन यात्राओं ने मुझमें संसार भर में चेतना जगाने की भावनाएँ भरी। मेरे अन्दर संसार व्यापी प्रेम तथा न्याय का जागरण हुआ।

सन् 1916 में जब मैं अफगान सरकार का महमाने मुहतरम था, ईश्वर ने मुझे प्रेम धर्म का प्रकाश दिया। प्रेम धर्म की पुस्तक के जर्मन तथा जापानी भाषाओं के अनुवाद छपे। यह सभी धर्मों में एकता सच्चे स्वयम सेवकों के समूह में चेतना जगाती है।

मैं ईरान से आसाम तक आर्यान संघ बनाने का कार्य करता हूँ। यह धार्मिक राज होगा। हमें समाज को सदाचारी बनाना हैं।

मेरे विचार से आधुनिक प्रजातन्त्र प्रणाली सड़ी गली प्रथा मात्र है। रुपया राजशक्ति तथा धोखाधड़ी की दक्षता चुनाव जीतने के अचूक साधन हैं। ठगी का बाजार गर्म है। मैं आजकल की संसदीय प्रणाली का उन्मूलन कर गाँव-गाँव तथा नगर-नगर में सुराज स्थापित करने का पक्षधर हूँ। मेरा कहना है, नियमों के रस्सों से समाज को मत कसो। मनुष्यों को सदाचारी बनाओ। आधुनिक न्यायालयों को समाप्त करो। इनमें वकीलों का खोपड़ा जीतता है। तथा धन न्याय खरीदता है। प्रत्येग ग्राम तथा नगर स्वायत्तता प्राप्त स्वतन्त्र राजनैतिक इकाइयाँ हों। जनता को एकजुट करो। कोई भी संगठन से बाहर न रहे। सिद्धान्त हो, उनन्चास इक्यावन विलीन हो। संघर्ष रहित सुखी समाज का निर्माण हो। लड़ें नहीं, लड़ाएँ नहीं। आजकल की चुनाव प्रथा समाज को फाड़ती है।

सभी धर्मों तथा दलों के विचारों की परख करो। निष्पक्ष परख अच्छे फल के लिए अनिवार्य है। संघर्ष कराने वाले विचारों को खोज कर सच्चाई के साथ निकाल फेंको। अपने पराए की भावना संघर्ष कराती है। त्याज्य है।

पापियों तथा अपराधियों के उपचार के लिए, हमें सदाचारी अस्पताल खोलने चाहिएं। जो स्वभाव से अपराधी है उन्हें सुधारने तथा सदाचारी बनाने के प्रयत्न किए जाएँ। किन्हीं भी परिस्थितियों में हत्या नहीं करनी चाहिए। यह अनिवार्य है। फाँसी की सजा गोली मारना तथा विद्युत से मारना बन्द होना चाहिए। हत्यारों, सिफलिस या एड्स के बीमारों तथा कुष्ठ रोगियों को नसुपंसक बना दिया जाय।

साधु, संन्यासी, योगी, पुजारी तथा उच्च धार्मिक समाज सेवियों को संगठित होकर समाज सेवा करनी चाहिए। उनकी वाहिनी बनाकर सदाचारी समाज का गठन हो। मनुष्य के अन्दर छिपी बुराई स्वतन्त्रता के विचार का दुरुपयोग करती है। स्वतन्त्रता को उच्छृंखलता नहीं बनने देंगे। सभी प्रकार की सनक को उखाड़ फेंको। आजकल देश पर अहिंसा की सनक सवार है। यह कहने मात्र की बात है। हमारी सरकार अहिंसा तथा शान्ति के गीत गाती है पर इसकी पुलिस मजदूरों को पीटती है, विद्यार्थियों पर गोली चलाती है तथा किसानों को सताती है। इसके सिपाही पूर्वी सीमाओं पर नागाओं पर गोलियाँ चला रहे हैं।

स्वार्थ तथा अँधे स्वार्थ के गर्तों में न गिरने के लिए मैं अपने संसार संघी

मित्रों को चेतावनी देता हूँ। यह सर्व विदित है कि किस प्रकार स्वार्थांध नेताओं ने महान सदाचार धर्म तथा दलों के नारे देकर अपना निजी लाभ तथा शक्ति प्राप्त की। लीग ऑफ नेशन्स पर फ्रांस तथा ब्रिटेन के साम्राज्यों ने एकाधिकार जमा लिया। अब राष्ट्र संघ संयुक्त राज्य अमरीका के हाथ की कठपुतली है।

हमें इस तथ्य को भी जान लेना है कि साम्यवाद के सिद्धान्त को रूसी गुट ने अपनी स्वार्थ-पूर्ति में प्रयोग किया है। इसी प्रकार संसदीय शासन प्रणाली तथा आधुनिक प्रजातन्त्रवाद से ब्रिटेन, फ्रांस तथा अमरीका अन्य राष्ट्रों को अपने नीचे लेने का प्रयत्न करते हैं।

प्रकृति राष्ट्रों, जातियों तथा उपजातियों को मनुष्यता के विकास करने को प्रोत्साहित करती है। प्रकृति के नियमों को समझने की क्षमता न होने के कारण संघर्ष होते हैं। अब तक तो लड़ते आए हैं, परन्तु अब समय ऐसा है जबकि सम्पूर्ण संसार को एक देश की तरह मिलकर रहना चाहिए जिसकी एक ही सरकार हो तथा एक न्यायालय तथा एक सेना हो। मेरा अभिप्राय राष्ट्रों का उन्मूलन करना या उन्हें मिटाने का नहीं है। मैं उनका एक संघ बनाना चाहता हूँ। जितने भी महाद्वीप हैं वे स्वतन्त्र राजनैतिक इकाई रहें या कहें प्राप्त करें। प्रत्येक महाद्वीप में तीन, चार या पाँच जनपद हों। आप यहाँ संसार संघ के एक जनपद के आर्यान में मिल रहे हो जो एशिया राज का उपविभाग है। मेरा कहना है कि हम स्थानीय पूर्ण स्वतन्त्रता देंगे पर सब गुथे रहेंगे संसार संघ राज में।

अन्त में मैं आपसे इस दृढ़ विश्वास के साथ काम करने की प्रार्थना करता हूँ कि संसार में संघीय शासन प्रणाली अकेली ही शान्ति स्थापित करेगी। युद्ध कहने को कहानी मात्र ही रह जायेंगे। संघर्षरत राष्ट्रों में शान्ति व्यवस्था बनाए रखना कोरी कल्पना मात्र है या बेचारे प्रजाजनों को धोखा देने का एक ढंग मात्र है। आप संसार को संघ राज की व्यवस्था देने की प्रतिज्ञा करें तथा इसके लिए प्रयत्न प्रारम्भ कर दें। क्षेत्रों तथा महाद्वीपों को संसार संघ राज में गूँथ दें।

जातीय, राष्ट्रीय तथा सांस्कृतिक तथा धार्मिक मान्यताओं का आदर करते हुए उन्हें मनुष्य जाति की एकता में साझेदारी बनाना है। प्रतियोगिता का स्थान सहयोग लेगा।

मित्रो, आगे बढ़कर संसार संघ राज की योजना को जगत में फैलाओ। संसार की एकता के लिए संसार संघ क्लब्स स्थापित करो।"

—"राजा महेन्द्र प्रताप प्रेसीडेंट वर्किंग कमेटी।"

संसार संघ राज की योजना गाँव से लेकर समस्त संसार की राजनीति का ध्रुवीकरण है। आज संसार के राष्ट्रों का सर्वाधिक ध्यान तथा धन युद्ध आयुधों के निर्माण तथा उनसे बचाव की विधियाँ खोजने में लगा है। युद्ध संघर्ष तथा

अलगाववाद देशों को फाड़ते हैं। मनुष्यों के मस्तकों में शैतान सवार है तथा संसार की रचना को क्षण मात्र में समाप्त करने के आयुध निकाले हैं। धनी राष्ट्र निर्धन राष्ट्रों पर सवार हैं तथा उनका शोषण करते हैं। लड़ाओ और राज करो ही राजनीति का स्वरूप है।

जो ईश्वर आज तक संसार को चलाता आया है वह आगे भी चलाता रहेगा। परन्तु मनुष्य को अपना कर्तव्य पालन करना चाहिए। ईश्वर की रचना को सुखी बनाना ही मनुष्य का कर्तव्य है। ईश्वर रचनाकार है। वह अपनी रचना की सेवा के लिए मनुष्य को भेजता है।

यदि संसार संघ राज की योजना चालू हो जाय तो संसार को आदर्श राजनीति के दाव पेच चलाने में सफल्ता मिलेगी। संसार में एक भी मनुष्य भूखा नंगा नहीं रहेगा। सबको स्वास्थ्य बर्द्धक रोटी कपड़े तथा घर मिलेंगे। सबल राष्ट्र निर्बल राष्ट्रों पर हावी नहीं होंगे। राष्ट्रों से सेना बल ले लिया जाएगा तथा संसार राज की सेना ही संसार के महत्त्वपूर्ण स्थानों पर रहेगी। राष्ट्र अपने प्रबन्ध को पुलिस रखेंगे।

सत्ता का विकेन्द्रीकरण कर दिया जाएगा। सभी राजनैतिक इकाइयाँ स्वतन्त्र होंगी। अपने-अपने क्षेत्रों में शासन चलाने में सरकारी ढाँचा कम खर्चीला होगा। विश्व राजनीति के भीष्म पितामह राजा महेन्द्र प्रताप ने तो मार्ग-दर्शन किया है। यदि संसार वाले उनके पद चिह्नों पर चलते संसार संघ राज बना लें तो पृथ्वी पर स्वर्ग उतर आएगा। योजनाओं को कागजों पर छापने से नहीं उसे साकार रूप देने से ही लाभ होगा।

प्रेम-धर्म प्रवर्तक : राजा महेन्द्र प्रताप

ब्रज बिहारीलाल शर्मा

प्रेम-धर्म की चर्चा करते समय यहाँ यह उल्लेख करना अभीष्ट समझता हूँ कि राजा साहब ने अपना Religion of Love मूल रूप से अंग्रेजी में लिखा था। इसका प्रथम संस्करण अंग्रेजी भाषा में बर्लिन में मुद्रित हुआ जो आज प्राप्त नहीं है। 1946 में राजा साहब जब भारत वापस आए उस समय अपने साथ अपनी अनेक पुस्तकों की हस्तलिपि पाण्डुलिपियाँ तथा कुछ छपी पुस्तकें लाए थे, उन्हीं में से ''Religion of Love'' का हिन्दी अनुवाद मेरे पिता श्री पं. दान बिहारी लाल शर्मा ने किया था। वही हिन्दी अनुवाद प्रेम-धर्म के रूप में आज प्राप्य है। राजा साहब से मेरी चार पीढ़ियों का सम्बन्ध था। मेरे दादा जी पं. चिन्तामणि शर्मा आपके शिक्षक थे, मेरे पिताजी आपके व्यक्तिगत मित्रों में से एक थे। इसी नाते मैं आपको ताऊ जी कहता था और मेरे बेटे उन्हें दादा जी कहकर आनन्दित होते थे।

राजा साहब ने अपनी प्रेम-धर्म पुस्तक में यह उल्लेख किया है "कि समय-समय पर मेरे मन में दैवी विचार उत्पन्न हुए, जिन्हें सिलसिलेवार लिखते रहने पर यह पुस्तक पूरी हुई।" एक अन्य स्थान पर आपने उल्लेख किया है कि "धर्म अनादि है, अनन्त है। धर्म हमेशा परमात्मा में निवास करता है, किन्तु दुनिया के समय और आवश्यकताओं के अनुसार वह विभिन्न सूरतों में प्रकट होता है।"

प्रेमधर्म प्रेम और धर्म। प्रेम क्रिया रूप होने पर सेवा युक्त क्रिया बन जाता है, जिससे मोह और क्रोध नष्ट हो जाते हैं, निज स्वरूप विशाल हो जाता है, शरीर तुच्छ लगने लगता है।

समर्पण यदि समर्पण ही है तो वह कभी प्रचार का विषय नहीं बनना चाहता, त्याग यदि विशुद्ध त्याग ही है तो वह कभी विज्ञापन बनने का प्रयास नहीं करता। चर्चा है आज देश की स्वतन्त्रता के अग्रगण्य सेनानी की जिसने स्वतन्त्रता-यज्ञ में तन-मन-धन से अपना सारा जीवन चुपचाप उत्सर्ग कर दिया। वह महान व्यक्तित्व समस्त प्रलोभनों से सदा दूर रहा। कभी उसने अपने बलिदान को भुनाने की चेष्टा

नहीं की।

समय की आवश्यकता के अनुसार 'प्रेम-धर्म' राजा साहब की लेखनी से प्रकट हुआ। समाज में विद्यमान बुराइयों की ओर राजा साहब ने 'प्रेम-धर्म' में संकेत किया है–

> *"जैसे मनुष्य ने अपने काम-भाव एवं अहंकार को परमात्मा बना लिया है, मनुष्य-मनुष्य में भेद हो गया है। जातियों में आपस में घृणा का भाव फैल गया है। महिलाओं और पुरुषों के अधिकारों में भिन्नता प्रचलित हो गई है। महिलाओं को पुरुषों ने गुलाम-सा बना लिया है।"* आदि-आदि।

मुख्य रूप से इन बातों को लेकर समाज में फैली भ्रान्तियों का निवारण कर देश को स्वस्थ बनाने की परिकल्पना प्रेम-धर्म में की गई है।

जीवन को सुखी, सन्तुष्ट आनन्दमय, सुचारू एवं परिपक्व बनाने के लिए प्रेम-धर्म में कुछ अनुकरणीय आदेशों को रखा गया है– जैसे *तन्दुरुस्ती, शिक्षा, ज्ञान, सेवा, आनन्द, परमात्मा और उद्देश्य।*

प्रेम का वास्तविक दर्शन तो भारत में ही देखने को मिलता है और शायद इसीलिए भारत दर्शनिकों की नहीं, सन्तों की भूमि रहा है क्योंकि भारत धर्म के बन्द घेरे में बन्दी नहीं है, वह तो स्वतन्त्र चिन्तन की उन्मुक्त अभिव्यक्ति है।

जहाँ तक मेरा विचार है धर्म का अर्थ स्वभाव ही होना चाहिए क्योंकि जब तक जो सिद्धान्त स्वभाव नहीं बनता तब तक वह सिर दर्द बना रहता है, इसलिए धर्म वही है जो धारण हो जाए या जिसे धारण कर लिया जाए।

मानसकार ने लिखा है कि–

> "पर उपदेश कुशल बहुतेरे, जे आचरहिं ते नर न घनेरे।" राजा साहब मात्र उपदेशक ही नहीं थे अपितु अपने सिद्धान्त की चलती-फिरती प्रयोगशाला थे। उनके सम्पूर्ण व्यक्तित्व में वही आचरण हू-ब-हू दिखाई देता था जैसा उन्होंने कहा था।

जन साधारण को उस समय आश्चर्य हो रहा था जब 1914 में आप भारत को स्वतन्त्र कराने के ध्येय से जर्मनी गए। ओह! वह युवक कितना त्यागी और विवेकी है। न जाने कितने दिनों से इसने विवेक-वैराग्य आदि का अभ्यास किया है। कोई योग-भ्रष्ट योगी है जो राजघराने में उत्पन्न होकर पूर्व संस्कारानुसार पुनः योग में प्रवृत्त हुआ है, नहीं तो क्या बन्धु-बान्धव, नव-विवाहिता पत्नी, दुधमुँहे कोमल बच्चे एवं सम्पूर्ण धन-वैभव विषवत् परित्याग कर देना कोई सरल कार्य है? दृढ़ देश-भक्ति, विवेक और प्रबल वैराग्य के सन्मुख माया कर ही क्या सकती थी।

गोस्वामी जी ने मानस में ठीक ही कहा है–

"तेहि बिलोक माया सकुचाई, कर न सकइ कछु निज प्रभुताई।

राजा साहब के अविद्याजन्य काम, क्रोध, मोह, लोभ, अहं, मत्सर आदि विकार समाप्त हो गए, उनकी आँखों में प्रेम, कानों में प्रेम, वाणी में प्रेम, मन में प्रेम, तन में प्रेम, बुद्धि, प्राण, रोम-रोम में प्रेम में समा गया था। इनमें से न कोई सम्प्रदाय है, न मत है, न वाद है, न देश, न काल है और न कोई वस्तु है इसलिए कि सब प्रेममय है, जैसा कि उपनिषद् में कहा गया है, 'सर्वमिदमहं च वासुदेवः"

"यह सब और मैं वासुदेव ही हूँ"–इसी के समरूप राजा साहब ने कहा :

"ॐ देवा प्रेम, अल्लाह, जीहोवा। सब जगह तू ही तू है। जो कुछ दीखता या बे दीखता है वह सब तेरा ही शरीर है, तेरी ही आत्मा है, तेरा ही चमत्कार है। सब केवल एक ही है।"

स्मृति में कहा गया है कि 'मन और इन्द्रियों की एकाग्रता परम तप है।' इसके अनुसार जब हम राजा साहब के सम्पूर्ण जीवन पर दृष्टिपात करते हैं तो उनके समान तपव्रती अन्यत्र कहीं कोई भी दिखाई नहीं पड़ता है। राजा साहब के एक-एक विचार को विमर्श हेतु प्रयोगशाला में रखा जाए तो हम एक इस प्रकार का संसार अपनी कल्पना में पाते हैं जहाँ साक्षात् राम राज्य दुहराया जाता है। कितनी सहजता, कितनी स्वाभाविकता, कितनी विनम्रता के साथ राजा साहब ने पर पीड़ा कातरता का समय-समय पर उदाहरण प्रस्तुत किया है। उनका सामीप्य प्राप्त कर एक विशाल जन समुदाय ने इसका दर्शन किया है, जिसकी स्मृति मात्र आज भी स्फुरण भर देती है, और उनके पद-चिह्नों पर चलने के लिए मानस उद्यत होता है तभी उसे व्यावहारिक विवशताएँ अवश सा बना देती हैं जिससे वह स्वयं पर खीज प्रकट करके शान्त सा रह जाता है।

राजा साहब का एक विचार जो मुझे बार-बार चिन्तन के लिए बाध्य करता है और जिससे मैं वास्तव में अपने विद्यार्थी जीवन से ही विशेष प्रभावित हूँ, और जिसे एक समय मैंने स्वयं राजा साहब के श्री मुख से श्रवण किया था, वह है–

"मनुष्य कुछ विचारों का गुलाम हो जाता है, जिसके कारण वह दूसरी कोई बात सुनना पसन्द नहीं करता।"

कहने का अभिप्राय यही है कि हम परवश होकर साम्प्रदायिक दंगे करते हैं; मानव जाति को विघटित करते हैं; हिंसात्मक रूप लेकर मात्र अपनी विचारधारा को आगे लाने के लिए दूसरों को पूर्णरूप से उखाड़ फेंकना चाहते हैं। यह कहाँ

तक न्यायसंगत है कि सभी यदि ऐसा सोचे कि मेरी सुनो, मुझे देखो, मेरी पूजा करो तो सम्पूर्ण समाज का क्या रूप होगा? विचार मात्र से मन की स्थिति विचित्र-सी हो जाती है।

इस प्रकार राजा साहब के प्रेम-धर्म में वर्णित विभिन्न विचारों पर चिन्तन किया जाए तो निश्चित रूप से शोध प्रबन्ध की रचना की जा सकती है, जो भविष्य के लिए एक निधि ही होगी। राजा साहब ने एक अन्य स्थान पर अपने विचार व्यक्त करते हुए कहा कि–

> *"आपका, हमारा सिद्धान्त होना चाहिए, जो विचार लड़ाए बुरा। जो विचार मेल मिलाप कराए–अच्छा।"* प्रेम-धर्म उक्त सिद्धान्त से सम्पूर्ण विश्व में प्रेम और शान्ति की अजस्र धारा अबाध गति से प्रवाहित होगी, जिससे समस्त वातावरण मुखरित हो उठेगा।

यद्यपि आधुनिक व्यक्तिवादी युग में यह सब कुछ असम्भव-सा प्रतीत होता है लेकिन उस महामानव की यह कल्पना कितनी सुखद, कितनी शीतल और कितनी सच्ची प्रार्थना है। प्रेम-धर्म के समस्त उपदेशों को पढ़कर, समझकर या अध्ययन करने के पश्चात् गीताकार की यह पंक्तियाँ स्मृत हो उठती हैं–

> मनुष्याणां सहस्रेषु कश्चिद्यतति सिद्धये।
> यततामपि सिद्धानां कश्चिन्मां वेत्ति तत्वतः ॥

राजा साहब अत्यन्त सरल व्यक्ति थे। वे आडम्बर को नहीं जानते थे। उन्होंने स्पष्ट कहा था कि–

> *"प्रेम-धर्म का सच्चा अनुयाई वही कहा जाएगा जो लोगों के कष्ट में सहायता देने को सदैव तत्पर हो, और जिस प्रकार की सेवा उससे बन सके वह करे। मस्तक पर धार्मिक चिह्न धारण करना, यज्ञोपवीत पहनना या अपने बालों को किसी विशेष ढंग से रखना, ये सब उसके लिए आवश्यक नहीं होंगे, यह पूर्ण स्वतन्त्र होकर 'प्रेम' ही अभिवादन में कह सकेगा।"*

इस प्रकार राजा साहब द्वारा प्रतिपादित 'प्रेम-धर्म' हमारे समाज के लिए एक ऐसी आचार संहिता के रूप में अनुपम देन है जिसको आचरण रूप में धारण कर हम न केवल अपने आप को समाजोपयोगी बना सकते हैं वरन् प्रेम-धर्म के अनुयाइयों का एक दिव्य समूह बना सकते हैं, जिसके द्वारा एक ऐसे समाज की संरचना सम्भव हो सकेगी, जिसमें न कोई ऊँचा-नीचा होगा, न कोई अस्पृश्य-स्पृश्य होगा, न जाति के आधार पर किसी की पहचान होगी बल्कि होगा प्रेम-धर्म के

अनुयाइयों का एक समाज, जो एक-दूसरे का सुख-दुःख में शरीर के विभिन्न अंगों की भाँति एक-दूसरे के सुख-दुःख को समझकर तत्काल यथाशक्ति मदद करने को तत्पर रहेगा।

अस्तु इस विवेचन के उपरान्त हम इस निष्कर्ष पर पहुँचते हैं कि राजा साहब में 'अहिंसा परमोधर्मः 'यथा याति त्रिविष्टपम् 'व' वसुधैव कुटुम्बकम्' के पाठ को न केवल दोहराया अपितु जीवन में ज्यों का त्यों उतारा। उनके आचरण में ही समस्त सिद्धान्तों का समावेश था। आंग्ल भाषा की एक उक्ति यहाँ मेरे मानसपटल पर उभरने लगी है–Coming Events cast their shadow before और अपनी वाणी को विश्राम देने से पूर्व उस गौरवान्वित, त्यागमयी मूर्ति महामानव को मेरा शत-शत नमन।

राजा महेन्द्रप्रताप से सम्बन्धित संस्मरण

(क) संस्मरण

ज्योतिस्वरूप सिंह

प्रेम महाविद्यालय की स्थापना

प्रेम महाविद्यालय की स्थापना का किस्सा बड़ा दिलचस्प है। राजा महेन्द्र प्रताप ने 1909 ई0 में अपने मित्रों, शुभचिन्तकों और सगे-सम्बन्धियों को पत्र लिखा कि "मेरे पुत्र हुआ, उसके 'नामकरण' संस्कार के अवसर पर आयोजित समारोह में पधारने का कष्ट करें।" फिर क्या था? सभी लोग नाच-बाजा और तोहफों के साथ शरीक हुए। राजा साहब के आदरणीय मित्र महामना श्री मदन मोहन मालवीय जी भी पधारे। उत्सव के अन्त में राजा साहब ने खड़े होकर ऐलान किया–

"सज्जनों! इस उत्सव में पधारने के लिए मैं आपका हृदय से आभारी हूँ किन्तु यह एक कटु सत्य है कि मेरे कोई पुत्र पैदा नहीं हुआ है। आज से यह महल और इसके साथ के भवन तथा तीस हजार रुपये सालाना आमदनी के पाँच गाँव प्रेम महाविद्यालय नामक इस टेकनिकल संस्थान को दान देता हूँ। मेरे लिए यह कालेज मेरे पुत्र से भी अधिक प्रिय होगा।" यह घोषणा सुनकर लोग भौंचक्के रह गए। उनके साले महाराजा रणवीर सिंह को तो गश आ गया।

राजा महेन्द्रप्रताप अपने विद्यार्थी काल से ही बड़े स्वाधीन विचारों के थे। देशभक्ति उनकी नस-नस में व्याप्त थी। अंग्रेजी हुकूमत से उन्हें सख्त नफरत थी। 1906 ई0 में वह कलकत्ता कांग्रेस में शरीक हुए थे। उसके बाद से उन्होंने स्वदेशी बाना अपनाया। छुआछूत के इतने विरोधी थे कि 1911 में आगरा में खुले आम भंगियों के साथ भोजन किया और उसी साल अल्मोड़ा के एक टमटा परिवार (हरिजन) में भी सहर्ष खाना खाया। किसी हिन्दु राजा के लिए उस समय ऐसा साहस दिखाना आश्चर्य की ही बात थी। उस समय कोई बड़े-से-बड़ा नेता या समाज सुधारक भी ऐसा करने को साहस नहीं कर सकता था। पण्डित जवारहरलाल नेहरू की माताजी श्रीमती स्वरूपरानी नेहरू ने 20 अक्टुबर, 1931 ई. को जब

हरिजनों के साथ खाना खाया तो उन्होंने कांग्रेस जनों से कहा कि इस बात का प्रचार समाचार पत्रों के माध्यम से होना चाहिए किन्तु हमारे राजा साहब ने यह कार्य बिना किसी प्रचार और विज्ञापन के उनसे 21 वर्ष पूर्व किया था।

चल पड़े अलख जगाने

हिन्दुस्तान छोड़ने के पहले ही उन्होंने घूम-घूम कर अंग्रेजी हुकूमत के खिलाफ व्याख्यान दिए और जनता को देशभक्ति और राष्ट्रीयता का पाठ पढ़ाया। मुल्क और कौम को जगाने के लिए *'प्रेम'* और *'निर्बल-सेवक'* नाम के पत्र निकाले। आखिर वह भी समय आया, जब वह देहरादून वाली कोठी से अपने बीबी-बच्चों को छोड़कर रात के सन्नाटे में निकल पड़े। जब वह अपनी जीवन संगिनी से अलग होने लगे तो वह पछाड़ खाकर जमीन पर गिर पड़ी। फिर कभी उन्हें अपने बागी शौहर से मिलना नसीब न हुआ। बेचारी अपने मायके में ही प्रभु को प्यारी हो गई। यह किसे मालूम था उनका यह विछोह चिर बिछोह होगा।

अस्थाई हिन्द सरकार

राजा महेन्द्रप्रताप ने 1 दिसम्बर, 1915 को अफगानिस्तान की राजधानी काबुल में प्रथम अस्थाई हिन्द सरकार की स्थापना की। इस सरकार के आप अध्यक्ष और मौलाना बरकतुल्ला भोपाली प्रधानमन्त्री तथा मौलाना आबेदुल्ला सिन्धी गृह व प्रचार मन्त्री बनाए गए। इस सरकार का सचिवालय बाग बाबर पैलेस में कायम हुआ। कई मुल्कों की सरकारों ने इस अस्थाई सरकार को मान्यता भी प्रदान की। यह बात बहुत कम लोगों को मालूम है कि राजा साहब ने ही नास्तिक देश सोवियत रूस और कट्टर सुन्नी मुल्क अफगानिस्तान में सन्धि कराई थी।

राजा साहब 29 अप्रैल 1979 को इस दुनियाए-फानी से 93 साल की उम्र में कूच कर गए। आलमी-शोहरत के लीडर राजा साहब हजारों राज़ सीने में छिपाए इस दुनिया से चले गए।

छुप गए वो साज़े-हस्ती छोड़कर,
अब तो बस आवाज़ ही आवाज़ है।

आदत और स्वभाव

उनके प्राइवेट सेक्रेटरी की हैसियत से मैंने उन्हें बहुत करीब से और हर हाल में देखा है। मैं अपने तजुर्बों को और लोगों को भी बताना अपना फर्ज समझता हूँ। वह बच्चों की तरह भोले एवं फरिश्तों की तरह मासूम थे। उन्होंने कभी किसी को कड़ी बात नहीं कही। उनके शब्द कोष में 'तुम' शब्द था ही नहीं। नौकरों

और सेवकों को 'आप' कहते और पुकारते समय नाम के साथ 'जी' भी लगाते। नेतरामजी, हरी-बहादुरजी, काजी-बहादुरजी वगैरह। अपने पौत्र को अमरप्रतापजी और पौत्री को हमेशा सरलाजी कहकर बुलाते। मुझे सेक्रेटरी साहब कहते थे। कभी किसी पर गुस्सा करते मैंने उन्हें नहीं देखा। उनके जैसा मानवता की इज्जत करने वाला मुझे दूसरा कोई इन्सान नहीं मिला। महाराजाओं, नवाबों, मिनिस्टरों और नेताओं से लेकर गाँव के किसानों तक के साथ एक-सा सलूक करते। जब भी कोई उनसे मिलने जाता फौरन कुर्सी से उठकर उसका स्वागत करते और जब वह जाने लगता तो फिर खड़े हो जाते। कभी-कभी दरवाजे तक छोड़ने भी आते थे।

वक्त के वह इतने पाबन्द थे कि कोई उनका प्रोग्राम फेल नहीं हुआ। भारी बरसात, कड़ाके की सर्दी और चिलचिलाती धूप में भी वह सफर के लिए निकल पड़ते थे। कभी वादा खिलाफी नहीं की। अपने कर्मचारियों को हमेशा पहली तारीख को वेतन देते थे। कभी-कभी पहले भी। बीच में कोई पेशगी माँगता तो जरूर दी जाती। ठीक चार बजे सुबह उठ जाते थे। बाथरूम से बाहर निकलते तो पूरे लिबास में निकलते। उनके जलपान, लंच और डिनर का समय निश्चित था। रात के बारह बजे तक लिखने-पढ़ने में व्यस्त रहते थे। दिन में सोते तो किसी ने उन्हें देखा न होगा। किसी किस्म का नशा उन्होंने हाथ से भी न छुआ। पान भी नहीं खाते थे। हाँ माँसाहारी अवश्य थे। खुराक बहुत कम थी, हर आदमी के खत का जवाब दिया जाता था। पत्रों के उत्तर देते समय नाम के पहले 'श्री या जनाब' जरूर लिखते थे। अक्सर चिट्ठियाँ सर्टिफिकेट ऑफ पोस्टिंग के साथ भेजी जाती थीं।

दरवेश-सिफत इन्सान

राजा महेन्द्र प्रताप सूफी तबीयत के दरवेश-सिफत इन्सान थे। उन्होंने 'प्रेम-धर्म' नामक एक नया मजहब भी कायम किया था। अपने महल के हॉल का नाम '*प्रेम-केन्द्र*' रखा था, जिसकी दीवार पर हिन्दी में प्रेम-केन्द्र, उर्दू में मरकजे-मुहब्बत और अंग्रेजी में लव-सेन्टर लिखा है। प्रेम-केन्द्र में प्रत्येक रविवार की रात में प्रेम-धर्म की सभा होती थी, जिसमें सभी धर्मों की प्रार्थनाएँ की जातीं। इस नए धर्म का पुजारी कोई ब्राह्मण नहीं बल्कि कालीचरण नामक एक हरिजन (जाटव) युवक था। राजा साहब ने इस प्रेमधर्म के अनुसार कुछ विवाह भी कराए थे। इन शादियों पर कुछ खर्च नहीं पड़ता था। राजा साहब की ओर से कुछ फल और मिठाइयाँ बाँट दी जातीं। बस शादी हो गई। हाँ, दूल्हे और दूल्हन का प्रेमधर्म के अनुसार 'शपथ' लेना आवश्यक था। यहाँ एक वाकया बयान करता हूँ। जब उन्होंने अपनी विधवा पुत्रवधू की पुनः शादी कराई तो मैंने ही पुरोहित का काम किया।

राजा साहब ने अंग्रेजी में 'रिलीजन ऑफ लव' पुस्तक रूस के महान नेता

लेनिन को भेंट की। लेनिन ने प्रसन्न होकर उसे पढ़ा और कहा कि टालस्टायवाद है। राजा साहब सभी धर्मों की इज्जत करते थे। बड़े प्रेम से दशहरा, जन्माष्टमी, बड़ा दिन और ईद मनाते थे। इस सूफी इन्सान ने दिल्ली की जामा मस्जिद में मुसलमान भाइयों के साथ ईद की नमाज अदा की और एक-दूसरे मौके पर भोपाल के नवाब सर हमीदुल्ला खाँ के साथ उनकी आलीशान मस्जिद में भी नमाज अदा की।

स्वर्गीय राजा साहब के गुणों का कहाँ तक वर्णन करूँ? सारी जिन्दगी वह इन्सानियत की खिदमत करते रहे। नाम-नमूद और इज्जत शोहरत से बिल्कुल बेनियाज थे। ऐसे लोग अब कहाँ मिलेंगे? सिरजनहार ने राजा साहब को बनाने के बाद फिर वह साँचा ही तोड़ दिया। अब दुनिया में राजा महेन्द्र प्रताप जैसे लोग नहीं पैदा होंगे।

ऐसा कहाँ से लाऊँ, कि तुझ-सा कहूँ जिसे?

(ख) संस्मरण

ब्रजबिहारी लाल शर्मा

भारतीय स्वतन्त्रता संग्राम के प्रयोधा राजा महेन्द्र प्रताप भारत को आजाद कराने के उद्देश्य से सन् 1914 में भारत से बाहर चले गए थे। 32 वर्षों तक अपने इसी उद्देश्य की पूर्ति के लिए आपने विश्व की पाँच बार परिक्रमाएँ कीं और अपना ध्येय पूर्ण हो जाने के उपरान्त जब 1946 में आपके वापस आने की सूचना भारतवासियों को मिली, विशेषकर वृन्दावन वासियों और उसमें राजाजी द्वारा संस्थापित उनकी औद्योगिक प्रशिक्षण संस्था प्रेम महाविद्यालय को, तब माहौल एकदम खुशी से भर गया। उस समय मेरे पिता श्री पं. दान बिहारी लाल शर्मा प्रेम महाविद्यालय वृन्दावन के मन्त्री थे। उसी समय की बात है–ट्रस्ट की बैठक में राजा साहब के स्वागत की तैयारियों से सम्बन्धित कार्यक्रम बनाने की महत्त्वपूर्ण मन्त्रणा चल रही थी। उसमें यह प्रश्न उठा कि राजा साहब पानी के जहाज से मद्रास उतरेंगे तथा उनके स्वागत के लिए मद्रास कौन जावे, प्रेम महाविद्यालय की ओर से। उस समय एक अहम प्रश्न भी उठा कि आदरणीय राजा साहब को तो जो भी यहाँ का प्रतिनिधि जाएगा पहचान ही लेगा परन्तु ऐसा व्यक्ति कौन हो सकता है जिसे राजा सहब 32 वर्ष के लम्बे अन्तराल के उपरान्त पहचान सकें। खोज करने पर वृन्दावन में ऐसे मात्र तीन व्यक्ति ही निकले जिन्हें राजा साहब पहचान सकते थे। एक मेरे पिता श्री पं. दान बिहारी लाल शर्मा, दूसरे प्रेम महाविद्यालय के मैनेजर बाबू श्री राम गुप्ता तथा तीसरे वहीं के कर्मचारी श्री पुरुषोत्तम लाल 'लल्लो जी'। यह तय

हुआ कि श्रीराम गुप्ता तथा श्री लल्लो जी मद्रास जाकर राजा साहब का स्वागत करेंगे, तथा पं. दान बिहारी लाल जी शर्मा महाविद्यालय पोलिटैकनिक, मथुरा में राजा साहब का स्वागत करेंगे।

निर्धारित समय पर राजा साहब का स्वागत करने मेरे पिता जी जाने की तैयारी कर रहे थे तभी राजा साहब के एक मात्र पुत्र कुँवर प्रेम प्रताप जी ने आकर उनसे अनुमति चाही कि 'मुझे भी साथ ले चलें तो अच्छा होगा क्योंकि मेरी प्रबल इच्छा अपने पिताजी के दर्शन करने की है।' कुँवर को राजा साहब करीब 1 वर्ष की अबोध अवस्था में छोड़कर 1914 में विदेश चले गए थे। मेरे पिता जी सहर्ष उन कुँवर साहब को अपने साथ ले चलने को तैयार हो गए। मैं उस समय 13-14 वर्ष का था तथा अपने पिताजी के साथ मथुरा गया था। वहाँ हम लोग कार से पहुँचे। उसके करीब पन्द्रह मिनट बाद राजा साहब की गाड़ी भी पहुँच गई। जीवन में पहली बार उस युग पुरुष के दर्शन कर मैं रोमांचित हो गया। जैसे ही राजा साहब कार से उतरे मेरे पिताजी ने उन्हें नमस्कार किया–एक क्षण देखकर राजा जी बोले, "आप तो दान बिहारी लाल हैं।" और दोनों एक-दूसरे से लिपट कर आनन्दित होने लगे। वे क्षण बहुत भावुक थे तभी पास में खड़े कुँवर प्रेम प्रताप जी की ओर मुखातिव होकर राजा साहब बोले यह तो प्रेम प्रताप हैं? इतना कहना था कि कुँवर की आँखों में अश्रुपात होने लगा और वे झपट कर राजा साहब के श्री चरणों में लोट गए। एक पिता पुत्र का एक दिव्य-मिलन, बिना बताए पहचाना इसे कहते हैं–"Blood is thicker than water"

समय के पाबन्द

बात सन् 1950 की है। राजा साहब प्रति वर्ष आर्यान दिवस दिनाँक 20, 21, 22 मार्च को मनाया करते थे। उस वर्ष यह उत्सव विश्व धर्म सम्मेलन के रूप में मनाया गया। इसके संयोजक मेरे पिता श्री पं. दान बिहारी लाल शर्मा थे। तीनों दिवसों में प्रत्येक दिन तीन-तीन बैठकों का आयोजन होता था। पूरे भारत से एवं कुछ एक विदेशी सज्जन इस सम्मेलन में अपना भाषण देने पधारे थे। अपूर्व संगम था धर्माचारियों का। दिनाँक 21/03/50 के शाम की बैठक जो 3 बजे से 6 बजे तक की थी उस सभा का सभापतित्व तत्कालीन अखिल भारतीय कांग्रेस कमेटी के राष्ट्रीय अध्यक्ष पट्टाभिसीतारमैया को करना था। बैठक का समय 3 बजे का हो गया प्रेम महाविद्यालय, वृन्दावन का विशाल प्रांगण श्रोताओं से तथा प्रेम-धर्म का विशाल बरामदा प्रतिनिधियों से खचाखच भरा था। राजा साहब ठीक 3 बजे प्रेम महाविद्यालय के ऊपरी कमरों से सभा स्थल पर नीचे पधारे और मंच पर विराजमान हो गए। 10 मिनट तक संभा के मनोनीत अध्यक्ष डॉ. पट्टाभिसीतारमैया का इन्तजार किया

गया। वे नहीं पहुँच पाए। तब राजा साहब ने किसी अन्य महानुभाव को उस बैठक का कार्यवाहक सभापति घोषित किया और सभा की कार्यवाही उन मनोनीत कार्यवाहक सभापति की अध्यक्षता में शुरू हो गई। बैठक सुचारू रूप से निर्विघ्न चलती रही। श्रोतागण मन्त्रमुग्ध से सभी विद्वानों के भाषण सुनकर आनन्दित होते रहे। अपने निर्धारित समय पर 6 बजे साँय बैठक विसर्जित भी हो गई। सभी लोग चले गए। प्रतिनिधिगण अपने-अपने आवासों पर चले गए। राजा साहब भी ऊपर अपने कमरों में जाने लगे-परन्तु उस समय तक डा. रमैया नहीं आ सके। जाते समय राजा साहब ने प्रेम महाविद्यालय के गेट कीपर को बोला कि, "सुनिए फाटक बन्द कर दीजिए और बाहर बैठ जाइए, एक सज्जन आवेंगे उनके साथ काफी कारों का काफिला होगा। वे सभा की बात पूछेंगे तथा मुझसे मिलने को भी कहेंगे। आप उन्हें कह दीजिएगा कि बैठक, जिसकी अध्यक्षता आपको करनी थी आपका काफी देर इन्तजार करने के उपरान्त तीन बजकर दस मिनट पर शुरू कर दी गई और छः बजे समाप्त हुई। राजा साहब छः बजकर दस मिनट पर ऊपर चले गए हैं। वे अब किसी से नहीं मिल सकेंगे क्योंकि वे आज के अपने अन्य पूर्वनिर्धारित कार्यों में व्यस्त हैं। कृपया क्षमा करें।" यह सुनकर गेट कीपर जी उस समय एक छींतर सिंह नामक व्यक्ति थे, कुछ संकोच से में पड़ गए। राजा साहब उनकी मनोदशा देखकर समझ गए कि शायद यह व्यक्ति डॉ. सीतारमैया जैसी इतनी बड़ी विभूति से यह बात न कह सकेगा। यह समझ कर राजा साहब ने यह सारी बातें कागज पर लिखीं और छीतर सिंह को दी। तथा कहा कि आप जब वे आवें उनका परिचय पूँछकर यह कागज उन्हें दे देना। रात्रि 8 बजे डा. सीतारमैया अपने काफिले के साथ प्रेम महाविद्यालय आए। छीतर सिंह ने उनका परिचय प्राप्त कर राजा साहब का पत्र उन्हें दे दिया। उसे पढ़कर क्षमा याचना करते हुए डॉ. रमैया वापस लौट गए। ऐसे थे समय के पाबन्द हमारे राजा साहब।

दानशीलता

वृन्दावन में राजा साहब का एक भवन झारगुदड़ी में स्थित था जिसमें उनके एक मात्र पुत्र कुँवर प्रेम प्रताप रहा करते थे। कुँवर की मृत्यु के उपरान्त भवन खाली था। बात 1964 की है। आसाम प्रान्त के एक महान सन्त 'पागल बाबा' वृन्दावन पधारे। उन्हें किसी ने यह भवन दिखाया। वे इसे खरीदकर इसमें अपना आश्रम स्थापित करना चाहते थे। 'पागल बाबा' के अनुयाइयों ने कहीं से मेरे पिता जी तथा राजा साहब के आपसी सम्बन्धों के बारे में जानकारी ली। तदुपरान्त 'पागल बाबा' अपने अनुयाइयों के साथ मेरे पिताजी के पास इस भावना से पधारे कि मेरे पिता जी राजा साहब से निवेदन करके यह भवन उन्हें दिलवा दें। बाबा के सन्त स्वरूप

तथा आचरण की भव्यता, विनम्रता से मेरे पिता जी प्रभावित हुए और उन्होंने कह दिया कि वे चेष्टा करेंगे। मेरे पिताजी इस कार्यसिद्धि हेतु देहरादून गए जहाँ राजा साहब उन दिनों निवास करते थे। उनके साथ 'पागल बाबा' के कुछ प्रमुख अनुयाई भी गए। वार्तालाप हुआ। 'पागल बाबा' के भक्तों ने राजा साहब से निवेदन किया कि महाराज का निवेदन है कि इस भवन की ऐवज में आपको पच्चीस हजार रु. भेंट करेंगे। तत्काल राजा साहब बोले, कि उस भवन की कीमत मुझे अब तक किसी ने सत्रह हजार रु. से ज्यादा नहीं बताई है। अत: में सत्रह हजार ही स्वीकार करूँगा। काफी देर इस बात पर विमर्श होता रहा। बाबा के भक्त पच्चीस हजार देना चाहते थे, राजा साहब सत्रह हजार रुपया लेना चाहते थे। आखिर मेरे पिताजी नें हस्तक्षेप करके राजा साहब से कहा कि भाई साहब, रजिस्ट्री होने दीजिए, आपकी भावना का पूर्ण रूप से समादर होगा। बिक्री पत्र राजा साहब के Power of Attorny Holder ने सम्पन्न कर दिया। इसके बाद जाड़ों में तीन माह के अवकाश के दौरान जब राजा साहब वृन्दावन पधारे तब 'पागल बाबा' ने उन्हें इस स्थल पर पधारने के लिए आमन्त्रित यह कहकर किया कि यह स्थान आपका ही है–मैं आपका अनुज इसकी देख-भाल की व्यवस्था करता हूँ कृपया पधारकर अवलोकन करने की कृपा करें कि व्यवस्था में कोई त्रुटि तो नहीं है। चार पाँच कारें राजा साहब को लेने भेजी गई। वे कृपा कर वहाँ पधारे। बाबा मय-परिवार के भवन के गेट पर उनके स्वागत के लिए फूल मालाएँ लेकर उपस्थित मिले। राजा साहब को मालाओं से अलंकृत कर प्रणाम आदि के शिष्टाचार के बाद अन्दर लाया गया। मेरे पिताजी और मैं भी राजा साहब के साथ उपस्थित थे। वहाँ राजा साहब ने मेरे पिताजी से कहा कि "शर्मा जी वह बात जो आपने कही थी कि मेरी भावनाओं का समादर होगा–मुझे तो बाबा ने पच्चीस हजार दे दिए हैं। अब मैं क्या करूँ?" उस समय मेरे पिताजी की सलाह पर राजा साहब ने आठ हजार रुपया बाबा को भेंट किया जिसे बाबा ने यह कहकर स्वीकार करने में अपनी विवशता प्रकट की कि यह आपका ही है। और अधिक देने की क्या आवश्यकता है। यह सुनकर राजा साहब ने यह धनराशि ठाकुरद्वारे में जो वहाँ स्थापित है–भेंट कर दी। ऐसे दानी थे हमारे चरित्र नायक राजा साहब।

परोपकारिता

गर्मी का मौसम था। राजा साहब अपने देहरादून के आवास '*धर्म*', 93 रामपुर रोड पर विराजमान थे। उस समय राजा साहब की आर्थिक स्थिति सुदृढ़ नहीं थी। उनके पास एक युवक आता है। सामान्य शिष्टाचार के उपरान्त वह युवक बड़े संकोच में राजा साहब के पूछने पर विनम्रतापूर्वक निवेदन करता है कि "मेरा सिलेकशन

इंजीनियरिंग कालिज रुड़की में हो गया है। परन्तु अपने परिवार की जटिल आर्थिक विपन्नता के कारण मेरे पास फीस जमा करने को धनराशि नहीं है। आपका शिक्षा-प्रेम एवं विद्यार्थियों के रहनुमा के रूप में देश-विदेशों में ख्याति सुनकर आया हूँ, कृपया मेरी मदद करने की कृपा करें।" उस युवक की बातें सुनकर तथा उसकी फाइल परिचय पत्र आदि देखकर राजा साहब ने पूछा, कि कितनी धनराशि से काम चल जावेगा? युवक बोला, "2000 रु.।" राजा जी बोले आप परसों आ सकेंगे क्या? युवक बोला, "हाँ।" और वह चला गया।

राजा साहब की आर्थिक स्थिति ठीक नहीं थी। उनके पास इतनी धनराशि उपलब्ध नहीं थी। युवक-विद्यार्थी की मदद करना चाहते थे। अतः उन्होंने दूसरे दिन अपनी राज घराने की एक पोशाक जो जरी की थी, बाजार में बेचने के लिए अपना नौकर भेजा। वह चार हजार रुपया उसको बेचकर लाया। निर्धारित समय पर युवक राजा साहब के पास आया। अभिवादन कर वह उनके सम्मुख खड़ा हो गया। दयालु राजा उसे बैठने के संकेत देकर अन्दर कमरे में गए और चार हजार रुपया उसे देने लगे। युवक बोला मेरा कार्य 2000 में चल जाएगा। इस पर राजा साहब बोले–भाई फीस के अलावा किताबें कहाँ से खरीदोगे। फिर अर्थ संकट आवेगा और आपकी शिक्षा निर्विघ्न सम्पन्न नहीं हो सकेगी। अतः यह चार हजार रुपया स्वीकार कर लो। राजा साहब की पर-पीड़ा कातरता पर युवक विह्वल हो रोने लगा। उसके पास धन्यवाद बोलने को शब्द नहीं थे। राजा जी ने उसकी भावाञ्जलि स्वीकार की और उसके उज्ज्वल भविष्य की कामना करके उसे विदा किया।

(ग) संस्मरण

प्रभुदयाल मैसी

राजा साहब की महानता, विशालता, व्यापकता तथा उनके बलिदानों की कहानी पर जब मैं दृष्टिपात करता हूँ तो तन रोमांचित तथा हृदय गद्‌गद होने लगता है। उनमें कितनी महान आत्मा का पूर्ण विकास था कि वह साँस-साँस पर दूसरों के लिए सर्वस्व निछावर करने सहज ही में तत्पर रहते थे।

एक संस्मरण ने हृदय को स्पर्श किया। सुनिये। सन् 1975 में अक्टूबर का महीना था। मैंने 22 अक्टूबर को अपने पुत्र के जन्मोत्सव को प्रेमधर्म के वार्षिक उत्सव के रूप में मनाने की योजना बनाई। इस उत्सव में सम्मिलित होने के लिए राजा साहब से पूर्व स्वीकृति प्राप्त की जा चुकी थी तथा उत्सव में उनके स्वागत हेतु तैयारियाँ की गईं। खुले मैदान में शामियाने लगाये गये। श्रोतागण एकत्र थे।

यकायक उत्सव के पहले ही राजा साहब को मूत्र रोग हो गया तथा उनको

वृन्दावन के श्रीरामकृष्ण मिशन सेवाश्रम अस्पताल में भरती कर दिया गया। डॉक्टरों ने हिलने-डुलने की मनाकर दी तथा पूर्ण विश्राम की मन्त्रण दी। उत्सव में सम्मिलित होने का समय आया। वे पलंग से उठकर बैठ गये। कहने लगे, "अवश्य जाऊँगा।" डॉक्टरों ने गम्भीर परिणामों की चेतावनी दी। बहुत अनुनय विनय करने पर भी जाने की बात पर अड़ गये। चले। डाक्टर साथ गया। सभा स्थल पर पहुँचे। जयकारों की ध्वनि हुई। भाषण दिया और लौट आये। कुछ ईश्वर ने इस प्रकार रक्षा की कि सकुशल अस्पताल पहुँच गये। रामकृष्ण मिशन के डॉक्टरों ने शल्य चिकित्सा की मन्त्रणा देकर देहली जाने की मन्त्रणा दी। प्रधानमन्त्री इन्दिरा गाँधी को राजा साहब की ओर से तार दिया गया। उंन्होंने राजा साहब के इलाज की तुरन्त व्यवस्था कर दी तथा वे अखिल भारतीय आयुर्वेद संस्थान नई दिल्ली में दाखिल हुए जहाँ आपरेशन द्वारा सफल उपचार किया गया। आपरेशन भी दो बार करना पड़ा।

मैं भी रामकृष्ण अस्पताल में उनसे प्रार्थना करने गया था कि "आपका स्वास्थ्य ठीक नहीं, आप डॉक्टरों की राय मानें तथा न आयें। उन्होंने कहा-'कोई बात नहीं। प्रेमधर्म का वार्षिक उत्सव मनाया जायेगा। ईश्वर ने चाहा तो मैं जरूर आऊँगा। सब कुछ ईश्वर पर निर्भर है।' 22 अक्टूबर को सायं सात बजे का समय था। वृन्दावन के गणमान्य व्यक्तियों के अनुरोध करने पर तथा रामकृष्ण मिशन के डाक्टरों के मना करने के बावजूद राजा साहब 6-30 बजे ही प्रेमधर्म के वार्षिक उत्सव पर आधा घण्टा पहले ही आ गये! मैंने नम्रतापूर्वक उनसे कहा-"आप ऐसी स्थिति में यहाँ पर आये हैं, मुझे बड़ा कष्ट हो रहा है। आप गाड़ी से उतरकर आराम से बैठ लीजिये। अभी संसद सदस्य श्री चकलेश्वरसिंह एवं पुलिस अधीक्षकजी भी नहीं आये हैं।" राजा साहब बोले-"आप अपना काम कीजिए, ईश्वर के कार्य में मैं आया हूँ। ईश्वर जो चाहेगा वही होगा। हमारे आपके सोचने से कुछ नहीं होगा।" इतनी तकलीफ और बीमारी की हालत में राजा साहब ने प्रेमधर्म की सभा को जिसमें भारी संख्या में लोग इकट्ठे थे सम्बोधित किया और देर तक बैठे। श्री चकलेश्वर सिंह तत्कालीन संसद सदस्य जो इस सभा की अध्यक्षता कर रहे थे उपस्थित जनों को सम्बोधित करते हुए बोले कि-"राजा साहब ने अपना सब कुछ इस देश की आजादी के लिए अर्पण कर दिया और आज भी जब डाक्टरों ने राजा साहब से निवेदन किया कि आपके मीटिंग में जाने से गम्भीर परिणाम निकल सकते हैं क्योंकि आप 20 दिन से बिस्तर पर बीमार पड़े हैं। आप न जाइयेगा। फिर भी राजा साहब प्रेमधर्म का उपदेश देने इस सभा में आये हैं। आश्चर्य है कि ईश्वर ने उनको कितनी शक्ति इस पावन कार्य को करने के लिए दी है। मेरी ईश्वर से प्रार्थना है कि वह उनको शक्ति दे कि वह इस राष्ट्र को अपना मार्गदर्शन कराते रहें।" मेरे लिए राजा साहब ने कहा था-"श्री प्रभुदयाल अक्सर प्रेम धर्म की सभायें कराते रहते हैं और जब भी ये बुलाते हैं, मैं इनकी सभा में जरूर आता हूँ।"

राजा महेन्द्र प्रताप : एक सम्पूर्ण व्यक्तित्व

अनूप शर्मा

राजा महेन्द्र प्रताप भारत को ब्रिटिश राज्य से मुक्त करवाने हेतु सम्पूर्ण विश्व में घूमे। अपने 31 वर्ष 7 माह के विदेश प्रवास के दौरान आपने विभिन्न देशों के राष्ट्राध्यक्षों से भारत की स्वतन्त्रता हेतु सहयोग माँगा और उसका प्रयोग किया। 9 अगस्त 1946 को वापिस भारत आए। राजा साहब के भारत आने के 1 वर्ष के बाद ही भारत स्वतन्त्र हो गया था। लेकिन भारत भूमि पर कदम रखते ही राजा साहब ने भारत के बारे में सामाजिक, राजनैतिक चिन्तन प्रारम्भ कर दिया।

भारत लौटने पर मथुरा की एक स्वागत सभा में आपने कहा कि "यह जो स्वतन्त्रता हमें मिल रही है यह तभी कायम रहेगी जब हम अपने कर्तव्य का पालन करेंगे तथा मिल-जुलकर रहेंगे। यह देश हिन्दू तथा मुसलमान दोनों का है।

राजा साहब पश्चिमी देशों की तानाशाही, साम्राज्यवादी, समाजवादी और साम्यवादी शासन की पद्धतियों को देख आए थे। लेकिन इससे वे सन्तुष्ट न थे। राजा साहब भारत लौटने पर कांग्रेस में बड़े उत्साह के साथ सम्मिलित हुए, लेकिन भारत वर्ष की जैसी कल्पना उन्होंने अपने मन में संजो रखी थी, कांग्रेस को उसको मूर्त रूप देने में उन्होंने अक्षम पाया। 1952 में पं. जवाहर लाल नेहरू के आग्रह पर वह कांग्रेस के टिकट पर चुनाव लड़ना चाहते थे, परन्तु जब उनसे कांग्रेस दल तथा संसदीय मण्डल के सभी निर्णयों, नियमों व व्यवस्थाओं को मानने के शपथ-पत्र पर हस्ताक्षर करने के लिए कहा गया तो उन्होंने मना कर दिया और इन्हें कांग्रेस का टिकट नहीं मिला।[1] उनके मन में कोई बहुत स्वार्थ या यश-कामना न थी। आप 57 से 62 तक लोक सभा के सदस्य रहे और हर सम्भव तरीके से जनसेवा की। लोकसभा में कोई ऐसा प्रसंग न था जिस पर उन्होंने अपनी प्रतिक्रिया व्यक्त न की हो।

राजा साहब ने शान्ति दल की स्थापना करके उसके द्वारा देश की दशा सुधारने का कार्यक्रम भी आरम्भ किया।[3] उस समय संगठन अथवा दल समय की

माँग थे इस कारण उन्होंने यह कदम उठाया। शान्ति दल का उद्देश्य प्रत्येक नगर व गाँव में स्वराज्य स्थापित करना था तथा सर्व सम्मति से कार्य करना था। आज की धूर्त व घृणा की राजनीति से तो कोसों दूर थे।[4]

राजा साहब ने एक बार मथुरा के पत्रकारों को राव कृष्ण पाल सिंह के यहाँ आमन्त्रित किया और राजनीति के चारित्रिक उत्थान, विश्व बन्धुत्व और पारस्परिक सद्भाव के विषय पर वार्ता की।[5] वास्तव में राजा साहब देश की परिस्थितियों से बहुत क्षुब्ध थे और उनका रुझान उस ओर हो गया था, जिसे हर महापुरुष के जीवन काल में 'पागलपन' या 'सनक' माना जाता है।

राजा साहब ने अपना नाम 'पीटर पीर प्रताप' रखकर यह सिद्ध किया कि जाति, धर्म तथा वर्ग-भेद से ऊपर उठकर एक नए समाज की रचना प्रारम्भ की जा सकती है। अपने 'प्रेम-धर्म' की सभा में, जो प्रत्येक रविवार को होती थी प्रार्थना ब्राह्मण पुजारी नहीं बल्कि कालीचरण नामक एक हरिजन सम्पन्न कराता था। भारत में जातिवाद से ऊपर उठकर सबसे पहले हरिजनोद्धारक का काम राजा साहब ने ही किया जो एक अनुकरणीय तथ्य बनकर समाज के सामने प्रस्फुटित हुआ।

आधुनिक भारत वर्ष के निर्माण में राजा महेन्द्र प्रताप की भूमिका बड़ी विशिष्ट थी। राजा साहब देश की स्वतन्त्रता के पश्चात् जो संविधान चाहते थे वो सीधा, सरल तथा सपाट हो जिससे प्रतिनिधियों पर प्रतिनिधि निर्वाचित न हो, *बल्कि निम्नतम संघीय केन्द्र सीधे गाँव और नगर होने चाहिए। उनके अनुसार जातीय आधार पर प्रान्तों का निर्माण अनुचित, अवांछनीय तथा अव्यावहारिक है।*

राजा साहब संविधान से **अंग्रेजी** को बाहर करने के पक्षधर थे। क्षेत्रीय भाषाओं के हिमायती थे। हिन्दी को ही वे केवल राष्ट्रीय भाषा के रूप में चाहते थे।

राजा साहब समाज के व्यापक आधार के निर्माण के लिए **अन्तर्जातीय विवाह** के पक्षधर थे। स्वयं अपना विवाह इसी के अनुरूप किया। इसी प्रकार उन्होंनें हिन्दू समाज में **विधवा विवाह** की व्यवस्था को बल देकर नारी की दयनीय सामाजिक स्थिति को उबारने का भरसक प्रयत्न किया। **मदिरा पान एवं जुआ** एवं इसी प्रकार की अनेकों बुराइयों का राजा साहब ने मात्र उल्लेख ही नहीं किया बल्कि उनके उन्मूलन के लिए प्रत्येक व्यक्ति के व्यक्तिगत स्तर पर प्रयत्न करके स्वस्थ समाज की संरचना का आह्वान किया। उनके स्वस्थ समाज की अवधारणा का मूल मन्त्र 'कार्य ही पूजा है' था। उनके सामाजिक कार्यों ने स्पष्ट कर दिया कि वे किसी एक जाति, एक धर्म अथवा किसी एक वर्ग से बँधे हुए नहीं थे। वे सबके लिए थे और सब उनके लिए थे। राजा साहब की हर धर्म, हर वर्ग, हर जाति में उनकी आस्था थी। राजा साहब ने एक ऐसे समाज की संरचना में सक्रिय भूमिका निभाई जिसमें प्रत्येक व्यक्ति के कल्याण से ही सम्पूर्ण समाज का विकास

सम्भव हो सकता था।

राजा साहब की राजनैतिक गतिविधियाँ भी एक अन्य महत्त्वपूर्ण पक्ष है। इस परिप्रेक्ष्य में उनका स्वकथन अति महत्त्वपूर्ण है जो उनकी राजनैतिक गतिविधियों की आधार संहिता थी। "मैं छोटी-छोटी बात पर अंग्रेज से लड़ता रहा, अंग्रेज कहता था उससे मिलने आओ तो या तो जूते उतारकर आओ या टोपी उतरकर आओ। मैंने प्रयत्न किया कि मैं न जूते उतारूँ न टोपी उतारूँ।"[6]

उनका प्रयत्न था कि राजनीति जो ढाँचा अंग्रेज देश को देकर गए उसमें व्यापक परिवर्तन आए क्योंकि वे मानते थे कि वह भारत की परिस्थितियों के अनुकूल नहीं था। उन्होंने ऐसी राजनैतिक व्यवस्था कायम करने के लिए प्रयत्न किए जिसमें गाँव-गाँव में पंचायत हो, मौहल्ले-मौहल्ले में पंचायत हो। सर्व सम्मति से नेता नियत किया जाए। उन्होंने संघर्ष विहीन राजनीति स्थापित करने का प्रयत्न किया। उनका प्रयत्न था कि जो सब सिद्धान्त की लड़ाई कराते हैं उन्हें पहचाना जाए और उन्हें सिर से निकाला जाए।

राजा महेन्द्र प्रताप ने अपनी राजनीतिक गतिविधियों से संसार संघ का नया अलौकिक राजनैतिक विचार देकर विश्व को संघर्ष विहीन प्रशासनिक प्रणाली का दिग्दर्शन कराने का प्रयास किया। संसार संघ का उनका सूत्र मनुष्य को एकमात्र ईश्वर का अनुयायी बनाना था। प्रत्येक जाति को अपने आप में पूर्ण स्वतन्त्रता हो, ये न हो कि कोई भी दूसरे घर का चौधरी बने। उनका कहना था कि हम सबको सुखी बनाने वाले हैं। हम बना देंगे समस्त संसार का संघ राज, बना देंगे मनुष्य जाति का एक कुटुम्ब[7] उनकी राजनैतिक गतिविधियों का लक्ष्य था। गुलाम मत रहिए, किसी को अपने सिर पर मत बिठाइए।

राजा महेन्द्र प्रताप की राजनीतिक गतिविधियों का एक और योगदान संसार के न्यायालय की योजना का विचार और प्रयत्न था। उन्होंने इस बात पर बल दिया कि संसार के न्यायालय के साथ संसार का कानून भी होना चाहिए।[8] किसी भी देश के पास सेना नहीं होनी चाहिए। केवल संसार संघ की ही सेना हो तभी देश संसार राज्य की आज्ञा मानेंगे। देशों में केवल पुलिस रहे। घरेलू स्वतन्त्रता सभी देशों को प्राप्त हो, परन्तु किसी की भी ऐसी शक्ति न हो जो संसार संघ की सेना से अधिक हो। इसी से देश सुरक्षित रहेंगे और संसार में स्थाई शान्ति सम्भव है।

राजा साहब का स्वतन्त्रता के पश्चात् भारत की आर्थिक आजादी का भी सपना था। वे अंग्रेजों द्वारा प्रदत्त आर्थिक ढाँचे को हटाकर ग्रामीण उत्थान के लिए बजट का 90 प्रतिशत धन गाँवों के सुन्दरीकरण, कृषि की उन्नति, ग्रामीण क्षेत्रों के बालकों के लिए औद्योगिक शिक्षा एवं महिलाओं की समानता की शिक्षा पर व्यय[9] करने का प्रावधान चाहते थे। राजा साहब कहते हैं कि "हमको आर्थिक

कार्यक्रम बहुत सतह से बनाने चाहिए। जन कल्याण के नवीन आर्थिक जीवन के लिए लोगों के दिमागों में एक कड़ी से कड़ी जोड़कर शृंखला की तरह से स्थिति बनानी चाहिए। विद्यार्थियों के अध्ययन के लिए ऐसे स्कूल होने चाहिए जहाँ वे अपने अध्ययन के साथ-साथ दैनिक आवश्यकता पूर्ति के लिए उत्पादन भी कर सकें। ऐसे स्कूलों के पास बड़ी इमारत तथा पर्याप्त मात्रा में बड़े कृषि फार्म होने चाहिएं। दैनिक आवश्यकता की वस्तुओं के निर्माण के लिए फैक्ट्रियाँ भी होनी चाहिए जिसमें छात्रों की संख्या के अनुसार उतनी मात्रा में उत्पादन हो सके, साथ ही अन्य उत्पादन जो वो नहीं कर सकते उसके बदले में अपना अति उत्पाद देकर प्राप्त कर सके।[10] इस प्रकार के विद्यालय समुदायों का प्रारूप होंगे, और एक बड़ी आर्थिक समस्या हल होगी। राजा साहब के शब्दों में किसी भी देश की प्रमुख समस्या 'भूख' है। भोजन की कमी ही अपराध है, एक पूर्ण आहार युक्त व्यक्ति ही एक पूर्ण व सही राष्ट्रीय व देश भक्त हो सकता है।

राजा महेन्द्र प्रताप स्वतन्त्रता आन्दोलन के पश्चात् सामाजिक, राजनैतिक व आर्थिक रूप से भारत को समृद्ध बनाने हेतु प्रयत्नशील रहे। लेकिन उससे पूर्व आन्दोलन के इतिहास में उनकी भूमिका अविस्मरणीय है। राजा महेन्द्र प्रताप ने जिस साहसिक तरीके से हिन्दुस्तान के बाहर हिन्दुस्तान की आजादी का बिगुल बजाया उससे ब्रिटिश सत्ता बुरी तरह हिल गई। राजा साहब के द्वारा हिन्दुस्तान के बाहर देश को आजाद करने का इतिहास में पहला कदम था। ये राजा महेन्द्र प्रताप के आसाधारण व्यक्तित्व का ही परिणाम था कि बिना किसी शक्ति व अपने देश के समर्थन के उन्होंने एक देश के राष्ट्राध्यक्ष के साथ सन्धि करने तक सफलता अर्जित की। उनके प्रयत्नों ने ब्रिटिश हुकूमत को चैन से नहीं बैठने दिया। लेनिन जैसे नताओं ने भारत की स्वतन्त्रता के लिए भरपूर सहयोग दिया। राजा साहब के कारण ही रूस की भारत की आजादी में रुचि बढ़ी। राजा साहब ने भारतीय स्वतन्त्रता आन्दोलन में साहित्यिक माध्यम से जो सक्रिय भूमिका निभाई उसके द्वारा जो लेख तथा पत्र विदेशों से आते थे उनके द्वारा अंग्रेज सरकार के खिलाफ जनमत तैयार होता था। वास्तव में जो कार्य लोकमान्य तिलक तथा गाँधी जी जैसे लोगों ने यहाँ रहकर किया, वे विदेशों में रहकर ही इसे अंजाम देते रहे। भारतीय राष्ट्रीय आन्दोलन में राजा महेन्द्र प्रताप की भूमिका इस दृष्टि से अविस्मरणीय तथा विलक्षण है कि उन्होंने देश की आजादी के लिए उस समय कार्य किया जबकि देश में सार्वजनिक राजनीतिक चेतना का अभाव था। हिन्दुस्तान की आजादी के लिए गाँधी, जवाहर लाल नेहरू और सुभाष से पूर्व उन्होंने देश को स्वतन्त्र कराने की राजनैतिक गतिविधियाँ प्रारम्भ कर दी थीं।

भारतीय स्वतन्त्रता आन्दोलन के इतिहास में राजा साहब की गतिविधियाँ

इस परिप्रेक्ष्य में अत्याधिक विशिष्ट हैं कि उनको अपनी योजनाओं और कार्यों में सभी धर्मों, वर्गों, समुदायों के व्यक्तियों से भरपूर सहयोग मिला। वैदेशिक गतिविधियों में प्रमुख रूप से हिन्दुओं के अतिरिक्त मुसलमानों, बौद्धों तथा ईसाइयों ने उनका साथ खुले दिल तथा निष्ठापूर्वक दिया। भारत की आजादी के लिए जो बीड़ा उन्होंने उठाया, उसमें बिना किसी भेदभाव के ऐसा योगदान किसी भी भारतीय राजनीतिज्ञ को नहीं मिला।

राजा महेन्द्र प्रताप का राजनीतिक व्यक्तित्व अद्‌भुत विलक्षण और अभूतपूर्व हैं। ये अकाट्य सत्य है कि जब हिन्दुस्तान की आजादी का आन्दोलन देश में गाँधी के निर्देशन में चल रहा था तो उस समय क्रान्तिकारियों के विरुद्ध जो क्रूर दमनात्मक कार्यवाही ब्रिटिश सत्ता ने की उसका समुचित उत्तर किसी भी मंच से नहीं दिया गया और राजनैतिक मंचों ने भी उनके दुःसाहस और मनोबल को तोड़ने में कोई विशेष भूमिका नहीं निभाई। विशेष रूप से कांग्रेस के शीर्षस्थ नेताओं ने क्रान्तिकारियों के बलिदान की न तो प्रशंसा की और न ही उन्हें किसी प्रकार का नैतिक संरक्षण, सहयोग अथवा सहानुभूति प्रदान की। सम्भवतः यह इसलिए हुआ कि दोनों दर्शन एक-दूसरे के विपरीत थे। लेकिन राजा महेन्द्र प्रताप ने हिन्दुस्तान की आजादी के लक्ष्य को प्राप्त करने वाले सभी वर्गों का स्वागत किया। उन्होंने अफगानिस्तान में हिन्दुस्तान से भागकर आए हुए हिंसात्मक गतिविधियों में संलग्न नवयुवकों को न केवल कारागार से मुक्त कराया बल्कि उन्हें संरक्षण भी दिया। इस दृष्टि से भारतीय स्वतन्त्रता आन्दोलन के इतिहास में राजा महेन्द्र प्रताप कांग्रेस के गाँधीजी सहित सभी अग्रणी नेताओं से आगे शीर्षस्थ स्थान पर प्रतिस्थापित प्रतीत होते हैं, क्योंकि एक साधन विहीन व्यक्ति एक तपस्वी की भाँति सारे विश्व में अकेला इक्कतीस वर्ष सात माह तक निरन्तर भारत की आजादी का संकल्प लेकर सभी राजसी ठाट-बाट छोड़कर मारा-मारा फिरता रहा। विदेशों में उन्हीं की सरकार, उन्हीं का धन, उन्हीं के व्यक्तियों के बलबूते पर भारत की अस्थाई सरकार का गठन किया जाना और अपनी शर्तों के आधार पर अन्य देशों के साथ सन्धियाँ करना विलक्षण, असाधारण एवं अकल्पित बात थी।[11]

अन्ततः देश के आजादी प्राप्त होने के बाद भी उनकी कोई राजनीतिक महत्त्वाकांक्षा नहीं थी। उन्होंने अपना सम्पूर्ण धन, वैभव समाज सेवा में अर्पित कर दिया। प्रेम महाविद्यालय की स्थापना करके ऐसे स्वतन्त्र भारत के संरचना की नींव डाली जो मानसिक रूप से परिपक्व और स्वस्थ हो, परन्तु उनका यह स्वप्न आज तक सम्भव नहीं हुआ। यदि उनके दर्शन तथा चिन्तन पर देश की राजनीति को थोड़ा भी नियोजित किया जाता तो वर्तमान में गिरते हुए राजनैतिक मूल्यों से सम्भवतः ये देश विमुक्त हो जाता।

सन्दर्भ

1. आदर्श और सिद्धान्तों पर सदैव अड़िग–दिगम्बर सिंह पृ. 30
(राजा महेन्द्र प्रताप अभिनन्दन ग्रन्थ)
2. दैनिक जागरण–2.12.96 आगरा संस्करण
3. जब मैंने राजा साहब को पहली बार देखा–सत्यभक्त पृ. 71
(राजा महेन्द्र प्रताप अभिनन्दन ग्रन्थ)
4. क्रान्ति कारी राजा महेन्द्र प्रताप–विजय कृष्ण शुक्ल पृ. 47
(प्रेम भारती–राजा महेन्द्र प्रताप स्मृति अंक)
5. राज साहब के चरणों में–मोहन स्वरूप भाटिया पृ. 6
(राजा साहब–जन्म शताब्दी स्मारिका)
6. अप्रैल 1979 के संसार संघ से उद्‌धृत–राजा महेन्द्र प्रताप
7. संसार संघ–सं. फनीलाल गोस्वामी पृ. 8
वर्ष 92 (अंक 5 से 8 मई 1985–अगस्त 1985)
8. संघ उद्देश्य–राजा महेन्द्र प्रताप पृ. 56
9. त्याग और क्रान्ति के जनक राजा महेन्द्र प्रताप, श्री हुकुम चन्द्र तिवारी एडवोकेट पृ. 37
(राजा महेन्द्र प्रताप जन्म शताब्दी स्मारिका)
10. ग्रेट प्राब्लम सोल्वड्–राजा महेन्द्र प्रताप पृ. 49
11. राजा महेन्द्र प्रताप : एक ऐतिहासिक अनुसन्धान–डॉ. बिशन बहादुर।

यह राज प्रथा

राजा महेन्द्र प्रताप

मनुष्य कुछ विचारों का ऐसा गुलाम हो जाता है कि वह दूसरी कोई बात सुनने को पसन्द नहीं करता। मैं इकत्तीस वर्ष से अधिक विदेशों में रहकर 1946 में देश लौटा अर्थात् अब बत्तीस वर्ष देश में लौटे हो रहे हैं।

हिन्दू मुसलमान लड़े। अब भी जहाँ तहाँ लड़ जाते हैं। इतिहास बताता है कि सात सौ वर्ष मुसलमान बादशाहों ने इस देश में राज किया। डेढ़ सौ वर्ष ईसाई अंग्रेज भी राज कर गये। यह बस इसीलिए सम्भव हुआ कि हिन्दू मुसलमान लड़े और हिन्दुओं ने कुछ जातियों को अछूत बनाया। अछूत जातियों ने मुसलमानों और अंग्रेजों की मदद की। सेवा की। मुझे अपने बाल काल की याद है। अंग्रेजों के बैरे भंगी होते थे। अब तो भंगी कहना अपराध है।

यह राज प्रथा अंग्रेजों ने बनाई। अंग्रेज कलक्टर जिले का सर्वे सर्वा होता था। राजे, राव, सेठ, साहूकार कलक्टर का बड़ा आदर करते थे। कलक्टर चाहे जिसका अपमान कर सकता था या खिताब दिला सकता था। पुलिस कलक्टर के हुक्म को मानती थी। पुलिस कप्तान अंग्रेज होता था।

मैं छोटी छोटी बात पर अंग्रेज से लड़ता रहा। अंग्रेज कहता था कि उससे मिलने आओ तो या जूते उतार करके आओ या टोपी उतार के आओ। मैंने प्रयत्न किया कि मैं न जूते उतारूँ और न टोपी उतारूँ।

जब 1915 में अंग्रेज और जर्मन लड़े तो मैंने देश छोड़ा। जर्मनी जा सका। वहाँ मेरा बड़ा आदर हुआ। जर्मन सरकार ने मेरे स्वतन्त्रता संग्राम में मदद की।

मैं विदेशों में हिन्दुस्तान के पत्रों में लेख भेजता रहा। 'प्रताप' समाचार पत्र, कानपुर ने सबसे पहले हिम्मत करके मेरे लेख छापे। बाद को लाहौर के समाचार पत्र मेरे लेख छापने लगे।

मैं चाहता हूँ कि यह राज प्रबन्ध बदले। जब नगर पालिका है तो नगर राज नगर पालिका को चलाना चाहिए और जब जिला परिषद् है तो जिले का प्रबन्ध जिला परिषद् को करना चाहिए। न्याय-पंचायतें करें न्याय।

यह तहसीलें, कलक्टरियाँ और जजी क्यों हैं? इनमें न्याय नहीं होता। रुपया या वकील की खोपड़ी मुकदमे जीतती है। प्रथा बदलनी है।

चारों ओर देखिए। कचहरियों में जाकर देखिये प्रतिदिन लड़ाई के, चोरी, डकैती के मुकदमे हो रहे हैं। जैसे जब तब रोग लग जाता है इसी प्रकार जब तब लड़ाई हो जाती है।

समाज का सुसंगठन हो तो लड़ाई न हो। हो भी तो बहुत कम हो। आज तो यह दशा है कि जहाँ देखो वहाँ लड़ाई है या तनाव है। हिन्दुस्तान जर्मनी और आयरलैंड के टुकड़े हुए। ईसाई रूस और बुद्ध चीन कम्युनिस्ट हैं।

सबसे बड़ी और बुरी बीमारी है लड़ाई। यह मेरी बड़ी खोज है कि लड़ाने वाले विचार लड़ाई कराते हैं। सदा हमारा सिद्धान्त रहना चाहिए–जो विचार लड़ाये बुरा, जो विचार मिलाये अच्छा।

मेरी इस खोज का बड़ा महत्व है। लड़ाई कराते हैं लड़ानेवाले विचार। इनको अभी तक पहचाना नहीं गया। मेरा नवीन विचार विज्ञान सिखाता है कि कैसे इनको पहचाना जाय और सिर से निकाला जाय।

इस राज प्रथा में आपस की लड़ाई को बढ़ावा मिलता है। त्रुटि आपकी हमारी है। हमने अपने बूढ़ों का आदर करना छोड़ दिया है। लड़े और कचहरियों को दौड़े। अपनी कमाई को वकीलों को और कचहरियों को दे आये।

ग्राम ग्राम में पंचायत हो। मोहल्ले मोहल्ले में हो पंचायत। सर्व सम्मति से अपने नेता नियत करिये। कैसे दुःख की बात है कि हम अपने बड़े बूढ़ों का कहना नहीं मानते और नवयुवक मुनसिफ तहसीलदार की आज्ञा मानते हैं। राज प्रथा का हमारे जीवन पर बहुत असर होता है। परन्तु हम इधर ध्यान नहीं देते। ध्यान देना और सुधार करना चाहिए।

(अप्रैल 1978 के संसार संघ से संकलित)

□□□

Contributors

1. Shri Ram Niwas Mirdha
   President, Surajmal Memorial Education Society
   New Delhi

2. Shri Manzoor Ahmad
   Vice Chancellor, Dr. Ambedkar University, Agra

3. Prof. Suhas Chakravarty
   Professor, Deptt. of History
   University of Delhi

4. Prof. Ashok Kumar Patnaik
   Professor, Deptt. of History,
   Utkal University, Bhubaneshwar

5. Dr. Rajpal Singh
   Reader, Deptt. of History,
   M.N. College, Yamuna Nagar

6. Prof. A.C. Bose
   Retd. Professor, Deptt of History,
   Jammu University

7. Mrs. Yuthika Mishra
   Lecturer, Deptt. of History
   Vivekanand College,
   University of Delhi

8. Dr. Vir Singh
   Director, Maharaja Suraj Mal Centre
   for Research and Publication, New Delhi

9. Shri Anand Mohan Sahay
   Former Indian Ambassdor in Japan

10. Shri Shiv Dhyan Singh
    Advocate, Mathura

11. Shri Hari Singh
    Retd. Principal,
    Prem Maha Vidyalaya, Vrindavan

12. Shri RameshVerma
    Weekly Sainik, Agra

13. Mohd. Hafiz Akbar Khan
    (Private Secretary to Raja Mahendra Pratap at Dehradoon)
    36, Indira Nagar, Dehradoon

14. Shri Shiv Kumar
    (Private Secretary to Raja Mahendra Pratap at Vrindavan)

15. Sadhvi Mahanandamayi Maa
    Shri Kaleshwar Mahadeva Math,
    Kaleshar, Yamuna Nagar

16. Swami Mahanand Maharaj
    Shri Kaleshwar Mahadeva Math,
    Kaleshar, Yamuna Nagar

17. Shri Brij Bihari Lal Sharma
    Shreedham Vrindavan

18. Shri Jyoti Swaroop Singh
    (Private Secretory to Raja Mahendra Pratap)

19. Shri Prabhu Dayal Messy
    (President Christian Community Mathura0

20. Dr. Anoop Sharma.
    A/7031, Suhag Nagar, Firozabad

●●●